HANDBOOK

FOR

Youth Evangelism

Dean Finley
Compiler/Contributor

BROADMAN PRESS
Nashville, Tennessee

© Copyright 1988 ● Broadman Press
All Rights Reserved
4262-56

ISBN: 0-8054-6256-2
Dewey Decimal Classification: 269.2
Subject Heading: EVANGELISTIC WORK WITH YOUTH // YOUTH
Library of Congress Catalog Number:

Printed in the United States of America

Contents

Foreword

Dean Finley

This book is designed to help youth leaders to get their ministry back on track. Evangelism must be the priority of any youth ministry. Despite the misunderstandings about evangelism, youth leaders must stop avoiding the task and begin to give themselves to proclaiming the gospel without reserve.

The following chapters have been designed according to a common format. Each chapter contains a section of introduction, biblical basis, youth culture, implementation, ideas, and resources. This group of authors has met together on numerous occasions in the process of working out a overall program of youth evangelism. Each chapter was written independently and, thus, can be read for information with little reference to the other chapters. However, because each chapter has the same basic structure, the book can be divided into at least five books. Typically, books are structured to be read straight through from cover to cover. This book, on the other hand, could be read by reading the identical sections from each chapter consecutively. For example—

Biblical Basis: The reader may want to read the section on biblical basis from each chapter along with the chapter on "Theology of Youth Evangelism" to gain insights for youth ministry in general. Also, these sections can be used as the basis for a course to train potential youth leaders in the biblical basis for their ministry.

Youth Culture: Each chapter in the book contains observations about the psychology and sociology of youth in America today. These insights are based on a combined total of two-hundred-plus years of ministry and experience with thousands of teens. It is suggested that the reader use this part of each chapter for a discussion starter with other youth leaders.

Implementation: Generally, if a you picked up this book and read the contents you would be drawn to a particular chapter because of your interest in that subject. The implementation section in each chapter deals with the chapter topic and practical applications of introducing the process into a church's youth ministry. This section contains information on developing strategy and guidelines for accomplishing the given task.

Ideas: This section alone in each chapter is worth the price of the book. A youth leader who has run his or her own "idea well" dry can find some of the finest ideas for strengthening their youth ministry in this section. The ideas are not fully developed but the basic idea is presented to start the reader towards implementation. The ideas have been collected from thousands of youth leaders and conferences throughout the United States.

Resources: Youth leaders are always in search of new materials. The resources section of each chapter will help the youth leader know where to search to find other materials related to the chapter topic.

Because of the unique design of this book the reader will not want to just read the information and then place the book on the shelf. This is a reference book to be taken off the shelf and used over and over again. Its purpose is to call youth leaders of America back to the ministry that God has given them. We must tell teenagers about the good news of Jesus Christ and call them to respond. This task is our calling.

Dean Finley
Stone Mountain, Georgia

1
Building an Evangelistic Youth Ministry

Dean Finley

Introduction

Youth evangelism is defined as the processes, procedures, and activities of any Christian sharing the *gospel* with a non-Christian age twelve to eighteen. In most churches the youth program includes grades seven to twelve, in some cases grade six.

The key to any successful youth ministry is reaching lost teenagers. Youth ministry is not just activities for youth. Sometimes activities have been mistaken or substituted for ministry. God has not called us to be a center for social activities. He has called us to be proclaimers of the gospel of Jesus Christ. This does not exclude activities. However, youth ministry activities must include evangelism. A common tension for the youth ministry is the relationship of ministry, evangelism, and socialization.

An easy trap for most youth ministries to fall into is the attempt to try to entertain youth. An evangelistic youth ministry happens when a church changes from an entertainment mode to a ministry service mode.

Youth evangelism must be a part of a church's overall evangelism strategy. An informal survey of your church members will reveal that 50 to 70 percent of them accepted Jesus as their Lord and Savior before reaching the age of twenty. Second, most of those will report that an adult prayed with them when they accepted Jesus as their Savior. This leads us to conclude that half of a church's evangelistic thrust should be towards reaching lost youth.

The most requested staff position in churches beyond that of pastor is minister of youth and music. It is logical to think that as churches grow larger this trend will continue. A church will do well to make building an evangelistic youth ministry a significant part of their strategy of growing an evangelistic church. The following materials are provided as a basis for planning to reach non-Christian teenagers for Jesus Christ.

Evangelism is a part of the goal of each youth church program organization and every youth ministry event. To talk of an evangelistic youth ministry is almost redundant. We should ask, How in the world could you have a youth ministry and not be evangelistic? The whole nature of ministry is to be redemptive in people's lives. Therefore, it is impossible to have a ministry and not be evangelistic. It may be that some things youth leaders in the church do are called youth ministry while, in reality, they are only youth activities. Let us not get caught in the argument that says you cannot reach youth and minister too. To many times we hear the philosophy of youth ministry that says, "I don't play games with youth anymore. Everything we do is going to be spiritual." Who said that these items had to be mutually exclusive? However, we must be careful to make sure that in the midst of youth activities and meetings we are presenting non-Christians the gospel and asking them to respond. If we fail in this, we fail in youth ministry.

The work sheet which follows will help youth workers evaluate their willingness to be involved in building an evangelistic youth ministry.

Personal Evaluation of Youth Ministry

Who is the most evangelistic person I know and why are they?
When in the past have I shared my faith the most? Why?
Name ten youth in your church.

1.   2.
3.   4.
5.   6.
7.   8.
9.   10.

Look at the list, underline the youth you know who are Christians.

When was the last time you personally prayed with someone and they accepted Jesus as Savior and Lord?

Can a person be a minister and never be involved in evangelism?

What keeps me from being more evangelistic?

What steps could I take to help the youth ministry in our church to be more evangelistic?

Name the persons who are more evangelistic because they have been involved in your youth ministry.

1.   2.   3.

Review the previous questions. How would you rate your involvement in evangelism from 10 to 1?

10. I'm doing everything God wants me to in evangelism.

9. I almost never miss a God-given evangelism encounter.

8. I miss a few of the evangelism opportunities I have.

7. I share with most non-Christians I've meet.

6. I've shared with about half of the non-Christians.

5. I've shared with less than half the non-Christians.

4. I've shared with a lot of non-Christians.

3. I have shared with a few non-Christians.

2. I shared with one or two non-Christians.

1. I have never shared my faith with a non-Christian.

Biblical Basis

The best way to define evangelism is biblically and the most evangelistic person in the Bible was Jesus. He invited His disciples to follow Him and learn how to be fishers of men and to evangelize the world (Mark 1:17).

There are five basic approaches to evangelizing youth that can be seen in the life-style of Jesus.

1. *Prayer for Spiritual Awakening:* Jesus was a person of prayer (Matt. 6:5-15; 11:25-26; 14:19; 15:36; 26:26-27; Mark 1:35; 6:46; 8:6; 14:33-36; 15:34; Luke 5:16; 6:12, 9:18; 22:31-32; 23:44-46; John 11:41-42; 12:27-28; 14:16; 17:1-26). Also the New Testament church was so

effective in its evangelistic efforts because of it prayer evangelism (Acts 1:14 to 2:47; 9:40; 10:1-33; 12:5-12; 28:8). The greatest awakenings in history have been directly related to the prayers of God's people for the lost. More often than not youth played a central role in these awakenings. Youth ministry must be evaluated in relation to prayer for the lost.

2. *Relational Evangelism:* Jesus was also busy relating to specific individuals and, as He did, He not only reached them with the gospel but reached through them to the relationships in their lives (Matt. 8:5, 14; 9:23; 15:21; 17:14; Mark 1:29; 2:14-15; 5:23; 7:24; 9:14; Luke 4:38; 5:18; 7:1; 8:2-3, 39-41; 9:37; 19:9; John 1:40-41; 44-51; 2:1; 4:9-53; 11:38). The early church also practiced reaching out through relationships (Acts 10:2-24; 16:15-34; 18:8; 1 Cor. 1:16; Heb. 3:6; 1 Tim. 3:15). A prime target for evangelism is the close relationships in our lives and in the lives of young people. Parents need to be sharing the gospel with their own children. Youth need to witness to their closest friends and to build trusting relationships with them.

3. *Environmental Evangelism:* Jesus made a regular practice of sharing the gospel as He went about, and He put the gospel into the language of the listener. One of Jesus' ways of presenting the gospel was to use a parable. He did this to clearly communicate the gospel message. In each case the parable was designed to fit the situation or environmental circumstances (Matt. 13:24-30, 31-33; 36-50; 18:23-35; 20:1-16; 21:28-44; 25:1-30; Mark 4:26-29; Luke 7:36-50; 10:25-37; 11:5-13; 12:13-21; 13:6-9; 14:15-24; 15:1-32; 16:14-31; 18:9-14; 19:1-27; John 3:1-16; 4:1-26; 19:7-12). The church needs to have a plan for sharing the gospel with youth wherever they can be found in the city. This is an informal sharing that takes place wherever youth are encountered. Youth also need to follow the example set by Jesus who shared with anyone He encountered in language they could understand.

4. *Presentational Evangelism:* Jesus not only shared the gospel as He went about, but He went out of his way to present the gospel to individuals on a regular basis. In many of these cases He did not just encounter a certain individual but He went out of His way to find them, in most cases interrupting His rabbical activities to care for the individual (Matt. 8:1, 28, 9:1, 20, 27, 32; 12:22; Mark 1:23, 40; 2:3-5;

5:1-15, 25-34; 7:31-37; 8:22-26; 16:9; Luke 4:33; 5:12, 18; 6:6; 8:26, 43; 11:14; 13:11; 14:1; 22:50; John 9:1-7). A time should be set aside each week when the goal is to seek out lost youth and present them the gospel in written or verbal form. This helps youth to develop the habit of setting aside a time each week to reach out to lost people.

5. *Informational Evangelism:* Jesus also sought to redeem all who would come to Him. He was continually attempting to reach the masses (Matt. 4:25; 5:1; 8:1, 18; 9:8, 33, 36; 11:7; 12:15; 13:2, 34, 36; 14:5, 15; 15:10, 32; 17:14; 19:2; 20:29-31; 21:8-16; 22:33; 23:1; 26:47; 27:24; Mark 1:33; 2:13; 3:9, 20-32; 4:1, 36; 5:31; 6:35; 7:33; 8:1; 9:14-17; 14:43; 15:8; Luke 3:7; 5:15-19; 6:19; 8:45; 9:10-16; 12:1; 14:25; 17:11; 18:36; 19:39; 22:6-47; John 5:13; 6:1-2). The Bible tells us God does not want anyone to perish. This means it is our responsibility to tell everyone the good news. We must work at ways of distributing the information so all have the chance to hear and respond.

Therefore, there are five approaches to youth evangelism based directly on the life of Christ.

Definition of Youth Evangelism Strategy Terms

Spiritual Awakening is the sovereign act of God responding to the fervent prayers of His people. Historically, youth have played an important part in spiritual awakenings. It is important to teach youth about the process of spiritual awakening and involve them in fervent prayer for a lost world.

Relational Evangelism: The materials and processes that train individuals to share the gospel in existing close relationships (that is, family and friends). Relational evangelism focuses on ministry, mission action, and incarnational theology.

Environmental Evangelism: The materials and processes that train individuals to share the gospel as they go about their daily activities. This evangelism brings together a theology of God, an understanding of the non-Christian, personal preparation, and draws upon the existing situation.

Presentational Evangelism: The materials and processes which train individuals how to present the gospel to a non-Christian. Youth learn to actively seek opportunities to present the gospel. They are led to set aside a time to participate in outreach/visitation/evangelism weekly.

Informational Evangelism: The materials and processes that are aimed at making the gospel message available to multitudes of people through revivals, crusades, rallies, tract and Bible distribution, audio-visual media presentations, and television programming.

Christ-style Evangelism: The process of integrating the preceding five evangelism approaches into an individual's life-style.

This biblical basis provides the framework for all of youth evangelism. The temptation will be to implement only a part of Jesus' evangelistic life-style. However, a balanced thrust of all five of these evangelism approaches will result in growth and evangelism. Therefore, it is suggested youth leadership implement all five approaches simultaneously. This strategy will lead youth towards a *Christ-style evangelism.* The structure for these approaches already exist within the existing church program organizations.

Youth Culture

In each chapter of this book you will find a section which gives insight into the youth culture. After reading these you will want to apply the insights you gain to a strategy of building an evangelistic youth ministry. However, there are at least three key ingredients that will affect your implementation of youth evangelism: time, psychological development, and socialization.

Teens' Time Reference

An important concept in understanding any culture is their concept of time. If you examine American youth today you will find that they are quasi-time conscious. Generally, only half of any given group of youth will be wearing a watch. Their attitude in programming any day is "I will take what comes to me." Most youth are not daily planners. They are more likely to plan one week at a time. Their management style is typically management by crisis.

Youth are more likely to respond to last-moment opportunities than adults. This is true for two reasons: one, their schedule is not already planned so they do not have to postpone planned activities;

second, they are free from demands and responsibilities. Teenagers have a time reference of now. Psychological testing of adults will show that they become past, present, or future oriented in their thinking. However, in the youth culture the key word is "What's happening? Now!" This emphasis on now must be taken into consideration implementing a strong youth-evangelism strategy. The chapter on creative evangelism will help you grab teens' attention. But, we must not make the mistake of forgetting that youth are people, too. The problems of youth are timeless.

In planning an evangelistic youth ministry you should start by getting in touch with and understanding youth. Allow me to suggest a couple of simple ways to do this. Ask a mixed-age group of adults to list the kind of problems they remember having as a teenager. Also ask them to list the several things that they enjoyed doing. Finally, ask them to list the year they became thirteen years old and the year they turned twenty. List these years on a piece of paper or chalkboard with the answers to the other questions underneath them. I believe if you ask a group of today's teens the same questions you would find they have many of the same difficulties and joys as did those adults.

Developmental Psychology

Every youth leader knows that there is a big difference between a seventh grader and a teen in the twelfth grade. The younger teen is likely to come home from school, watch cartoons, and play in the backyard with some toy. The older teen is maybe a young girl who is already engaged and who is thinking about getting married. In many youth groups these two teens are thrown together. They do have some things in common. However, they have many differences caused by physical, intellectual, social, and spiritual growth. Therefore, in many cases it will be good to have separate training opportunities for these teens. Their psychological developmental stages are quite different.

Developmental psychology must, however, be balanced by an intergenerational mix. Younger teens have a real need to associate with older teens. All of us can remember how we looked up to older youth. In some cases older teens have protested that they do not want to have younger teens around. Often this is a type of prejudice. What they mean is they do not want to be bothered with the responsibility of younger teens. It is possible for older teens to become so selfish that they refuse to take the responsibility of modeling the right way to live for younger youth. Their shirking of responsibility is a sign of their own immaturity. It will cost older teens something to have younger teens around but a good strategy of youth evangelism will help them to see the cost and commit them to loving their peers.

Youth Socialization

With the recognition of adolescence in American society, a totally new set of problems developed. A host of books are available on the subject of youth peer pressure. In most cases these books deal with negative peer pressure and rightly so. The peer pressure is negative because the youth culture so deeply reflects the total society. The authority structure for youth is their peer group. They are learning to work out relationships within that group. From their peer group they will eventually develop support systems for life and choose a mate. If you listened to some seminars and books you would get the feeling the best thing we could do for youth is eliminate peer pressure. However, peer pressure is the society at work. We could not have a society without peer pressure.

The key to building an evangelistic youth ministry is to turn peer pressure in the right direction. Peer pressure can be positive. The ultimate peer pressure for the Christian is the church. A Christian must be a part of a local body of believers to stay on track with the will of God. Each part of the body of Christ, the church, is held in place by the other parts. These parts put pressure on each other to stay in place and work with the other parts. Youth leadership should never be afraid of positive peer pressure.

Implementation

Developmental Phases of Youth Evangelism

These phases are guidelines for the process of introducing all forms of evangelism into a youth ministry. They are derived from the biblical context. A study of the phases will aid youth leadership in implementing a complete and balanced evangelism emphasis. Each of the five approaches to youth evangelism have been divided into sequential phases. These phases are not hard and fast divisions but are like colors of the spectrum partly blended together. It would be wrong to assume that time is a key ingredient in the progression of the phases. In many cases the phases take place almost simultaneously. Youth leaders who want to fully implement a particular evangelism approach should see that all phases are included.

Spiritual Awakening Evangelism Strategy

Phase 1: Realization. Awakening begins when individuals begin to be aware of the lost and dying condition of the world and dependence on God's intervention for salvation.

Phase 2: Aspiration. The strong desire for the world to be reconciled to God, and a willingness to be drawn into the process as an instrument of reconciliation.

Phase 3: Integration. This phase brings Christians in fervent contact with God through prayer, ends separation caused by sin, and causes a union of power.

Phase 4: Expression. This phase of spiritual awakening happens when the presence of God is manifested, embodied, and experienced in a unique outpouring of the Holy Spirit in a specific place and time.

Phase 5: Dispersion. The act or process of scattering, diffracting, and spreading the news of the expression phase to other Christian communities.

Phase 6: Mediation. The interposing, intermediary, actions of God's people to promote reconciliation and the application of spiritual awakening resulting in individually changed life-styles, resulting in new organizations and ministries.

Relational Evangelism Strategy

Phase 1: Investigating. Investigating is a consultation between a church and a renewal consultant.

Phase 2: Initiating. This phase focuses on an event like a lay renewal weekend or youth retreat. These events give participants new spiritual insights and call for a commitment to grow in Christ.

Phase 3: Sharing. The sharing phase develops from the initiating phase. The sharing phase involves meeting in small groups for personal growth and ministry evaluation.

Phase 4: Commissioning happens when the group turns from self-evaluation and growth to outreach and ministry. A ministry evangelism weekend is one way to begin the commissioning phase.

Phase 5: Penetrating is the wholistic result of the previous four phases. Penetration is an invasion of the community through ministry in the name of Jesus Christ.

Environmental Evangelism Strategy

Phase 1: Personal Preparation. During this phase youth examine the meaning of discipleship and evangelism. They realize all areas of their lives belong to God. They study the total life as a witnessing tool. They begin a regular quiet time, systematic Bible study, devotions, daily prayer, Scripture memorization, and fellowship with other believers.

Phase 2: Witness Training. At this phase youth study the Bible's message and learn how to give a personal testimony. They will learn what it means to "win the right to be heard" and receive some training in advance witnessing techniques.

Phase 3: Witness Experience. The witness experience phase helps youth to develop and refine witnessing skills with the support of other Christians. They will be involved in taking the leadership in witnessing roles and develop a plan for evangelism.

Phase 4: Spiritual Development. Spiritual development helps youth to review the basics of Christian growth and observation of good role models while learning to encourage new Christians.

Presentational Evangelism Strategy

Phase 1: Injection. This phase introduces as an element or factor the plan of God to reconcile all individuals.

Phase 2: Internalization happens when one or more individuals incorporate the plan of God within as a guiding principle. The plan becomes intrinsic and inherent as a part of domestic affairs and usually depends on leadership to organize for presentational evangelism.

Phase 3: The Motivation phase happens when the Christian community at large commits itself to act and this serves as an impulse, incentive, inducement, and stimulus for consistent presentational evangelism.

Phase 4: Actualization. This phase involves the actual training of the Christian community, moving from the potential presentation of the gospel to fulfilling the God-given commission.

Phase 5: Presentation. This phase is the weekly involvement of youth in setting forth, giving, bestowing, and offering the gospel for the attention and consideration of others.

Phase 6: Evaluation measures the response of listeners to the presentation of the gospel. If the non-Christian accepts Jesus then evaluation leads to follow-up growth. If the non-Christian rejects Jesus, plans are made for future presentations of the gospel to that individual.

Informational Evangelism Strategy

Phase 1: Examination. During this phase prospect discovery techniques are used to analyze, interrogate, test, inquire, and investigate the community.

Phase 2: Identification. This phase identifies and orients ways, means, and resources for reaching every individual in the community, resulting in a feeling of close emotional association.

Phase 3: Constitution is the establishing of laws, customs, and ordinances providing for the distribution of power in an organization of resources and developing a plan for reaching the community with the gospel.

Phase 4: Proclamation. This phase involves declaring, announcing, showing, praising, glorifying, solemnly, officially, formally, and publicly the gospel to the total community. This proclamation may be video, audio, or in printed form. The aim is to proclaim the gospel to everyone without exception.

Phase 5: Invitation. The job of informational evangelism is not completed until an invitation has been extended. This invitation is to offer, solicit, urge, request, suggest, and encourage a person to respond to the gospel in repentance and belief.

Phase 6: Consultation is a dialogue, conference, council, or deliberation with a non-Christian about his response to the gospel invitation. At this phase the new Christian is given basic guidance for Christian growth and someone is assigned to be their encourager.

Evangelizing Youth Through the Church Program Organizations

The primary way to reach non-Christian youth is through the church program organizations. There is a direct relationship between each of the youth church program organizations and a strategy for building an evangelistic youth ministry. These church program organizations are not limited to a particular evangelistic approach; but, by the nature of their assigned task, are the natural leaders for a particular approach. Each church program organization makes a contribution to each of the five evangelistic approaches. Each organization must contribute to each of the evangelism approaches in order to maintain the balance of their own expertise. The chapter titled "Church Program Organizations" outlines how to reach youth. In reading this chapter you will want to harmonize these organizations with the five youth-evangelism approaches.

Spiritual Awakening and Relational Evangelism: Evangelizing Through Missions Organizations

Missions organizations focuses uniquely on missions study, missions support, and missions action. These missions organizations also are charged with leading our churches in prayer.

Environmental Evangelism: Evangelizing Youth Through Church Training

Youth Church Training should offer three approaches for evangelizing non-Christian youth. The three approaches include: discipleship celebration, discipleship labs, and discipleship centers. A description of these strategies are given in chapter 6. Each of these approaches are designed with evangelism content.

Presentational Evangelism: Evangelizing Youth Through Sunday School

There are three avenues for reaching youth in Sunday School. These three strategies are weekly Bible study during the church Sunday School hour, special projects, and outreach Bible studies. First, the Sunday School lessons should be presented in such a way that non-Christian youth in the classes not only hear the gospel but also are given the opportunity to respond. Second, there is a need for a set of ideas and projects that help youth grow and share their faith. This includes regular church visitation and outreach. Third, the Sunday School should be responsible for conducting "Outreach Bible Studies." These Bible studies are conducted in homes of youth Sunday school members and are led by an adult.

Informational Evangelism: Evangelizing Youth Through Youth Choir

The youth choir provides a platform for youth to share their faith, along with the support of other youth. Outside of the regular weekly meetings of the youth choir are special events. For example, a youth musical can be presented by youth in the public arena. Youth choirs can be used in rallies and revivals.

Youth program organizations are always given a high priority in an evangelistic youth ministry. The use of church program organizations for evangelism will result in a strong ministry that multiplies itself. This emphasis will produce a lasting ministry that avoids duplications and is balanced in its approach. Furthermore, a focus on these organizations brings a continuity and unified direction for youth as they grow into adulthood. This emphasis on evangelizing through the church program organizations helps youth have a basis for leading their church to be evangelistic when they become adults.

Ingredients for Building an Evangelistic Youth Ministry

A church should consider and plan to include each of these ingredients in their process of building an evangelistic youth ministry. These can also be used as a evaluation tool as a church continues to reach lost youth in their community.

Determine Needs and Direction—The purpose of any youth ministry is to make sure that lost teenagers have a chance to respond to the gospel of Jesus Christ. The ultimate question is, "If we do not declare God's redemptive act, who is going to?" To build an evangelistic youth ministry a commitment must first be made to evangelism. To point up the need to evangelize, youth should conduct a survey and ask church members at what age they became a Christian. You will find between 50 to 70 percent of them became Christians before leaving their teen years. Also survey the church's effectiveness in reaching non-Christian youth.

Vision—A second ingredient in building an evangelistic youth ministry is to impart a vision of reaching the lost teenagers in the community. Lost teenagers must be identified and located. Sometimes they go unseen as we go about our daily routine. One youth minister began by driving around at night looking for youth and their "hangouts" and where they were "cruising." He then began to ask key leaders in the church, including other church staff, to go with him and they began to get a vision for reaching those lost teens. Another suggestion is to ask the congregation as a whole to list the young people they have come in contact with the last week (that is, the check-out clerk, the bag carrier at the supermarket, the waitress or server in the fast food restaurant). Ask them for suggestions on how to reach these teens for Jesus.

Church Organizations—A third ingredient is to make sure that the existing organizations are healthy, organized, and functioning. The basic approaches to evangelizing youth are centered in the church program organizations: Sunday School, Church Training, music, and the missions organizations. These organizations should be evaluated for their evangelistic content and methods. One might begin by asking, "When was the last time someone accepted Jesus as their Savior during one of these ventures?" and, "Would it be all right for someone to accept Jesus during these activities?" Finally, the question needs to be asked, "How would we go about making sure that teens involved in any of our church program organizations have the opportunity to become Christians?"

Youth Activities—A fourth ingredient is to evaluate every youth activity to see if it is in harmony with the primary purpose of evangelism. Is the puppet ministry evangelistic? Does the skating party next week have a time when youth can hear the gospel and respond to it? Is it possible for a youth to become a Christian at the lock-in next month? If the answers to these questions are all, "Well, we think so." maybe the youth and youth leaders need to take a closer look at why they have planned these special events.

Some may argue that youth need to have fun and not be preached at all of the time. Youth activities are social functions for youth. However, as mentioned earlier, evangelism and social activities are not mutually exclusive. These two goals can be accomplished at the same time. Just because a person is skating does not exclude the possibility of evangelism taking place. Evangelism is more than preaching. The best evangelism often takes place within a social context.

Youth activities also need to be evaluated to see if they contribute to the building of relationships. We are familiar with the week-long youth camp shaving-cream fight. This kind of activity teaches youth to live by the law of revenge. It also distracts from the purpose of the camp and builds barriers between individuals. Every effort should be made to turn youth ministry activities away from a competition basis towards a cooperative joint effort. A major contributor to isolating individuals and destroying their self-image is uncontrolled practical jokes. Youth should be challenged to grow up and minister to each other rather than act as children playing games and satisfying their own egos. Youth ministering to each other will build strong lasting relationships. Once ministry is a regular part of youth activities, youth will agree that they have far more fun than the alternative.

Discover Resources—An evangelistic youth ministry must make use of all available gifts, resources, and talents. A study of the biblical gifts will be very beneficial in discovering youth's talents and gifts. A survey directly related to talents and interest will provide a basis for a multi-dimensional ministry. Ministry and events should be built around the interest of the particular individuals in the church. It is not wise to start a puppet group if no one is really interested in puppets. However, if there are computer hackers, clowns, auto mechanics, sports enthusiasts, or Indian chiefs, then each of these talents should serve as the basis for ministry evangelism. It is best to pursue the gifts and talents that God has put within the congregation rather than just pursuing some interest of the leaders.

Balanced Approach—The leadership needs to have a commitment to using all approaches to evangelism. Physical buildings are made up of different substances (that is, brick, wood, mortar, tile, nails, and so forth). A strong evangelistic youth ministry has more than one approach to evangelism. We have seen that there are five basic approaches to evangelizing youth based on the life-style of Jesus.

One way to bring this balance is to conduct a parent/youth/youth leader/staff dialogue. The dialogue should include a discussion about evangelism and brainstorming about how to reach lost teenagers in the community. Also, an evangelism plan should involve all youth. The planning will need to consider the different levels of commitment for all the young people.

Leadership Training

An evangelistic youth ministry cannot be built on one individual. It will depend on teaching others to take leadership roles and model evangelism. Furthermore, it will be necessary to teach current leadership how to share the gospel in their regular contact with youth. Each of the five evangelistic approaches will need qualified leaders.

This means that the youth ministry will attempt to involve everyone in the church in some way. Every individual will be asked to contribute something according to his or her commitment level.

Evangelistic Events—Plan events that are "overtly evangelistic." Some youth ministry events should be unremittingly evangelistic, such as weekly youth visitation. Another example of wholly evangelistic events are found in the chapter on "Revivals." It is obvious that these events and others like them are primarily evangelistic. One of these events should be included in the youth programming each quarter.

Discipleship—Youth ministry must not only be committed to baptizing youth, but it must disciple them. This means designing follow-up events for new Christians. All of these are Church Training materials.

Evangelism always results in discipleship. If it does not, then it is not evangelism.

Attempt to Reach All Youth—The youth ministry must be dedicated to reaching lost teenagers both inside and outside the church building. Youth leadership should make plans to find out which youth in the church are non-Christians. However, they must feel that their responsibility does not end there. They must be willing and encouraged to serve in positions outside the church.

Priority of Jesus' Example

It has been said, "Miracles can happen if we don't worry about who gets the credit." Youth leadership must be committed to youth ministry based on God's truths and not personalities. The youth ministry should have a unique emphasis on the person of Jesus and a desire to help youth follow His example. Evangelistic youth ministries are ones that place much emphasis on the work and example of Jesus.

Simplicity—There must be a continual evaluation and commitment to attaining simplicity in the organizational structure. This includes discontinuing methods and programs that are no longer needed.

Recognition—Recognize outstanding efforts made by youth and their leaders publicly.

Family Relationships—The total ministry will seek to encourage family relationships. The attempt will be to include family members rather than exclude.

Prayer Support—Build a churchwide basis of prayer support.

Launch Events—A church needs to plan events that motivate youth to be involved in evangelism. Each of these events need to offer youth a chance for further evangelism training. These events will become launch pads for ongoing evangelism emphasis.

Annual Planning Retreat

The key to implementing an evangelistic youth ministry is conducting an annual planning retreat. This retreat must include a time of evaluation and planning. The evaluation will point out the evangelism areas not being developed in the overall program. If a church is interested in building an evangelistic youth ministry, they should conduct a Friday and Saturday night retreat with the key leadership of the church. This retreat should involve all of the following where possible:

The Youth Council	A few youth
The pastor	A few parents
The minister of youth	Acteen leaders
Youth mission leaders	Youth choir leaders
Youth Sunday School leaders	Youth activity leaders
Youth Church Training leaders	Minister of music
Minister of education	Others

Before the retreat each of the following tasks should be accomplished:

1. Someone should be assigned to collect data related to past evangelism efforts and their success.

2. Collect as many of the youth evangelism resources as possible.

3. Purchase a copy of this book for each person and ask them to read it in preparation for the retreat.

During the retreat, the objectives of the group will be:

1. To evaluate the youth ministry and the priority of evangelism, using the resources, ideas, and concepts of this book.

2. To gain insights into youth evangelism.

3. To set a course of action that will lay the basis for an evangelistic youth ministry.

After the retreat, when the group returns to the church they will want to implement a strategy that will lead to building an evangelistic youth ministry.

The following is a sample retreat schedule:

Friday

7:00—Introductions and overview of youth evangelism. Divide into five groups and ask each group to study the Scriptures in the five basic approaches listed in the section "Biblical Basis." Let groups report their findings and discuss.

8:00—The pastor, youth minister, or youth worker, will lead a Bible study. See the chapter "A Theology of Youth Evangelism." Include discussion of the idea and the texts.

9:00—Discussion based on chapter, "Church Program Organizations." Let the entire group discuss the idea of stressing church program organizations. They need to evaluate the current organizations on the intensity of their evangelism.

Saturday

8:00—Breakfast

9:00—A Bible study based on the chapter on "Leadership." Introduce the idea that there will be an intense effort to prepare for launching into building an evangelistic youth ministry over the next two months.

10:00—Break

10:30—Group discussion of section in this chapter; "Ingredients in an Evangelistic Youth Ministry."

11:30—Begin calendar planning for implementing plan

12:00—Lunch break

1:00—Calendar planning, as long as necessary. Include in this session a brainstorming time based on each evangelism approach and calendar the best of these ideas. The chapter on "Creative Evangelism" can be used to guide this process.

4:00—Closer

Ideas

This is not intended to be a comprehensive list, nor are the ideas completely spelled out. The best ideas can be found by brainstorming with the youth and youth leaders of your church. Once they understand the particular evangelism approach, then one or two of the following ideas might help them to begin identifying ideas of their own.

Prayer for Spiritual-Awakening Ideas

Note: All of the following ideas should be sponsored by the missions organizations of the church.

1. Have a special all-night prayer meeting at the church. Youth sign up with their parents as prayer partners for one hour.

2. Conduct a retreat around the theme of prayer and fasting.

3. Conduct a prayer and candlelight service at the local high school (if possible) one evening.

4. Conduct a study of historical spiritual awakenings.

5. Conduct a survey of how much time people spend in prayer each week in your church. Publicize the findings and tell them you will survey again in a month to see if it increases.

6. Have five-minute prayer meetings at the sanctuary altar before the worship service for one month.

7. Provide table placards for homes with listing of non-Christians on it.

8. Place a sign over every water fountain in the church that says, "Pray . . . the Lord of the harvest, that he will send forth labourers" (Matt. 9:38, KJV).

9. Conduct a prayer breakfast.

10. Ask the officials of the city to declare a day of prayer for problems in the schools.

11. Ask the youth group to wear their watches upside down for a month. Every time they look at their watch they will be reminded to pray.

12. Have youth list five people they know who are lost and use this list as a bookmark in their math book at school.

13. Place a sign below every clock in the church that says, "It is time to pray."

14. Appoint five different youth to each youth leader. During one week ask them to call the leader and pray with them about some lost people they know.

Relational Evangelism Ideas

Note: All of the following ideas should be sponsored by the missions organizations of the church.

1. Have a kinship fellowship. Youth are given a list of kin they might have (that is, Mom, Dad, cousin, Grandma, younger brother). They are then to fill their list with real or adopted people and invite them to the fellowship.

2. Conduct life-style meetings as described in the quarterly issue of *equipping youth* magazine.

3. Check with a local high school coach about providing cold-drink break during August football practices.

4. Conduct a bring-a-friend event. Youth who are members of your church will not be allowed to attend without a non-church member.

5. Conduct monthly birthday parties for youth and their guest(s).

6. Ask youth what clubs they belong to at school. Ask them to host a party at their house for the club and you will provide the entertainment and the refreshments.

7. Involve youth in ministry to senior citizens.

8. Have youth write love letters to their parents with a gospel tract or a request for them to go witnessing with them.

9. In January have youth collect the birth dates of all their friends and relatives. Have them make up birthday cards with a gospel presentation, address and return them to the youth leader. Each month the youth leader can put the appropriate cards in the mail.

10. Host give-a-friend-an-ideal-date. Youth identify friends that are dating and design an ideal date for them. They could ask their parents and the parents of their friend to help. The date should be complete with chauffeur.

Environmental Evangelism Ideas

Note: All of the following ideas should be sponsored by youth Church Training departments.

1. Get names of all teens who have been admitted to hospitals and visit them, especially during holiday seasons.

2. Get a video camera and tape needs in the community to show at a youth meeting. Let them organize to meet those needs.

3. Make a list of youth "hangouts" and organize to invade these with the gospel.

4. Conduct a letter-writing campaign over several weeks. Ask youth to choose a different community personality to write to each week.

5. Take the church bus to the local high school and offer free rides home after school.

6. Enlist youth to help with one of the school club projects, like the annual drama.

7. Help a couple of youth run for class officers.

8. Have T-shirt day at school. All the youth of the church wear a T-shirt with the same logo.

9. Use the church bus to transport one of the athletic teams to a local or out-of-town game.

10. Design a tract that includes the testimony of youth in your church to be distributed at the high school.

11. Find a wall-size map of your city along with some stick-on notes. Gather a group of youth and begin to identify where youth are gathered in your city during any given time of the day, week, month, and/or year. Your map will have notes stuck on it over the school, swimming pool, concert hall, fast-food hangout, athletic field, and so forth. Then write on each note when youth are gathered at that place. Be as specific as possible; include month, date, day, time, and so forth. Then plan a strategy to reach the youth who are going to gather there.

Presentational Evangelism Ideas

Note: All of the following ideas should be sponsored by the youth Sunday School departments.

1. Give each youth a Bible and ask that person to give it away in the coming week, then to give a report in the next meeting.

2. Provide youth with a shoe-shine kit and let them find a busy corner to shine shoes and share the gospel.

3. Conduct a census of the community door to door about church attendance. Teach youth how to share with non-attenders.

4. Provide coffee breaks for local firemen and policemen.

5. Host one of the school clubs in a party or recognition banquet.

6. Provide free refreshments at a local park and share the gospel.

7. Begin a weekly evangelistic visitation program.

8. Let youth conduct one-day children's clubs on dead-end streets. Present these children with the gospel.

9. Ask youth to provide the names and address of high-school employees. Target these individuals to be visited by witnessing teams.

10. While youth are attending an amusement park ask them to present the gospel to each person who stands next to them in line.

Informational Evangelism Ideas

Note: All of the following ideas should be sponsored by the youth choir organization.

1. Conduct an outdoor concert with a Christian message.
2. Send Bibles to all of the teachers in the local high school.
3. Provide free baggers for a local grocery store and place a tract in each bag.
4. Have youth and adults work together to make tract racks. Ask business owners to make use of these.
5. Place a big-screen TV in the back of a van with double-wide doors. Drive the van to an appropriate place like a beach and play Christian videos for those around to view.
6. Videotape ball games and invite teams to come and see selected portions. Place a testimony on the tape from several ball players.
7. Get permission for the youth choir or puppet group to perform inside a mall or shopping center.
8. Find out if the ACTS network is on your cable stations. Choose a program to view some evening and have youth gather to see it.
9. Design cheer placards for the athletic teams with the school mascot on one side and the gospel presented on the other side.
10. Enter your youth group in a holiday parade. Let them carry crosses and signs and pass out tracts along the parade route.

Resources

If your church would like to host a Building an Evangelistic Youth Ministry Seminar for other churches in your area contact the Specialized Evangelism Department at the Home Mission Board, 1350 Spring Street, Atlanta, Georgia 30367

2
A Theology
of Youth Evangelism

Hal Poe

Introduction

Whenever the title of this chapter has been mentioned, someone has asked "What distinguishes a theology of youth evangelism from a simple theology of evangelism?" The question arises because people tend to confuse the theology of evangelism with the theology of the atonement, justification, sanctification, and all the other great doctrines related to salvation.

The latter doctrines explain why evangelism must take place. They explain what is wrong with the human race as it plunges headlong toward destruction. They explain how God provided a remedy for the problem of sin. They explain how God applies that remedy to the human heart. These doctrines deal with the simple, universal, unchanging gospel message of salvation.

The gospel applies to all people of any age, race, or nation. The gospel applies to everyone in every time. The gospel is the message of evangelism. Every soul needs to hear the gospel and respond positively to escape the pain of sin and death, and to receive God's gift of righteousness and eternal life. Evangelism presupposes the problem (sin) and the answer (Christ). These realities are the foundations of evangelism, but evangelism goes beyond understanding the message to confrontation.

A theology of the atonement seeks to understand what God has done to save the world from sin and death. A theology of evangelism seeks to understand what God is doing about those who are lost in sin and separated from His love. Christians often see evangelism as something they do, but a theology of evangelism focuses attention back on what God does in evangelism. A theology of evangelism presupposes God is preparing nonbelievers to receive the gospel message. A theology of youth evangelism seeks to understand what God does in the lives of youth with which Christians may cooperate when presenting the gospel to young people.

Biblical Basis

God made us as we are for a purpose. The Bible says "He has made everything appropriate in its time. He has also set eternity in their heart, yet so that man will not find out the work which God has done from the beginning even to the end" (Eccl. 3:11). God has placed a longing within each person that only He can satisfy. Sin perverts that longing, driving people to satisfy that longing in other ways, but nothing works. Yet, in every stage of life, the longing takes on a new form as God creates a new situation in which the gospel can be heard. God reigns sovereignly over every stage of human life from childhood to old age. God has set a compelling need in the hearts of people in every stage.

Human aging occurs as a natural process, but not in the sense that it occurs accidentally. It happens as an intentional part of God's creation, "There is an appointed time for everything. And there is a time for every event under heaven" (Eccl. 3:1). Each stage of life has its own crisis and heartfelt need. Those of old age differ from those of youth. Those of childhood differ from those of middle age. God is the positive ingredient in each crisis which He uses to lead us to Him.

Only Christ truly answers the heartfelt need God places in each stage of life. Though God determines the need, sin causes the need. The need comes from our separation from God, even though we do not know it until He saves us. Even after we belong to Him, the needs arise to draw us closer to Him throughout our lives.

A Theology of the Human Condition

Because of the human capacity for creating idols, people can find some substitute for God regardless of the need they feel. A country-music song of several years ago contained the thought that even something less than real love isn't too bad. Human life is a catalog of attempts to find something to substitute for what only God can give. Romance, fame, wealth, and power have all figured in the idol making. People try to supply what is missing in life by devoting themselves to family, job, or some worthy cause.

A theology of youth evangelism examines the particular needs God has placed in the hearts of youth. The gospel speaks directly to the most basic human spiritual needs. To say that Jesus is the answer is not a simplistic cliche. It is a profound reality of life. The surface conflicts of youth are only outward expressions of deep turmoil where God is stirring the young heart to seek Him. A theology of youth evangelism must include an understanding of youth needs and determine how best to present gospel related to those needs. Youth are perhaps in the age of life most open to the gospel because of the intensity of their questions and needs.

A Theology of the Gospel

A Christian must know the gospel message before attempting to show a young person. Every Christian knows the gospel because their own salvation came from hearing and believing the gospel. Unfortunately, many Christians have learned so much more that they have forgotten what is gospel and what is not. The gospel is not everything a Christian believes. Instead, it is that simple, basic message about Jesus that even a child can understand.

In one seminar for youth workers, I asked them to explain the gospel to me. One person said, "God is love." Another said, "It's being committed." Someone missed my entire presentation because I assumed they understood the gospel, but they did not. It lay buried in all the many things they knew about religion.

The apostle Paul said; "For I am not ashamed of the gospel, for it is the power of God for salvation to everyone who believes, to the Jew first and also to the Greek" (Rom. 1:16). He insisted, "For since in the wisdom of God the world through its wisdom did not come to know God, God was well-pleased through the foolishness of the message preached to save those who believe" (1 Cor. 1:21). Peter explained that salvation came through the gospel message which the prophets of old expected and angels longed to understand (1 Pet. 1:8-12). In Hebrews we learn that God's rest awaits those who believe the word of the gospel (Heb. 4:2-3). The gospel that brings salvation consists of the essential elements of the Christian faith, and it focuses on Jesus.

In 1 Corinthians 15:1-5 Paul gave a brief outline of the gospel. He mentioned that, (1) Christ died for our sins, (2) He was buried, (3) raised the third day, (4) and He appeared to Cephas, the twelve, and many more. Later in the same chapter he explained that, (5) Christ reigns and, (6) will come again (1 Cor. 15:23,25). Through the New Testament, these same fundamental points appear again and again with slight variations in emphasis.

Since Paul wrote 1 Corinthians to Christians, they knew who Christ was. When Peter preached, he first explained that Christ was the descendant of David for the benefit of his Jewish audience (Acts 2:14-39). In writing to the Gentiles, John and Paul explained the deity of Christ by calling Him the Son of God (John 3:16; Rom. 1:1-3, Galatians 4:6, 1 Thess. 1:10, 1 John 1:1-3, 7). The gospel message is simple in its barest form. Nevertheless, some aspects of it require explanation for those who have never been exposed to the Christian faith or who have a poor understanding of what they have heard.

A Theology of Response

The gospel message in the New Testament also calls for a response. On the Day of Pentecost Peter cried, "Repent and let each of you be baptized in the name of Jesus Christ" (Acts 2:38). In the next chapter, after presenting Christ, Peter called on the crowd to "Repent therefore and return" (Acts 3:19). Peter also called on Simon to repent (Acts 8:22). Paul preached that God commanded all men everywhere to repent (Acts 17:30). Before King Agrippa, Paul explained he had devoted his life to declaring that everyone should repent and turn to God (Acts 26:20).

Sometimes the apostles called for a response and never mentioned repentance. Instead, they spoke of faith or belief, not mentioned in any of the passages that called for repentance. Paul promised freedom to those who believed in Christ at Antioch of Pisidia (Acts 13:39). Peter reminded the council at Jerusalem that he preached the gospel to the Gentiles in order that they might believe (Acts 15:7). Paul urged the Philippian jailer to "Believe in the Lord Jesus" (Acts 16:31).

Though some passages call for repentance and some for belief, everyone who repented, believed, and everyone who believed also repented. In the New Testament, repentance and faith are not two things that a person can do in stages. They are one thing that happens in a person's life—two sides of the same coin. Unfortunately, many people think of repentance as something we *do* to deserve salvation, like the medieval idea of penance. Others think of faith as simply believing a few basic facts about Jesus. Both ideas present a distorted view of how salvation comes to a person.

Throughout the New Testament, Abraham serves as the example of faith, but he is also an example of someone who repented. Abraham followed God by faith, not knowing where he was going, but believing the promises of God. (Heb. 11:8-12,17-19; Rom. 4:1-25; Gal. 3:6-9,14,16,18,29). The Bible says that Abraham "believed God, and it was reckoned to him as righteousness" (Gal. 3:6, KJV; Rom. 4:3, KJV; Jas. 2:23, NASB; cf. Gen. 15:6). Abraham left his family, his native land, his friends, his language, his culture, and everything he had known to follow God. Repentance means turning from one thing to another thing or changing one's mind about something. By believing God, Abraham repented. He turned from his way of life to trusting God. A person cannot repent from his old life of sin and death unless he has faith in Jesus Christ. A person does not have faith if he will not turn from his sin and trust Jesus as "the way, the truth, and the life" (John 14:6 KJV).

A Theology of Promise

When the apostles preached the gospel they also offered the promise of God. On the Day of Pentecost Peter promised the forgiveness of sins and the gift of the Holy Spirit (Acts 2:38). This promise deals with both the negative and positive dimension of eternal life with the Lord. The Bible tells us that without holiness, we cannot see God (Heb. 12:14). By dying for our sins on the cross, Christ takes away our sin, but that does not leave us holy. We become holy when His Holy Spirit comes to abide in our hearts. Negatively, He takes away the sin that keeps us from God. Positively, He gives us His Spirit which brings us to God. By receiving Jesus a person becomes a child of God and inherits eternal life and a place in the Kingdom.

The promise of the gospel stands absolute and unchanging for all people at all times. Nevertheless, the apostles explained the promise differently to different people. The Jews who heard Peter on the Day of Pentecost knew the prophecies. They knew about the Holy Spirit, ceremonial law, the importance of atonement, and forgiveness of sin. In contrast, the Gentiles had never heard about the Holy Spirit (Acts 19:2). The Gentiles' pagan religion had taught people to bargain and negotiate with God, rather than seek forgiveness. When the apostles presented the gospel to Gentiles they did not change the promise, but they explained it in terms the pagans could understand. God inspired John to write a Gospel that uniquely suited the Gentiles. The first three Gospels assume an understanding of the Holy Spirit, but John devoted chapters to explaining the Spirit and the meaning of the sacrifice.

A Theology of Communication

A theology of youth evangelism recognizes that young people who have not grown up in a church have little understanding of spiritual things, just like the Gentiles of the first century. We have the responsibility of explaining the gospel in simple terms, but we do not have the freedom to change the message to make it more acceptable. At first a young person may not understand the doctrine of the vicarious substitutionary atonement, but they can understand that Jesus came into the world and died so they would not have to experience the consequences of sin.

Some Christians strive to share the gospel to young people without explaining the concept of guilt lest the young person be manipulated into making a response. While the issue of manipulation is real, guilty feelings are an unavoidable element of the gospel. The gospel exposes the guilt of people as they behold the love and righteousness of Christ. The problem of human sin comes to light in the presence of Christ. When Isaiah had his vision of the Lord, he understood his own sinfulness and guilt in contrast to the majesty and holiness of God (Isa. 6:1-7). The Bible clearly states that we all are guilty of sin and breaking God's laws (Rom. 3:23).

Guilt and guilty feelings are two different things, sometimes closely related and at other times experienced independently of the other. Guilt is one of the common experiences of the human race. Psychologists and existential philosophers have observed and written about the problem of universal feelings of guilt, and they have suggested many reasons for and solutions to the problem. Guilt cannot be created by another person, but a manipulative person can take advantage of guilty feelings someone feels to transfer it from one situation to another. The gospel does not take advantage of a person's guilt to manipulate them into making a response. On the contrary, the gospel helps a person fully experience their guilt regardless of their feelings. This brings it to the surface where it can be forgiven and cleansed from a person's life. Only Christ can forgive guilt and send it away. Hebrews makes clear that the blood of Christ not only frees us from the penalty of sin, but also cleanses our consciences from the guilt of sin (Heb. 9:14; 10:2,22; 13:18). So young people who are going through a time of life particularly characterized by feelings of guilt often have a deepened emotional response to the promise of the gospel. Rather than imposing guilty feelings, the gospel relieves the guilt a young person feels by atoning for the guilt.

A Theology of Confrontation

The beauty and glory of the power of the gospel comes when someone clearly sees Jesus. The confrontation with the gospel is not an argument or an attack. In the Bible the idea of coming "face to face" best expresses the idea of confrontation. A person presenting the gospel does not present himself. Instead, he helps someone else come face to face with Jesus as well as with herself. How one confronts another person with the gospel depends very much on the recipient.

In the New Testament, Jesus confronted people in a variety of ways, but always appropriately for each individual. Sometimes He used a parable to help someone see his need. Sometimes He told people directly. Sometimes He told them to do something to show that their imagined righteousness was an illusion. He did this with the rich young ruler. The principle is that people are different, and God deals with people according to their differences. A theology of youth evangelism considers the ways in which youth differ from other age groups to determine the most effective way to reach them.

Anyone who has worked with youth between the seventh and twelfth grades realizes that they have more than just one group on their hands. In the years between childhood and young adulthood, youth go through three distinct stages of growth. These adolescent years are marked by rapid change and a number of issues the young person has never faced before. If these issues remain unresolved, they may become problems throughout the rest of their lives. Paul said, "When I was a child, I used to speak as a child, think as a child, reason as a child; when I became a man, I did away with childish things" (1 Cor. 13:11). The adolescent years are a time for growing up. The gospel is the answer for all the crucial questions a young person asks.

A Theology of Maturation

In the first couple of years of adolescence, a young person experiences rapid change in several areas of life. We are told "Jesus kept increasing in wisdom and stature, and in favor with God and men" (Luke 2:52, NASB). Most obviously, the body grows and changes dramatically. This is the age of awkwardness at its most embarrassing. A young man may feel like he is all legs. Little girls suddenly have the bodies of women. Acne creeps across faces that long to be pretty. Peach fuzz appears on the chins of boys who long to have real whiskers. The body seems to be in total rebellion. To make matters worse, emerging sexual changes give occasion for guilt and shame when the young person first discovers those changes. Whether through experience or fantasy, sex changes the way young people feel about themselves.

Emotional changes accompany the physical changes. Until now, boys usually played with boys and girls played with girls. Boys and girls had little time for one another, and if they did have contact it may have been a brawl. With the physical changes, however, comes a growing awareness that the opposite sex has an attraction. As young people become concerned with the opposite sex, they grow increasingly sensitive about their physical appearance and social ability. They compare themselves constantly with their peers. They are painfully aware of their clumsiness and social backwardness, often exaggerating the situation. The young person whose legs or arms have grown suddenly out of proportion may slump the shoulders and attempt to be smaller. No one knows what to do with hands or arms, or how to stand so as not to look as gawky as one feels!

At this early stage of adolescence, youth are particularly susceptible to insults and rejection by the group. The self-centeredness produces unrealistic standards of success, acceptability, and self-worth during these years. Self-centeredness also leads to an amazing capacity for cruelty, almost as though pointing out another person's unattractiveness eases the pain of one's own. Each school class has its boy or girl who has been singled out as the misfit. They go by different names in different generations and locations: *nerd, zorp, lizard, geek, square,* or *turkey.* Everyone in school knows who they are, but they may feel no one is their friend. They live a lonely life, and, to a certain degree, they represent this stage of life in its extreme case. They have believed the propaganda that they are unworthy human beings. At this stage of life, sin assaults the self-esteem to destroy what remains of the image of God.

Low self-esteem is not simply a psychological problem. Because it stands contrary to the purpose of God (that people should become children of God, joint heirs with Jesus, and recipients of abundant life), low self-esteem is a sin problem. People cannot solve their own sin problems. Ultimately, only Jesus can solve the problem of low self-esteem when He frees persons from all their sins. The problem of low self-esteem needs to be resolved early in life or it will follow a person throughout life.

Perhaps Zacchaeus is a biblical example of a person who still lived with the problems of youth long into adulthood. Even in the songs little children sing today, we still make fun of Zacchaeus:

Zacchaeus was a wee little man,
And a wee little man was he.

People have always found a substitute for their need, could it be Zacchaeus found power and money as a substitute for self-esteem? Some people substitute self-pity and enjoy feeling sorry for themselves. Self-pity is just as sinful, however, because it runs away from the joy and the life God offers. When Zacchaeus met Jesus, he found what was missing in his life, and the substitute was not needed or wanted anymore. When Zacchaeus turned to Jesus, he turned from the sin that bound him. Jesus saved him.

The gospel speaks directly to the issue of self-esteem and places a person's value and worth on a new level. Jesus came into the world to die for us because of His great love for us. God places the highest value on each individual. Jesus frees young people from the value system of egocentric teenagers as He accepts them, blemishes and all. The promises of the gospel give a young person hope for growing up and surviving the painful years of early adolescence.

A Theology of Authority

The middle years of adolescence form the backdrop for much of the open warfare between youth and their parents. To live as a mature adult, a person must be able to stand on his own two feet. The struggle for independence begins in earnest during the middle adolescent years and often takes the form of rebellion. The youth has a compelling urge to be free, yet lacks the maturity to live as a responsible adult.

The desire for independence from parents leads to curiosity and experimentation in areas where the parents have traditionally controlled practice and belief. Experimentation in decision making includes hair, clothes, music, sex, and money. This age group wore the duck tail in the 50's, long hair in the 60's and 70's, and the spike haircut in the 80's. Though they may live under the same roof with their parents, youth show by the styles they follow that they have declared their independence from Mom and Dad. The token symbols

of independence often come only after hard-fought battles with parents or out-and-out defiance.

Not all youth have a stormy battle with authority, but all youth
deal with the struggle for independence. In some families the maturing process happens with mutual respect as parents prepare their
children to assume more and more decision-making responsibility in
their life. In some families, the parents so control and dominate their
children that the youth never makes an attempt to grow up. It is
possible to go through life and remain totally dependent on parents
until they die, and then not know how to make decisions. A primary
cause of divorce in America arises from the number of people who
remain tied to Momma or Daddy after they marry. Daily parental
intrusion leads to the destruction of the marriage of the one who
never grew up and cut the apron strings.

As young people distance themselves from their parents, belonging
to a group becomes increasingly important. Peer pressure replaces
parental instruction as the dominant influence in decision making.
The group provides a sense of security and belonging during the
struggle with the family. Some groups are as informal as two or three
friends who spend all their time together. Other groups have a more
formal nature like the members of the band, the football team, or the
cheerleader squad. Young people develop a rigid caste system that
allows no mobility of groups. Part of the sinfulness of this age lies
in its egocentric exclusivity and jealousy.

The youth of middle adolescence in the search for independence
tend to conform to the dictates of the group. The individual does not
decide to wear peculiar clothes, listen to outlandish music, or wear
their hair a certain way because of their own originality. They do it
to be like the other members of the group. Teenagers who hear this
usually smile broadly as they look at themselves and see the girls all
wearing the same hairstyle and necklace and fellows with the same
shirt and shoes. The dress code helps identify someone as part of a
group, and to deviate by being out of uniform risks being dropped
from the group.

Jesus gave the classic biblical account of the rebellious struggle for
independence in the story of the prodigal son. The son not only

separated physically from the father but also broke with the values of the father. He kept his new friends as long as he had money, but when his ability to keep up ended, they dropped him. The prodigal's experiment with independence ended disastrously. The young man's true freedom came when he understood he was going about life in the wrong way and needed someone who could help him put his life back on track. Salvation came when he turned to his father and turned his back on his self-centered approach to life.

The gospel speaks directly to the issue of freedom and independence. Jesus said "You shall know the truth, and the truth shall make you free" (John 8:32) Jesus is "the way, the truth, and the life" (John 14:6 KJV). Only Jesus can satisfy the thirst for freedom. Throughout life, someone always has authority over people, long after parents are gone. The responsibilities of life alone comprise a far more rigid disciplinarian than parents ever were. The only true freedom in life comes when Jesus frees us from sin and death. Jesus gives the power to be free of the fearful urge to be conformed to the world.

In the plan of God it is appointed that people should leave their parents and begin a new family (Gen. 2:24). While every young person must learn to give up the protection of the family and the dependency it creates, independence does not have to happen in a sinful way. Through Jesus it can happen in a holy way. Instead of leaving parents for egocentric reasons, Jesus said to leave them for His sake (Matt. 19:29). He then becomes the new basis and means of loving the family. In giving up the family through Jesus, a young person can begin to love and be a part of the family as a responsible adult for the first time.

Because of the search for independence, young people open themselves to new ideas. Their curiosity leads them to ask questions. This searching drive which God has placed in young people makes them more open to hearing the gospel than perhaps any other age group. A youth must make a decision not based on parental wishes but a personal one. Because salvation is a uniquely personal experience, receiving Christ as Savior is the ultimate independent decision anyone will ever make. Receiving Christ answers the longing in the heart for independence.

A Theology of Purpose and Self-Image

In the last couple of years of adolescence, the drive for freedom relaxes as youth assume more and more responsibility for themselves. The great day of emancipation for American teenagers comes when they get their driver's licenses. While restrictions will remain for a few years, the ability to drive oneself rather than rely on one's parents eases the intensity of the conflict at home. Simply being trusted with the car gives a young person a sense of responsibility and independence.

Instead of demanding independence, the late adolescent youth has the problem of knowing what to do with independence. The late adolescent struggles with what might be called an identity crisis. Soon they will graduate from high school, but then what? After struggling for the right to make their own decisions, they suddenly have to decide what they will do with their life. Do I go to college, get a job, join the army, get married, go to vocational school, or bum around? Throughout life parents had been the reference point that provided identity, but the youth in late adolescence has no reference point.

Because of human sinfulness, people consistently make the wrong thing a point of reference, or they wander aimlessly. In either case, they ignore God's purpose for their life. The rich fool made wealth and success his reference point throughout his life. His philosophy worked for a while but ultimately failed him (Luke 12:16-21). Some young people have a wild, almost frantic, desire to get married in the last year of high school to supply the security of a point of reference. Others simply grow depressed as they look out into life and wonder if there is anything out there for them.

During the 1960s the baby-boom generation reached this stage of late adolescence with a fury. Raised in the highly materialistic, overindulgent days of postwar prosperity, the baby boomers had everything but direction. They tried drugs, free love, transcendental meditation, social protest, organic food, and after twenty years the baby boomers still make news with their current fads designed to help them find themselves.

They have built a life out of going in search of themselves. In this same period of social upheaval, however, many found Christ in what was called the Jesus Movement. Jesus settled once and for all their identity crisis. He put the false methods and symbols of fulfillment to rest.

The apostle Paul developed an identity that worked for awhile, but it was not the identity God intended for him. His identity could not supply true meaning to life. Paul said of himself:

> circumcised the eighth day, of the nation of Israel, of the tribe of Benjamin, a Hebrew of Hebrews; as to the Law, a Pharisee; as to zeal, a persecutor of the church; as to the righteousness which is in the Law, found blameless. But whatever things were gain to me, those things I have counted as loss for the sake of Christ (Phil. 3:5-7).

When Paul came face to face with Christ, he realized how empty his plan of success really was. He had devoted his life from the time of his youth to what King Solomon called "vanity," but Christ satisfied the longing of his soul.

The purpose of people, the reason for their presence in the universe, is to become the children of God. If they fail in that one essential, nothing else matters. Jesus asked, "What does it profit a man to gain the whole world, and forfeit his soul?" (Mark 8:36). The purpose of life is not to do something to assure that we will be remembered. The purpose of life is to receive God's gift of eternal life as we receive His son Jesus (John 1:12). Once a young person settles his identity as a child of God, he has a basis for deciding all the other issues of education, vocation, and marriage. Jesus promised to give guidance through His Holy Spirit. And He said we do not need to worry about the future. He has prepared a place for us, not just in heaven, but in the path we walk until death brings us to heaven.

A Theology of Evangelism

The evangelist is the person who tells someone the gospel. The evangelist to youth may be an adult or another young person. Another young person will be in settings that the adult will never be a part of, but the adult can fill a need that another young person cannot.

Christians of all ages have a part to play in God's plan for total evangelism. Many people will probably have some part to play in each conversion, as Paul explained: "I planted, Apollos watered, but God was causing the growth" (1 Cor. 3:6).

Jesus constantly created evangelistic opportunities based on the needs of the people He met. Whether healing, feeding five thousand people, or talking with an outcast, Jesus met the needs of people out of His deep compassion for them. His ministry did not end, however, until He had also given the word of life. Youth ministry should meet the needs of youth in such a way that it creates an opportunity to present Jesus Christ as the ultimate answer.

The youth worker, whether paid professional or volunteer, plays a vital part in the openness of youth to the gospel. The most important thing a volunteer can do to lead a young person to Christ is to genuinely care about that youth. Youth sense who helps them because they care and and who helps them because its their job. Youth accept the people who accept them for better or worse. A drug pusher often takes time to talk with the lonely eighth grader. Tenth graders who want freedom from their parents have not rejected adults as a class. They are looking for answers to questions, and they want the opinion of someone older who takes them seriously. The drug pusher often takes them seriously. Young people tend to accept the ideas of the people who accept them for better or worse.

A Theology of Evangelistic Youth Ministry

In many youth groups, the youth worker has been raised to almost idolatrous levels. At a time when young people are at odds with parents, they still need the role model and advice of significant adults who care about them. The people who work with youth because they want to create an evangelistic opportunity.

The youth group of a church, in whatever form it takes, provides an evangelistic opportunity by its very nature. The youth group satisfies the need to belong. The youth group offers an alternative set of values based on the gospel of Jesus Christ. The youth group provides a sense of security while the family goes through the turmoil of the teenager's rebellion. The youth group provides a setting for spiritual questions as well as the other deep concerns of young people in a troubled world. By giving youth a forum to share their concerns the leader has gained insight into their lives and a basis for later private conversation about the Lord.

In order for the group to be evangelistic, it must be open to outsiders. The members of the group must see themselves as the evangelists. An effective ministry of youth evangelism depends upon the desire of the Christians in the group to want others to know Christ as personal Savior. This desire runs counter to the natural youth tendency to have an exclusive group, but through a consciously planned program of study and ministry the exclusiveness can change to openness. Focusing on Christ instead of on itself will help a youth group remain open. Though youth have deep needs, the focus of youth ministry should not be on the need, but on how Christ answers the need.

This handbook explores practical ways to develop a broad strategy for reaching youth with the gospel. The message of salvation has remained the same for two thousand years, but the context in which we must preach has changed constantly. This handbook presents a variety of approaches to evangelizing youth that effectively communicate the gospel to youth. These approaches recognize the differences between youth and adults as well as the differences between youth and children. God is doing some special things in the lives of youth to make them more open to hearing the message of salvation. Youth workers must learn to cooperate with God.

Resources

Dave Bennett, *Keep Giving Away the Faith* (Nashville: Convention Press, 1979).

James Dobson, *Preparing for Adolescence* (Ventura, California: Regal Books, 1980).

C. H. Dodd, *The Apostolic Preaching and Its Developments* (New York: Harper & Row, Publishers, 1964).

Lewis A. Drummond, *Leading Your Church in Evangelism* (Nashville: Broadman Press, 1975).

Theodore Lidz, *The Person* (New York: Basic Books, Inc., 1968).

Glen C. Smith, ed. *Evangelizing Youth* (Wheaton, Illinois: Tyndale House Publishers, Inc., 1985).

Richard Ross and G. Wade Rowatt, Jr., *Ministry with Youth and Their Parents* (Nashville: Convention Press, 1986).

3
The Task
of Youth Evangelism
Phillip Hunter

Introduction

The major concern of today's youth is what others say. How do we proclaim the gospel so they are more concerned with what God says? Today's youth are full of talent, ready for a challenge, hungry for experience. How can we proclaim the gospel so they will commit themselves to pick up their cross and follow the lordship of Christ? Today's youth are criticized for their laziness, ungratefulness, disrespect of parents and others in authority, their music, manners, dress, hair, and drugs. How do we proclaim the good news so it will change their lives for their own good and the glory of God? Today's youth are distraught from sexual, emotional, and physical abuse; worried about personality and pimples; anxious because of their height and weight; confused and scarred by world affairs; groping to see if life does have any meaning. How can we help them to see that life in Jesus is worth living?

Today's youth are each seeking "abundant life" in their own way. They believe abundance rests in the American way: beauty, bucks, and brains. How can we proclaim the gospel so they see Jesus Christ "is the way, and the truth, and the life?" (John 14:6)

The purpose of this chapter is threefold:

1. Remind discouraged youth leaders that God is still in the business of redeeming messes—the bigger the mess, the greater the glory.

2. Inform those inside the walls of our churches of what is going on outside the walls. Our youth are being destroyed in today's cul-

ture and many youth leaders seemingly are unaware of "what is going on."

3. Suggest some ways in proclaiming the gospel that could make a dramatic difference in the lives of youth for the glory of God. Seeing the ever-growing need of youth today, demands we be at our best and do our best, always relying on His best.

"Do you not say, 'There are yet four months, and then comes the harvest'? Behold, I say to you, lift up your eyes, and look on the fields, that they are white for harvest" (John 4:35). We must proclaim. If we do not tell them about Jesus, who is going to?

Biblical Basis

Regardless of the complexities or the uniqueness of their problems, we, as youth leaders, still have in the gospel of Jesus Christ the message that can transform anyone. "Therefore if any man is in Christ, he is a new creature; the old things are passed away; behold, new things have come" (2 Cor. 5:17).

In spite of all their wrongdoing, the good news is still,

> He saved us, not on the basis of deeds which we have done in righteousness, but according to His mercy, by the washing of regeneration and renewing by the Holy Spirit, whom He poured out upon us richly through Jesus Christ our Savior, that being justified by His grace we might be made heirs according to the hope of eternal life (Titus 3:5-7).

Often youth are locked in the prisons of low esteem, laziness, arrogance, selfishness, ungratefulness, disrespect, guilt, bitterness, aimlessness, alcohol-and-drug addiction. Still the Son, Jesus Christ, can set them free. "If therefore the Son shall make you free, you shall be free indeed" (John 8:36).

What often though is our attitude? Frustrated by low attendance in Sunday School and youth choir; anxious over the discouraging comments of pastor and parents; underpaid, overworked, and misunderstood; do we not sometimes become defensive, cynical, and passive? Unaware, we can even become as an elder brother. Remember that familiar parable?

And He said, "A certain man had two sons; and the younger of them said to his father, "Father, give me the share of the estate that falls to me." And he divided his wealth between them. And not many days later, the younger son gathered everything together and went on a journey into a distant country, and there he squandered his estate with loose living. Now when he had spent everything, a severe famine occurred in that country, and he began to be in need. And he went and attached himself to one of the citizens of that country, and he sent him into his fields to feed swine. And he was longing to fill his stomach with the pods that the swine were eating, and no one was giving anything to him. But when he came to his senses, he said, "How many of my father's hired men have more than enough bread, but I am dying here with hunger! I will get up and go to my father, and will say to him, Father, I have sinned against heaven, and in your sight; I am no longer worthy to be called your son; make me as one of your hired men." And he got up and came to his father. But while he was still a long way off, his father saw him, and felt compassion for him, and ran and embraced him, and kissed him. And the son said to him, "Father, I have sinned against heaven and in your sight; I am no longer worthy to be called your son." But the father said to his slaves, "Quickly bring out the best robe and put it on him, and put a ring on his hand and sandals on his feet; and bring the fatted calf, kill it, and let us eat and be merry; for this son of mine was dead, and has come to life again; he was lost, and has been found." And they began to be merry (Luke 15:11-24).

Meanwhile, the elder brother "became angry, and was not willing to go in: and his father came out and began entreating him" (v. 28).

Many youth are like the prodigal son. They, too, are using God's precious gift of choice unwisely. They, like the prodigal have chosen to go their own way in life (v. 12). They have also squandered not only their substance but also the purity of their lives (v. 13). They, likewise, have found themselves in the pigpens of drug and alcohol addiction, pregnancy, abortion clinics, detention centers, and prostitution. Like the prodigal, they have found themselves in places they never imagined themselves being (v. 15-16). Yet, they are there.

Should we despise and condemn? Should we "throw in the towel" and give up in despair?

Jesus said,

> A new commandment I give to you, that you love one another, even
> as I have loved you, that you also love one another. By this all men
> will know that you are My disciples, if you have love for one another
> (John 13:34-36).

Of such love, Jesus said, "For the Son of Man has come to seek and
to save that which was lost" (Luke 19:10).

Considering the needs of the youth of today demand us to seek in
love: "love covers a multitude of sins" (1 Pet. 4:8). Through such love,
there is the possibility that, just like the prodigal, they too will come
to their senses, (Luke 15:17) and come home to our Heavenly Father.

Youth Culture

The Situation

A study of today's youth culture outside the confines of the church
has led me through the stages of shock, denial of the facts, acceptance, heartbreak, prayer, and a determination by God's grace to
change some of the following statistics. Their only hope is new life
in Jesus Christ.

The traditional family with both parents at home and close relatives now represents less than 7 percent of American families.[1]

A decade from now, the majority of seventeen-year-old teens will
come from broken homes. The number of families maintained by
women alone grew almost 90 percent between 1970 and 1985.[2] The
growth is attributed to more divorces and more unwed mothers. By
1980, women headed 56 percent of poor families with children.[3]

Thirteen-million children live in single-parent homes,[4] and 59 percent of all children live in a home where both parents or the sole
parent is working. Two thirds of all mothers now work.[5] Presently,
there are an estimated seven-million "latchkey kids" (that is, children who come home to empty houses after school.)[6]

With parental involvement and supervision at an all-time low,
consider these pressures and temptations confronting our youth.
Punk and heavy-metal music rather than melody and rhythm, this

new brand of music now employs acts which are violent, sexually explicit, vulgar, and profane. Like a toxic waste dump, this subculture is poisoning the minds of our youth beyond estimation. Many rock stars include such explicit content that if their recordings were movies, they would be rated X or at least R for their language, lewdness, and violence.

When youth are not listening to rock music, think what they are seeing in their homes on television—not only continuous sex and sexual innuendoes, but a steady diet of violence. Based on studies, more youth watch television from 8 to 9 PM than during any other evening hour. This time frame, the "family hour," is also the most violent. Some researchers recorded 168 violent acts in one week during this hour, the highest ever in the nineteen years they have conducted this survey.[7]

If punk, heavy-metal music, television, and movies were not enough to totally distort the minds of our youth, consider the impact of pornography. It is now an estimated $8 billion-per-year business.[8] This flood of explicit material has led to an increasing depersonalization, commercialization, and trivialization of sex. Advertisers, recognizing the sex craze of America now employ the "look of sex" to market anything to everything.

Since 1970 alcohol advertising budgets have jumped 490 percent on television and 300 percent on radio.[9] From their preschool years on up, children are bombarded by thousands of catchy jingles and captivating images, courtesy of the alcoholic-beverage industry. These ads drum home the point that good times, success, and friendships are the rewards of drinking.

Even though drugs and alcohol claim more young victims each year, according to *Parade* magazine, in the past five years at least sixty major motion pictures, many of them favorites with youngsters, included scenes showing recreational drug use.[10]

The Results

The Bible says; "For the wages of sin is death" (Rom. 6:23). Drugs have replaced lack of discipline as the main problem facing public education, according to the annual Gallup Poll on education.[11] Only

23 percent of American teenagers say they don't drink or use drugs. Alcohol-related disasters will affect 50 percent of all Americans during their lifetime.[12] The projection is that nine out of ten youth eighteen years of age by 1993 will have at least experimented with drugs.[13] Out of a total of 24,353,421 teenagers,[14] one million will run away from home this year.[15] Many are lured into cults. Others are involved in crime and prostitution. Many missing are never found alive or positively identified.

Our teen pregnancy rate is the highest in the industrialized world. More than a million American teenagers, about one in ten, get pregnant each year.[16] Some thirty-thousand girls ages fifteen and under get pregnant.[17] Teenage sexual activity has doubled since 1971. About 50 percent of unwed teenagers are sexually active.[18]

Some twenty-seven thousand new cases of sexually transmitted diseases occur every day in the United States, including genital herpes, gonorrhea, syphilis, venereal warts, and AIDS.[19] The abortion rate for teenagers in the United States stands as high or higher than the combined abortion and birth rates in countries such as Sweden, France, Canada, and England.[20]

Suicide is now the second major cause of death among adolescents. In the fifteen-to twenty-four-year-old age bracket, suicide has increased by 300 percent since 1950.[21] Our youth suicide rate is among the highest of all other industrialized nations. An estimated five thousand youth kill themselves each year (that is, thirteen teens a day). Half a million others try but fail, according to Charlotte Ross, director of the Youth Suicide National Center in Washington, D.C.[22] A who's who survey of high school students found 31 percent of high achievers had contemplated suicide, and 4 percent had tried it.[23]

The Church's Role

Where is the church in the midst of this crisis? Southern Baptists are the world's largest Protestant denomination. A comparison of the number of youth, ages thirteen through eighteen, in America with the number of youth in the Southern Baptist Convention glaringly points to the dire need for us to proclaim the gospel to the youth of our nation.

Age in	Number America[24]
13	3,109,095
14	3,273,052
15	3,394,998
16	3,760,120
17	3,716,530
18	3,580,644

20,834,439 total population

Compare these statistics to the following outreach efforts of Southern Baptists.

	Number in 1985	Number[25] in 1986
Baptisms	86,499	85,218
S.S. Enrollment	1,137,341	1,086,209
S.S. Attendance	551,500	530,400
C.T. Enrollment	333,240	317,610
C.T. Attendance	181,800	168,000

Based on these statistics Southern Baptists only baptized 0.4 of the youth in America in 1986. Only 5.2 percent were enrolled in Sunday School but less than half those—2.5 percent—attended. One-and-a-half percent were enrolled in Church Training, but only 0.8 percent attended. Even a comparison of the combined efforts of all denominations is not encouraging.

Like never before, we must commit ourselves by His grace and power to raise up a generation of youth willing to overcome the barriers of intimidation and peer pressure to stand together for the Lord in living and being the witnesses He has called them to be. We must dare to reach out to those youth outside the walls of our churches who are ungovernable and totally blinded by sin in knowing right from wrong.

We must challenge a culture that arrogantly declares, "Whether right or wrong, I did it my way," with the message that Jesus Christ is the only Way. You may be thinking, "What can we do that we have not already tried?" Here are six suggestions for proclaiming the gospel to youth.

Implementation

Prayer Before Proclamation

Can you think of one great youth ministry known as a pillar of prayer? Usually, youth ministries are evaluated by other standards than prayer. Good looks, charm, wit, personality, games, and programs cannot change a youth for life. That is God's business. Maybe if we would pray more, we would reach more youth for Jesus.

Only God can bring conviction of sin. Only God can convince a youth Jesus is the right Way. Only God, by His Spirit, can cleanse and indwell a youth creating in him new desires. You're thinking, *I know that,* but are we practicing what we know? How often are you praying for lost teenagers? You know the saying, "little prayer, little power." Whether you are proclaiming to one, ten, a hundred, or thousands—pray. "For though we walk in the flesh, we do not war according to the flesh, for the weapons of our warfare are not of the flesh, but divinely powerful for the destruction of fortresses" (2 Cor. 10:3-4). Neither you or I will ever win the battles that only He can win.

We must begin to spend as much time praying as we do planning. We must begin to spend as much time praying as we do in activities. We must accept the fact that we can't change lost youth, but God can. We must make prayer a priority in our lives and ministries to see the realization of our Lord's promise, "Now to Him who is able to do exceeding abundantly beyond all that we ask or think, according to the power that works within us" (Eph. 3:20). Pray before you proclaim.

Walk the Talk

Until someone becomes a living demonstration of the Christian life, most youth will have deaf ears to our verbal explanations of the gospel. The old saying continues to ring true: put up or shut up.

The apostle John said it this way, "the one who says he abides in Him ought himself to walk in the same manner as He walked" (1 John 2:6). The Greek word for *walk* is *peripateo* which literally means walk around; it is a metaphor for the way we live.

T.B. Maston underscored the importance of how we live by declaring, "the proof of what we believe is in the lives we live."[26] Reflecting the principle of "more is caught than is taught," Maston suggests: "We should recognize that many whose lives we touch will only know as much about the Lord and Savior as we reveal to them in the lives we live. Dare we ask the question and seek to answer it honestly: What kind of representative of Jesus are we to loved ones, neighbors, friends, and casual acquaintances? Possibly many of them never read the Bible except what they read in our lives. How accurate a translation are we of the kind of life Jesus lived while He lived on earth the kind of life He still attempts to live in and through you and me? Do they read in us an accurate or a garbled translation?"[27]

Let us so "walk in the same manner as He walked," that we will not only live out the power of the gospel but also possess an unexplainable boldness and contagious joy in proclaiming the gospel. Walk your talk.

Wounded Healers

This way can transform your life and ministry. It is the way God chose for His Son to redeem the world. "But He was pierced [wounded] through for our transgressions,/He was crushed for our iniquities;/The chastening for our well-being fell upon Him,/And by His scourging we are healed" (Isa. 53:5).

It's unrealistic to think anyone has all the answers or has it "all together" every moment of every day. Yet, how many of us live in the prisons of disguise and denial, pretending we have it "all together"? Pharisees never have nor ever will experience and enjoy the power of God.

The apostle Paul declared,

that I may know Him, and the power of His resurrection and the fellowship of His sufferings, being conformed to His death; in order that I may attain to the resurrection from the dead. Not that I have already obtained it, or have already become perfect, but I press on in order that I may lay hold of that for which also I was laid hold of by Christ Jesus. Brethren, I do not regard myself as having laid hold of it yet; but one thing I do: forgetting what lies behind and reaching forward to what lies ahead, I press on toward the goal for the prize of the upward call of God in Christ Jesus (Phil. 3:10-14).

Today's teenager has great difficulty trusting people who act like they have all the answers. Are you that kind of youth leader? Some pastors and many parents would like for their youth leader to have it all together with all the answers. However, it is not our strength that makes the difference in people's lives. It is His strength. When Jesus Christ is Lord of our lives, there is the recognition we cannot fight our own battles. Christ, and He alone, must keep us. We in our own strength are unable to do battle with the enemy and win. "Be strong in the Lord, and in the strength of His might" (Eph. 6:10) is the only way to win the battles of life.

Once we discover His strength, we can dare to share our needs, struggles, fears, and tears with the attitude, "Not that I have already obtained it, or have already become perfect, but I press on in order that I may lay hold of that for which also I was laid hold of by Christ Jesus" (Phil. 3:12). Oh how God blesses His strength so much more than our feeble efforts to be strong. As I have been willing to be honest with youth in my weaknesses, always dependent upon His strength, I have been amazed with the results. But isn't that what Jesus meant when He said, "Let your light [Jesus is the Light] shine before men in such a way that they may see your good works, and glorify your Father who is in heaven" (Matt. 5:16). Be a wounded healer.

Challenge and Expect the Best

Is it any wonder our half-hearted challenges of, "If you would like Jesus as your Savior, lift your hand while no one is looking" only results in half-hearted commitments. Why not ask with no music playing, and everyone looking, "who will be willing to stand up saying, I give my life to Jesus Christ. If no one else stands, I will stand alone. If no one else lives a pure life at school, I will in Jesus Christ. If no one else will witness, I will. My life is His. If that is your commitment, stand. Of course, many will not stand to such a challenge. Yet, the ones that do will "[turn this] world upside down" (Acts 17:6, KJV) even as those first disciples of Jesus did.

To challenge, expecting the best, is to challenge even as our Lord:

And he was saying to them all, "If anyone wishes to come after Me, let him deny himself, and take up his cross daily, and follow Me. For whoever wishes to save his life shall lose it, but whoever loses his life for My sake, he is one who will save it. For what is a man profited if he gains the whole world, and loses or forfeits himself? For whoever is ashamed of Me and My words, of him will the Son of Man be ashamed when He comes in His glory, and the glory of the Father and of the holy angels" (Luke 9:23-26).

Whoever does not carry his own cross and come after Me cannot be My disciple. For which one of you, when he wants to build a tower, does not first sit down and calculate the cost, to see if he has enough to complete it? Otherwise, when he has laid a foundation, and is not able to finish, all who observe it begin to ridicule him, saying, "This man began to build and was not able to finish." Or what king, when he sets out to meet another king in battle, will not first sit down and take counsel whether he is strong enough with ten thousand men to encounter the one coming against him with twenty thousand? Or else, while the other is still far away, he sends a delegation and asks terms of peace. So therefore, no one of you can be My disciple who does not give up all his own possessions. Therefore, salt is good; but if even salt has become tasteless, with what will be seasoned? It is useless either for the soil or for the manure pile; it is thrown out. He who has ears to hear, let him hear (Luke 14:27-33).

Giving our lives to Jesus Christ as Lord and Savior is the highest privilege of life. He is a King who saves us lost and condemned sinners from the penalty and power of sin. By His infinite grace and mercy, Jesus gives us the opportunity to tap His infinite resources. In those resources, we then can move from lives of mediocrity to lives of eternal significance.

We are saved from the impossibilities of life to "I can do all things through Him who strengthens me" (Phil. 4:13). Such a high privilege demands the high cost of our lives. Challenge, expecting the best.

Check Your Life-Style

Could it be the attitude of rebellion that says, "God, I don't need You or anyone else to tell me how to live my life," is the foundation for all sin? Consider how it robs each of us of our potential. How many times have you intended to accomplish something good and great only to quit because the costs were higher than at first anticipated?

You might prefer the word *unyielding* to *rebellion*. Whatever you want to call it, do something about it. Don't use the excuse, "I don't have time." We must differentiate between the urgent and the important.

Let's evaluate. Are you spending time alone daily with your Heavenly Father, learning of Him in the study and meditation of His Word? If you are married and have children, when was the last time you spent quality time with those you say you "love the most?" How long has it been since you shared a verbal witness of Jesus to a lost person, one on one? When was the last time you prayed with your children; with your wife; with a special friend, other than at mealtimes? When was the last time you relaxed with friends? What was the last book you read for personal growth other than the Bible? What youth strategy have you recently studied that could help you more effectively proclaim the gospel to youth?

God did not intend for any of us to become a museum piece, placed and anchored on an old shelf to collect dust. Let's make an impact on a world that isn't quite sure which end is up. Give yourself a checkup.

Never Give Up

Growing up, I often heard my parents, teachers, and pastors talk about potential: the potential of a child, the potential of a program, or the potential of a church. I have learned as important as potential is, it is persevering discipline that produces potential's fruit. Otherwise, potential is only worth about five cents a ton.

How long has it been since you felt like quitting? Consider your obstacles: arousing a sleeping church, immature saints, an indifferent world, Satan's opposition, and inward discouragement. *Youth leaders quit all the time,* you may think, *why not me?* No wonder the little voice that whispers, "I think I will just quit" is no stranger.

If you are in the pit of despair and discouragement, change your perspective. Look at Jesus. Set your heart and mind once again upon Him rather than the circumstances that defeated you.

When I was twenty-six, I nearly "quit the ministry." Graduating from seminary with all my ideas and "vast" part-time experience of college and seminary days, I knew I would change the world in less than five years. Following the first year of growth and "honeymoon excitement" at my church, attendance stunted and gradually critical remarks began to come. After almost three years, one brother informed me "that I should leave the church, because I was the poorest example of what a music and youth minister could possibly be." It amazes me now, how I allowed a few negative remarks to deafen my ears to the positive comments and to the good things God was doing. Yet, there I was, feeling sorry for myself: unappreciated, overworked, and underpaid. I was ready to quit.

After a few weeks of complaining, contemplating, and crying, God finally changed my perspective. He got my heart once again set upon Him. He reminded me how, "He came to His own, and those who were His own did not receive Him" (John 1:11). God reminded me that He remained faithful and loving, regardless of inconsistencies and failures. Even though others had failed and would fail me in the future, He assured me that He never had and never would.

I heard His words, "Follow Me." I said, "Yes Sir." Through the tough times of life, the unexpected crises that knock us down and cover us in doubt and discouragement, He still calls, "Follow Me." We must say, "Yes Sir."

Because we are called of God to proclaim the gospel to the youth of America and this world, the only way we can possibly fail to fulfill our calling is:

1. If we do nothing about accomplishing our task;
2. If we quit somewhere along the way;

3. If we accept failure as final.

Yes, it seems impossible. That's great! We have a God who specializes in the impossible. Let's grow up in Christ and leave doing the easy or comfortable for what He has called us to do, proclaim the gospel.

If we should dare to make a difference for Jesus Christ in this world, be assured, all of hell will break loose (as if it hasn't already). But remember, the good news is that all of heaven is backing us up.

Remember Paul's challenging command: "Therefore, my beloved brethren, be steadfast, immovable, always abounding in the work of the Lord, knowing that your toil is not in vain in the Lord" (1 Cor. 15:58). Don't ever give up!

Ideas

If you are serious about the task of youth evangelism then consider implementing one or more of the following. Do not just read the list and say "I wish I could do that," but get your calendar before reading the list and say "I am going to do something in order to better reach youth for Jesus."

1. Attend a youth evangelism school or other training that will help you make evangelism a priority in your church's youth ministry.

2. Set a goal of reading several books on evangelism between now and next year.

3. Get into your car, drive around your community, and observe the places you see youth. Do this a second time, only invite another youth leader to go with you. Write these places down and begin to ask God what would He have you do to reach these youth.

4. Conduct several private interviews with youth, parents, and youth leaders. Ask these individuals what they would do as a youth leader to reach lost youth.

5. Conduct an anonymous survey through the schools in your area. Ask teens to reply to the following questions. Share the answers with other youth leaders in your church.

   a. Do you know anyone who takes drugs?
   b. Have you ever taken drugs?

c. Have you ever tried alcohol?
d. How often do you drink alcoholic beverages?
e. Have you ever been drunk?
f. Have you ever thought about suicide?
g. When was the last time you went to church?

6. Conduct a deductive Bible study on the life of Jesus in a home near the local school. Identify the youth who are leaders in the school and personally invite them.

7. Decide to take some classes from a college or seminar near your home in the area of theology or counseling.

8. Find an organization in your community that works with teenagers and get involved.

9. Ask another youth leader to be your prayer partner to pray specifically over the names of lost teenagers.

10. Organize and teach a potential youth leadership class in your church. The focus of the class should be: "How can we do a better job of evangelizing lost youth?"

Resources

Home Mission Board, 1350 Spring St., NW, Atlanta, GA.
Prayer for Spiritual Awakening: Youth Edition
WOW Event Leader's Guide,
Promise of Life: Youth Adult Partnership Revival Planbook
Baptist Sunday School Board, 127 Ninth Ave. N., Nashville, TN.
DiscipleYouth I Kit and *DiscipleYouth II Kit,*
YouthSearch: A DiscipleYouth Witnessing Plan

Notes

1. Tipper Gore, *Raising PG Kids in an X-Rated Society,* (Nashville: Abingdon Press, 1987), p. 43.
2. "Women Who Maintain Families," *Facts on U.S. Working Women,* U.S. Department of Labor, Women's Bureau, Fact Sheet no. 86-2, 1986.
3. Daniel P. Moynihan, *Family and Nation,* (San Diego: Harcourt Brace Jovanovich, 1986), p. 46.
4. "Women Who Maintain Families, *Facts on U.S. Working Women.*

5. "Half of Mothers with Children Under 3 Now in Labor Force," New, Bureau of Labor Statistics, U. S. Department of Labor, 20 August 1986.

6. Gore, p. 44.

7. *Group* Magazine, "News, Trends and Tips, *Family Violence,* Vol. 11, No. 8 October 1985), p. 10.

8. Nelson Price, "Pornography and Sexual Violence: Booming Business Victimizing Children, Women and Men," *Engage/Social Action* July/August 1985, p. 13.

9. Gore, p. 137.

10. Gore, p. 166.

11. *Group* Magazine, "News, Trends and Tips, *Drugs #1 School Problem,* vol. 13, no. 2 January 1987), p. 25.

12. Gore, p. 137.

13. Conversation with Dr. Arthur Mallory, Commissioner of Education for the State of Missouri, January, 1987.

14. United States Summary, May 83 Series, PC80-1-B1. U.S. Department of Commerce, Bureau of the Census. U.S. Government Printing Office.

15. Gore, p. 162.

16. Jan Fowler, *Teenage Pregnancy: Statistics, Current Research, Federal Legislation,* Congressional Research Service, 1 June 1982, p. 6.

17. Jean Seligmann et al., "The Game Teen-Agers Play," *Newsweek* (4 February 1985), p. 72.

18. David Gelman et al., "A Nasty New Epidemic" *Newsweek* (1 September 1980), p. 48.

19. Seligmann, "A Nasty New Epidemic," p. 72.

20. Jane Murray, "Teen Pregnancy: an international perspective," *Planned Parenthood Review* (Winter 1986), p. 20.

21. Alfred B. DelBello, "Needed: A U. S. Commission on Teen-Age Suicide," *New York Times,* 12 September 1984, section A, p. 31.

22. Gore, p. 103.

23. Group Magazine, "News, Trends, and Tips," High Achievers Consider Suicide, Vol. 13, No. 4, March/April 1987), p. 12.

24. United States Summary, May 83. series PC 80-1-B1. By the U.S. Dept. of Commerce, Bureau of the Census. U. S. Government Printing Office. Based on a 1980 census of ages 6-12 which would be today's teenagers.

25. Based on the Uniform Church Letter. Data supplied by the Research Division of the Home Mission Board, May 1987.

26. T. B. Maston, *To Walk as He Walked* (Nashville: Broadman Press, 1985) p. 30.

27. Maston, p. 46.

4
Youth Leadership in Evangelism

Richard Everett

Introduction

The paragraphs that you are about to read are a reflection of nearly twenty-three years of ministry; ten years in the pastorate working closely with youth, and thirteen years as director of personal evangelism in North Carolina. This chapter reflects many sources. I am grateful for their impact on my life. These individuals are too numerous to name, and so I give credit to all of them.

There is a lot of talk about how to win our youth to Christ. How do we help them face today's world? How do we disciple them in the teachings of Jesus? How do we to talk to youth about such key subjects as love, dating, sex, friendship, and peer pressure? How will we help youth cope with their world without turning to drugs? Youth, for the most part, are going to model themselves after the world. Articles appear weekly in the leading newsmagazines dealing with youth problems. Almost without exception adults are involved in leading youth into these alternate life-styles. All too frequently we read the stories of youth turning to drugs, prostitution, theft, and sometimes murder because of neglect or abuse by parents. In some cases youth see their parents participate in such life-styles. Adults seem completely to blame. However, the Scripture says "Train up a child in the way that he should go: and when he is old, he will not depart from it" (Prov. 22:6 KJV).

Therefore, adults who live in the same world as youth must demonstrate a personal life-style that is evangelistic. If our youth are to learn to be evangelistic in their life-styles, they must have some role models. Youth are not involved in personal evangelism because they lack role models. If a youth leader does not share his or her faith, then how can we expect youth to do so? It is extremely difficult to lead someone where you have not gone.

Biblical Basis

Our biggest problem is we believe but we don't live what we believe. Jesus said, "Not everyone who says to me, 'Lord, Lord,' will enter the kingdom of heaven; but he who does the will of My Father who is in heaven" (Matt. 7:21). This is not referring to a salvation by works. Jesus does not teach we gain salvation because we work. We work because of our salvation. Our task is not to do just anything but to do the will of God.

A Christian is one who not only believes the teachings of Christ, but also one who behaves like Christ. We are defined by what we do. Suppose someone asks, "What are you doing?" You would answer, that you are talking, walking, or whatever it happens to be. We define ourselves by what we are doing. A Christian is under the lordship of Christ, doing what the Lord commands. Today we have an abundance of beliefs. The question, however, that really makes the difference is: Do your actions indicate your beliefs?

One theologian told about walking down the street in his home-town one day. As he walked past a store, he noticed a sign that said, "Fresh Bread for Sale." He thought, *The last thing I need is bread because I just had breakfast,* but as he walked his mind raced. He could see that loaf of bread being taken from the oven, butter and jelly placed on it. It got the best of him, so he turned around and went back to the store. He entered and asked the lady behind the counter, "I would like to buy a loaf of fresh bread." She replied to him that they did not sell fresh bread. He said, "But the sign in your window said there was fresh bread for sale." She laughed and said, "Oh, we don't sell bread; we paint signs." Do we just wear signs that say we are Christians or do our lives indicate that this is what we are?

Jesus' Plan of Leadership

Let's look now at several characteristics of our Lord's plan of leadership. Jesus truly was the Master Leader. In the New Testament, leadership is synonymous with discipleship. Remember discipleship is not something about which we have a choice. It is a direct commandment of the Lord.

> And Jesus came up and spoke to them saying, "All authority has been given to Me in heaven and on earth. Go therefore and make disciples of all the nations, baptizing them in the name of the Father and the Son and the Holy Spirit, teaching them to observe all that I commanded you; and lo, I am with you always, even to the end of the age" (Matt. 28:18-20)

Jesus' commandment was to make disciples. If we do not do this we are only making people, like newborn babes, long for spiritual milk (1 Pet 2:2). We have enough shallow Christians today. New Christians need some solid Christian role models to follow. Joseph was a godly man and he followed God; yet, he didn't train anyone to take his place. The result was that Israel became a nation in slavery. Joshua learned from Moses but failed to intentionally model leadership for anyone else. Therefore, when Joshua died Israel entered into a devastating era of weak leadership. Jesus, on the other hand, poured His life into His disciples. Paul also trained those who followed him. They, in turn, went out to establish new churches and to grow more disciples. "And the things which you have heard from me in the presence of many witnesses, these entrust to faithful men, who will be able to teach others also" (2 Tim. 2:2).

If this style of leadership is so important, then what are its basic characteristics?

1. *I do it.* Jesus let His life reflect that He walked with God. He lived dynamically. He helped people, prayed, performed miracles, loved, and touched people. Jesus taught by example. If youth are going to learn to minister, they must see leaders living a ministry in their daily lives.

2. *I do it and they watch me.* Not only did Jesus do things alone, but He gathered the twelve around Him and every place He went, they

went. Every time He performed a miracle, they were with Him. When He loved someone, they were with Him. When He prayed, they were with Him. Why do you think they asked Jesus on an occasion, "Lord, teach us to pray"? Of course they had been with Him when He prayed. Jesus said, "Follow Me" and they followed Him.

3. *They do it and I am with them.* "And He called the twelve together and gave them power and authority over all the demons, and to heal diseases. And He sent them out to proclaim the kingdom of God and to perform healing" (Luke 9:1-2) He later sent out the twelve "as lambs in the midst of wolves" (Luke 10:1-20) Jesus was never really far away. If they failed, they could have come back to Jesus for help; but they succeeded. They realized their real power was in the name of Jesus, and they came back with joy. It did not mean they were ready to turn the world upside down yet, but they had come a long way from fishing boats and tax tables to serving alongside the Lord. There is also a very important principle to learn in this passage from Luke. If you examine it carefully, you would not have any written confirmation that, as those people went out, they led one person to Christ. However, it is recorded that they had power over demons (v. 17) and that Satan took a fall (v. 18). They came back rejoicing because they had done what Jesus had commanded them to do. Youth leaders can always rejoice when they have been obedient to the commandment of Jesus.

4. *They do it.* In the three years the disciples followed Jesus, they experienced much. They knew the joy of casting out demons in Jesus' name, and they also knew the disappointment of the cross. They had experienced real life with Him; however, one final step had to be taken before Jesus' leadership/discipleship ministry was to be complete. As Jesus ascended into heaven, He gave them the promise that there was more to come. He promised His Holy Spirit to empower them, to motivate them. The disciples were left in the power of the Spirit to do the ministry that Jesus had done. He is in the background giving power to carry on His ministry, a ministry even greater than His. "Truly, truly, I say to you, he who believes in Me, the works that

I do shall he do also; and greater works than these shall he do; because I go to the Father" (John 14:12).

Implementation

Life-style Evangelism

While the term life-style evangelism has been used frequently it may be a misnomer. However, can evangelism be anything but a life-style? By using this term, we may be admitting a very serious problem among our concepts of the Christian faith. It may be that we have attempted to make evangelism something other than our day-to-day experience. While we have many witness-training programs, we are not to limit evangelism to those special times of training, a single night of visitation each week, or especially a time in the spring or in the fall prior to a revival.

We disavow the fact we are interested in people only as numbers; yet we visit lost people only during a revival meeting. Long before we ever confront them with the gospel, they know we are having a special meeting because this is the only time they are visited. We would be angry if someone suggested that all we were trying to do was to carve a few notches on our spiritual guns. However, our actions indicate that is exactly what we are doing.

The term life-style evangelism can be defined by the fellow who said "evangelism is one beggar telling another beggar where to find bread." Before evangelism becomes my life-style, I must understand what has taken place in my life. I must come to grips with the fact I have sinned and disobeyed the law of God. Because Jesus Christ has extended life to me, I then want to extend life to others through Him.

In the 1960s a very common expression was, "I witness by living the Christian life." Nevertheless, when was the last time you led a person to faith in Jesus Christ strictly through your actions? How long has it been since someone came running up to you out of breath saying, "I have been watching your life for six months and I am now ready to be saved." That experience has never happened to me. My life is simply not good enough that a person can view my actions alone and be led to Jesus Christ. I must put the words of the gospel with my actions to help them to understand who Jesus Christ is and what He can do for them.

It takes both my words and my actions to give the complete picture. One without the other may well give a person the wrong idea. Today we see people saying the right words but their actions do not support their words. Other people have good actions but never inject the gospel into those actions.

In July 1976 I left my office in downtown Raleigh, North Carolina. As I pulled onto the street at a busy intersection, I noticed the telephone company was working in a manhole in the middle of a busy, six-lane intersection. The traffic lights were of no use because the traffic was being detoured. Standing in the middle of the intersection was a Raleigh policeman. It was amazing! There we were at five o'clock in the afternoon in the middle of the summer with traffic more congested than the Exodus from Egypt. Thousands of people were anxiously leaving the big city to get to the beaches of eastern North Carolina. Many others were anxiously trying to get home for the long weekend.

As I sat and waited my turn in line, I noticed an interesting development. This young policeman, standing in the middle of tens of thousands of tons of steel and anxious people rushing to get where they wanted to go, was actually controlling all of those people by the wave of an arm and the blowing of a whistle. I sat and watched the picture unfold. He would hold up his hand in one direction, wave his arm in another, and the cars would move. With the simple uplifting of an arm, he could stop six lanes of traffic and six others would begin to move. I thought about it. *What would happen if that same young man, instead of wearing the gray-and-blue uniform of the police department, dressed in blue jeans, a T-shirt, tennis shoes, and sunglasses?* Although still a member of the police department, he would not have lasted a minute. He may have been run over! The reason he was able to stand in that position was his *uniform*.

Our lives must wear the "uniform" of Jesus Christ. "Put on the full armor of God, that you may be able to stand firm against the schemes of the devil" (Eph. 6:11). When we do not wear the whole armor of God, then we place ourselves in jeopardy. People will not listen to us, and although they may hear our words, our actions contradict them. If we merely seek to live our faith, people do not know why we do what we do.

Evangelistic Leadership

Perhaps the first question that many of us would ask when approached to lead youth would be, "Who me, a leader? What do I have to say? How can I be prepared to lead youth?"

Every leader in the church has one task. It is the major task and everything—building, activity, and meeting—is designed to accomplish this task. If the church ever stops accomplishing this task then it has stopped being a church. It is the task of evangelism. Thus, the task of all youth leaders is to lead youth to faith in Jesus. We must understand the very basic premise of all Christian work, the salvation experience. What in fact does it mean to be saved? Such words as *regeneration, reconciliation, satisfaction,* and others help to define what it means to be saved. However, have you considered what Jesus did on the cross? Why did He die? He did not die for Himself. He is perfect, He never sinned. He had no need to die. Why did He do this? Jesus died on the cross to make me just like Himself.

Leadership in Christ's Image

"Beloved, now we are children of God, and it has not appeared as yet what we shall be. We know that, when He appears, we shall be like Him, because we shall see Him just as He is" (1 John 3:2). God is in the process of making us like Himself. The first thing a leader must understand is we are created in God's image.

> Then God said, "Let us make man in Our image, according to Our likeness; and let them rule over the fish of the sea and over the birds of the sky and over the cattle and over all the earth, and over every creeping thing that creeps on the earth." And God created man in His own image, in the image of God He created him; male and female He created them (Gen. 1:26-27).

On Sunday evening, March 24, 1974, my wife Linda and I went to the Anni Penn Hospital in Reidsville, North Carolina. We went to the hospital for a specific purpose. Linda was about to give birth to our child. Beth was born and our purpose was accomplished at 3:01 AM, March 25. At 7:00 AM, Linda and I decided that we both needed some rest. I left her room and began walking down the hall. As pastor of Calvary Baptist Church in Reidsville I had walked that hallway many times after visiting other patients. As I walked, I was compelled to stop once more at the big nursery window. While gazing upon that small mass of flesh, nine pounds, fourteen ounces, whom we had named Beth, I felt a hand on my shoulder. I turned and saw a nurse. She spotted Beth on the baby bed, paused momentarily and then said some of the greatest words any father could hope to hear, "Richard, she looks just like you." Bless Beth's heart, she could not help it, but I would not take anything for those words.

Approximately five months later while working on a study in Christian evangelism and discipleship and seeking to understand what the Great Commission in Matthew 28:18-20 really meant, I began to understand in a new way what God was saying to me. In the passage to which we referred in Genesis 1:26-27, we noted that we were created in God's image. Jesus expanded this when He said to His disciples we should make other disciples. Therefore, to fulfill God's image in my life I must be a disciple of Jesus Christ. This means not only that I do certain things He taught for my own life, but I must help make disciples of others as well. Our youth need Christian models and must see Jesus in us.

Adults are unwilling to accept youth leadership positions because they do not understand the concept of being created in the image of God.

Now the word of the Lord came to me saying, "Before I formed you in the womb I knew you,/And before you were born I consecrated you;/I have appointed you a prophet to the nations."/Then I said "Alas, Lord God!/Behold, I do not know how to speak,/Because I am a youth."/But the Lord said to me,/"Do not say, 'I am a youth,'/Because everywhere I send you, you shall go,/And all that I command you, you shall speak./Do not be afraid of them./For I am with you to deliver you," declares the Lord (Jer. 1:4-8).

The late W. E. Richardson, chairman of the Bible Department at Carson-Newman College, made Jeremiah live for me. God explained to Jeremiah that before his parents ever knew they would give birth to a child, God had a plan. The words "I knew" in verse 5 are very powerful, denoting the most intimate of relationships. Realizing God knew me before anyone else helps me to understand I am important.

Leadership Guided by God

God is watching over me to carry out His work. "Then the Lord said to me, 'You have seen well for I am watching over My word to perform it' " (Jer. 1:12). "Behold, He who keeps Israel Will neither slumber nor sleep" (Ps. 121:4). As a leader God has created you in His image to do His work, and He will never leave nor forsake you.

God gave His son to redeem us. Therefore we have no right to put down ourselves or any other person. There is nothing greater than knowing and seeking to carry out God's will. A youth leader must be willing to do anything God wills.

I have never done well on what is commonly called a standardized test. The last time that I took an I.Q. test my score was reported as 92. During my high school years, I took every aptitude test available. During college I took the Graduate Record Examination for entrance into graduate school. I was a grader for W. E. Richardson. I went to his office to grade papers one day, and he was waiting to discuss my G.R.E. scores. Jokingly I said, "My two scores added together would not equal 800." He looked at me with a certain amount of surprise and said, "Have you already seen these scores?" I said, "No, sir, but I have been seeing them for the eight years. I've found I scored low on an aptitude test." My classroom work was at a high level but I had to accept that I had a slower learning ability. This made it difficult for me in school, because I am not a good reader. God gives to each of us what we need to accomplish His purpose. The point is we should not seek to compare ourselves with another person. We are not to try to overcome or to defeat another person. We must seek to be what God had in mind when He created us.

Self-Accepting Leadership

Each of us must learn to receive ourselves. Rejection breeds rejection. If you reject me; I am going to reject you. We reject other people if they come to us in a way that rubs us wrong. If you want to be a good leader, it is necessary to receive people. You meet them where they are, and you seek to lead them to a higher plane. If, however, you do not like yourself and do not receive yourself, it is nearly impossible for you to receive anyone else except superficially. You may have a working relationship, but you will never fully appreciate that person. You will never be open and honest because you are afraid to be open with yourself.

The greatest thing a person can do outside of his personal relationship with Jesus Christ is to receive himself and thereby to open himself to other people. The principle of receiving one another is one of the greatest traits any leader can have. So salvation does not merely get us entrance into heaven. It revolutionizes our life. As a leader, let your salvation experience carry you into exciting new dimensions.

Right Theology and Motive

Why did God create mankind and what is His desire for all people? God wants all people to have eternal life. "For God so loved the world that He gave His only begotten Son, that whoever believes in Him should not perish, but have eternal life" (John 3:16). "But the gift of God is eternal life through Jesus Christ our Lord" (Rom. 6:23, KJV). It is God's will that lost youth be saved. A youth leader must be totally consumed with the task of declaring the gospel so youth can respond and be saved. A youth with the gift of eternal life has something to live for. Each day is new and exciting.

If there is one area that has been greatly misunderstood, it is the New Testament concept of repentance. Disciples of Jesus Christ must have a firm conviction of their repentance from sin, a certainty of their faith in Jesus Christ, and their commitment to the lordship of Christ in their lives. People think of repentance as "don't do this" or "stop doing that." This is too superficial and that is probably the reason that we are not growing as we should in the Christian faith. Repentance means to turn away from one's sin. Without repentance there can be no salvation. Repentance taken literally from the Greek means to change your mind about who Jesus Christ is. "Have this attitude in yourselves which was also in Christ Jesus" (Phil. 2:5).

Christians are to take on the mind of Christ. If you have the mind of Christ you will stop doing some things not because someone says don't but because you cannot have the mind of Christ and continue to do things that would destroy His body. If we truly repent of sin and take on the mind of Christ, we will learn how to live like Jesus. As we study the Bible, we learn the body is the temple of the Holy Spirit. God dwells in me, and therefore, if I really want to follow Jesus I cannot do anything to my body that would seek to hinder it, because this is where God lives.

Perhaps you are thinking, *but I would never drink alcohol or take drugs.* If we fill our bodies with junk food, never exercise, and cause fat to accumulate around our hearts, thus shortening our lives, we are guilty of sin. *Repentance* is not a negative word but a positive one. We must take a look at sin and repent. "For all have sinned, and come short of the glory of God" (Rom. 3:23, KJV). A youth leader must lead youth in repentance by being a model.

Another important area that youth leaders need to consider is motive. "Why am I attempting to lead youth?" "What really is your motive?" "Are you doing your youth work in an effort to promote yourself?" "Are you working with youth as a stepping-stone to so called greater areas of ministry?" "Are you working with youth simply in order to have the largest youth group in your association or perhaps the state convention?" Are you ministering to youth out of a genuine experience of repentance or is it for some other motive?

Right Priorities

What is your number-one priority? Is it to have that largest youth group, or is it to be totally open and available to what God wants you to do?

But whatever things were gain to me, those things I have counted as

loss for the sake of Christ. More than that, I count all things to be loss
in view of the surpassing value of knowing Christ Jesus my Lord, for
whom I have suffered the loss of all things, and count them but rubbish
in order that I may gain Christ (Phil. 3:7-8).

Paul said his priority was to know Christ. You might assume Paul
knew God because he was a Christian. Paul was not referring only
to salvation but a day-to-day relationship with Him. There is no
more intimate relationship between husband and wife than to know
each other. This is what Paul was trying to get across. To know Christ
is the number-one priority in our lives. What do the youth in your
group see and hear each time you stand before them, sit with them,
or lead them in other ways?

Too many leaders are trying to grow in their relationship to Jesus
Christ in light of their ministry. To put it another way, some are
trying to be intimate with Jesus through ministry. The opposite is
true. We must be intimate with Jesus so we have something for
ministry. It is an expensive risk to try to teach youth while trying to
hear God's Word. We must commit ourselves to a time alone with
Him to know precisely what to do and say at those valuable times
of working with youth.

Paul set an example in saying his number-one priority was to know
God. Unfortunately, we live in a day that assumes as long as I am
busy doing church work I must be all right. Our biggest sin is we get
too busy doing good things for God, not the things He wants done.
This is dangerous because we don't have any guilt feelings; after all,
we did something good for God today.

The real issue is not whether I was doing something good for God,
but was I permitting God to do through me what He really wanted
to get done in my life? We have made action or activities synonymous with obedience. It is good for us to be active ourselves and to
involve youth, but we must remember that just because we take
youth on trips does not mean we are making disciples of them. Youth
need a leader who will not model working for the Lord but one who
does works that are God given.

Leaders Need a Current Relationship

Some churches have great youth mission trips, but years after those events the youth and leaders still labor under the shadow of those experiences. If we go on big mission trips and do work in other parts of the country, and yet return not involving ourselves in ministry to win the lost of our own high schools and communities back home, have we really been obedient to the Master? Some of us are guilty of living on a past experience only instead of growing.

A man painting stripes by hand on a highway after three days was called in by his boss. The boss noted that the first day the man had painted five miles of stripes. The second day he had painted three miles and the third day one mile. He asked the worker if there was some problem. The worker responded that there was no problem; why did he ask? The supervisor then recounted the man's work record. The worker looked back at his supervisor and said, "I can explain that. You see, each day I just keep getting farther and farther away from the paint bucket."

I'm afraid that this may well be the case in many of our lives. We are trying to minister today out of an experience that happened years ago. We are trying to excite our youth out of something that happened a long time ago.

The Christian life is dynamic. It is exciting every day and, if you are going to be the kind of leader that your youth need, you must be growing in your relationship every single day. Your number-one priority is knowing God. When youth listen to you, they will listen to someone who has an up-to-date relationship with Jesus Christ. We need to remember that, in the Gospels, Jesus taught us that He spent time with the Father and then came back to the people to share what the Father wanted them to hear. It is no different today. If the real message that people need to hear, and especially youth, is what God the Father wants them to hear, then the leaders must spend time with the Father. He is the only one who knows what youth really need.

Steps to Evangelistic Leadership

We must spend time alone with God every day. This means not only time away from the day-to-day routine, but it must be a time in which we concentrate upon Him. This is not preparing a lesson for the youth meeting. In the spring of 1977 a Southern Airways DC9 Jetliner was on a flight from Huntsville, Alabama, to Atlanta, Georgia. Near the northwest Georgia town of Dallas, the plane encountered a severe hailstorm. The hail was so large that eventually it knocked out both engines on the DC9 jet. Losing altitude it made a turn, went back, and attempted a landing on a two-lane highway near Dallas. In the crash almost everyone on board died as well as a few people on the ground.

The next night as national news media described the scene, they said had the plane not made its turn and continued straight ahead it could have made it to Dobbins Air Force Base near Marietta, Georgia. Now the question immediately arises, Did the pilot make an error? The answer is no. You see, when both of those jet engines stopped turning there was no power on board the aircraft, but it only took less than a minute to get the aircraft converted over to the back-up system. During that sixty seconds of no power they made the fateful turn. It was also during that sixty seconds that the Atlanta air-traffic controller was radioing, "Don't turn, go straight ahead, we calculate you can make it to the air force base." But with no power, the radio was silent and the pilot never received the message.

When we don't spend time alone with the Father every day, we place ourselves on a collision course. If I don't spend time with Him, He cannot prepare me today to face the next event. We must spend time alone with God if we would know Him.

Secondly, grow in your relationship to Jesus Christ to the point you have a broken spirit. A broken spirit means you are willing to say yes to God before He ever poses the question. When you trust Jesus Christ as your Lord, then there are some horizons in your Christian life that defy description.

Third you must seek God with a pure heart. All of us have sinned, but we have also been redeemed. However, there is also a problem in the lives of many Christians. They refuse to confess their sin and ask for forgiveness. It is impossible for one to know God as Paul was referring with unforgiven or unconfessed sin in their lives.

We must not blame our sin on someone else. Have you ever been guilty of saying, "I would not have said that if she hadn't made me mad," or, "I wouldn't have done that if he hadn't done this?" As a Christian, and especially as a Christian leader, you must be willing to recognize, acknowledge, and confess your sin. We all like to blame our sin on someone else. If we sin, we *choose* to sin. There is no one anywhere who can make us sin. Regardless of what it is, no one can make us sin. The only thing another person can do is to bring out of us a sin that we have permitted to have a breeding ground.

If we don't permit the sin of lust to get a foothold, then we are stronger when sexual temptation comes. What is the best way not to spill water out of a glass? The answer, "Have an empty glass." If the glass is empty you could turn it upside down and no water will spill. If we do not permit sin to have a foothold or a breeding place in our lives, we are not going to do those things.

> You brood of vipers, how can you, being evil, speak what is good? For the mouth speaks out of that which fill the heart. The good man out of his good treasure brings forth what is good and the evil man out of his evil treasure brings forth what is evil (Matt. 12:34-35).

If we don't let these sins grow in our lives, we are not going to do them.

Fourth, seek God's face and not just His hand. God is not a giant aspirin. Some try to keep God in their spiritual medicine cabinet and break off a chunk of God to get a solution to their problems. God wants to solve our problems. He wants to help, but He wants us to appreciate Him and love Him. When my daughter was two years old she would meet me at the door as I arrived home from a trip and say, "Daddy, what did you bring me?" Do we treat God like that? Do we really care about God before we have a hurt or want something?

Youth need a leader who will model for them the practice of seeking God's face and not just His hands. The Bible says, in order to have power we must learn to rejoice in Him. "Wilt Thou not

Thyself revive us again, That Thy people may rejoice in Thee?" (Ps. 85:6) Could it be the reason we are not experiencing growth in our spiritual lives is because the only time we approach God is when we want something? If God only gives us our wants we will only talk about what God has done instead of rejoicing in Him.

Conclusion

In the 1920s, a young man was working in a switch tower beside the Southern Railway in the little town of Philadelphia, Tennessee. There was a side track that he operated for the switching of cars. One night, two locomotives pulling passenger trains full of people passed Knoxville and Chattanooga heading toward each other on the same track at full steam. The man in the switch tower had to make a decision. You might think, *Well, he had the side track; let them pass each other.* The only problem was that the side track was loaded with railroad work cars full of sleeping workmen. So he had to make a decision. *Do I let two passenger trains fully loaded at full steam hit head on or do I run one train in on the side track?* Either way someone was going to die. How did he make his decision? Were there fewer workmen than there were passengers on the other train? What consolation is it if you make that kind of decision?

He made his decision. He threw the switch to run one of the trains in on the work train. A lot of people were injured and killed that night. How did he make his decision? Did he decide there were fewer people on the work train than there were on the fully loaded passenger train? What real consolation is there to that? I have often wondered why and how he made that decision. The town was my hometown and the man was my great-grandfather. My great-grandfather held in his hands the lives of all of those people. His choice meant death to some but life to others. As a youth leader you will also present choices to your youth. You have a chance to offer eternal life to youth.

The essence of our ministry must be to present the gospel of Jesus Christ to youth in a clear and effective manner. A manner that would help them to become obedient and in time become leaders of others. We must help youth to understand that Jesus is not a mere additive to life, but He *is* life. You and I must confront youth with the gospel of Jesus Christ because we know that without Christ priorities are not in order. We must make whatever commitment is necessary so that they will have the opportunity to respond to Jesus. "I can do all things through Him who strengthens me" (Phil. 4:13). You are motivated by the highest of motives—truth and love. Go teach, lead, model, and disciple that someday we see reproduced another person who follows Jesus Christ. Remember the words of God to Jeremiah. "Be not afraid of their faces: for I am with thee to deliver thee, saith the Lord (Jer. 1:8, KJV). "And they shall fight against thee, but they shall not prevail against thee; for I am with thee, saith the Lord, to deliver thee" (v. 19, KJV).

Ideas

1. Take a piece of paper and write down the place and time you will meet God each day and attach this to your bathroom mirror.
2. Write on your calendar a time in the next six months for a personal retreat with God.
3. Write out a list of sins and confess these to God.
4. Make a list of the ten youth you know best. Beside each name write something you observe in their life they have learned from your life's model.
5. Conduct a study of this chapter with other youth leaders in your church.
6. Do a Bible study on the word *servant* and see if it gives you any insights into leadership.
7. Write out a list of the biblical characters who were evangelistic and study their leadership qualities.
8. Make a list of people in your church who are evangelistic. Ask them to help you model for youth evangelism.
9. Choose someone you know who has an evangelistic life-style. Interview and spend time with this person.
10. Make a list of youth who need evangelism models.
11. Write out some action plans that will allow youth to watch you as you go about. They need to be with you at times other than church activities.

Resources

Cunningham, Luvern L. and William J. Gephart, *Leadership: The Science and Art Today* (Illinois: F.E. Peacock Publishers, 1973).

Burns, James MacGregor, *Leadership* (New York: Harper and Row Publishers, 1978).

Greenleaf, Robert K., *Servant Leadership* (New York: Paulist Press, 1977).

5
Church Program Organizations
Lonnie Riley

Introduction

The problem of blending church program organizations (CPO's) and youth evangelism has become increasingly apparent. Youth leaders have voiced their frustration with the existing organizations of the church: Bible study, discipleship, missions, and choir. The task is to include evangelism as an integral part of these organizations, which often has been a seemingly insurmountable problem.

In some churches where there is a youth minister or youth director, they have been viewed as an activities coordinator and nothing more. When it is time for a retreat, camp, or mission trip, the youth minister is the one to secure personnel, place, and program. However, when it comes to having input into reaching other youth through these church program organizations, the youth minister is often accused of "stealing turf."

Evangelism is the key that makes a church program organization more than just an organization. When evangelism is added, a church program organization comes alive with growth and excitement. Evangelism helps the organization to look beyond what it is to what it can become. Also, evangelism becomes the common link between the church program organizations.

The key to powerful church program organizations is understanding their role in evangelizing lost young people. This chapter seeks to bring existing church youth organizations together with youth evangelism. Combining the two could bring about one of the greatest spiritual revolutions for youth in many years.

Biblical Basis

God has historically been a God of order and organization. This can be clearly seen in the creation account of Genesis. Mankind, being the crown of God's creation, stands as a living monument to God's order and organization. With all the body's systems and organs, it moves and functions with unparalleled precision.

God uses order and organization to accomplish His purpose of redeeming mankind unto Himself. Both Old and New Testaments attest to the organizational structure and its use in relating us to God. Likewise, working to reach youth through the organizations of the church is God's design and demand if winning youth to Christ is to be effective.

God used organizational structure in the Old and New Testaments to bring about His purpose and plan. In this way, the organizations of the church are a continuation of God using organizational structure. These organizations help to bring lost youth to know Him personally and then grow in the grace of our Lord Jesus Christ.

Old Testament Examples of Using Organization

Organizational use is vividly illustrated in the Old Testament. Moses continually faced complaints from the people of Israel (Num. 11). They were hungry and wanted meat to eat. God had an organizational plan and the need of the people was met.

Joshua succeeded Moses and led the people of Israel on their conquest of the Promised Land. Many obstacles were encountered. In Joshua 6, God again sent His divine directive for the demise of Jericho. This directive contained the organization necessary for God's success. As the people of God used the organization, the purpose of God was accomplished.

More examples are David killing Goliath (1 Sam. 17), Joshua's strategy for destroying Ai (Josh. 8), Elijah's defeat of the Baal prophets (1 Kings 18), Hezekiah's remedy for reformation (2 Chronicles 29), Nehemiah's bold building of the wall (Neh. 2—3), Jeremiah's unusual utterances portrayed in life (yoke, Jer. 28; potter, Jer. 18). God has always organized His people for the redemptive task.

New Testament Examples of Using Organization

Organization was clearly a part of Jesus' strategy during His ministry. In the choosing of the twelve, Jesus' organization and its use are beautifully demonstrated. Mark 6:7; Luke 9:1; and Matthew 10:1 record Jesus' use of organization as He sent out His twelve to minister in His name. We, too, should organize in our efforts to evangelize youth.

On another occasion, Jesus was surrounded by hungry people. After viewing the problem and collecting His resources, He asked them to sit down in groups. (Mark 6:39-40). Youth are hungrily seeking purpose and direction and the use of existing church program organizations is a natural avenue for reaching the youth of a given community or area.

Organization, as seen in Scripture, is a necessity for accomplishing a goal. We must not, however, lose sight of the purpose of evangelizing and teaching youth. Evangelism must be the primary intent of organization.

The first-century churches were in themselves organized for the objective of evangelism. People who became a part of the church according to Acts 2:41-47 were involved in worship, Bible study, and fellowship. However, their primary task was to reach out with an unparalleled evangelistic fervor.

The New Testament never separates the concept of evangelism and ministry. Evangelism is to be the central part of all we do. Certainly, with the youth organizations of the church, we are without excuse in our lack of evangelistic activity toward the youth culture. Christ's commission to "go into all the world" includes its youth.

The use of church program organizations for evangelism will lead to the discovery of new, fresh, and exciting ways of winning youth.

Youth Culture

The wild, wonderful world of youth revolves around organization and fulfillment of purpose. To effectively reach youth, youth and adults must be equipped to win youth within the structure of their life patterns. This is our task because the needs of youth demand it and the existing church system provides the means for accomplishing it.

When youth enter junior high school, they are, in most cases, deeply involved in the organizational structure of the world, home, and school. Organizations and functioning within them is a part of where youth are. The family plays, lives, and enjoys life together. At school they are involved in organizations of all types. Some are involved in athletic team competition. Some are involved in scholastic organizations such as National Honor Society and the debate team. Further, others are a vital part of band, cheerleading, and student government. Apart from home and school, youth are also involved in organizations. They shop in organized malls and department stores. They view the fast-food restaurant and the local gasoline station as organizations and willingly function within the rules and limitations of each organization they encounter.

When we invite them into the church, it is often difficult for youth to identify the function of an organization. For example, Sunday School is typically the Bible study and evangelistic outreach arm of the church. If youth come and see very little teaching or evangelism they soon learn that this is not a serious organization. All of us have dropped out of organizations because they were nonfunctioning. Ask yourself if missions education is important and are the missions organizations of your church vital and functioning?

Christian stewardship demands that we use existing church program organizations for evangelism. Any given Sunday there will be more youth involved in your Bible study program than any other activity. We do not need to create another vehicle. Simply stated, we need to refine the function of each organization and its relationship to evangelism and translate this to the youth who could readily function within the guidelines. Youth desire to serve. When they see the how and why of organization and outreach, they will enthusiastically hold to and increasingly be involved in outreach/evangelism. The existing organizations we need to reach youth are presently in place in most churches. The task is to move the organization within the church out to reach lost young America.

Implementation

Stewardship of Existing Organizations

To maximize the use of the organizations of the church in evangelizing youth, youth leadership must have a working knowledge of each organization. Some may assume the mission organizations, for example, are for social action and not evangelism. A planning and training retreat may be necessary to help youth workers discover that they are part of the youth evangelism team. Church program organizations may do many things but, if they do not do evangelism, they have failed to achieve the primary reason for their existence. Evangelism will not be the primary objective of church organizations unless a strategy is developed to intentionally make evangelism the priority. Youth leadership should make this transition to evangelism by defining the function, discovering the possibilities, determining the future, and knowing and using available resources.

Define the Function

The shortest distance between two points is a straight line. This is, of course, assuming that one knows where the two points are. Leadership may know where they are but many times do not know where they want to go. The first step is to define the function of youth evangelism with an intended purpose in mind.

A statement of purpose can be defined in a reasonably short period of time. It must have input from all the organizational leadership of the church. As you review the purpose of each organization, if known, you can define the function of each. The function is what they are actually involved in on a continual basis. The doing of ministry may not coincide with the stated purpose. Organizations often schedule a lot of events and projects and hope for results. When they evaluate, they are discouraged because they accomplish very little.

Every event or project must have a stated result before they are actually conducted. This stated result must be in support of the overall statement of purpose. In the process of completing a statement of purpose, you will have defined the function of youth evangelism in church organizations.

The next step is to evaluate these organizations in achieving their defined task. This evaluation is not an inquisition and should not be based on personalities. The key ingredient in the evaluation must be a focus on the future and the improvement of each church program organization. The following questions are a sample of some that need to be asked during this evaluation:

1. How can missions, Sunday School, discipleship training, and church music be more evangelistic?
2. Are there lost youth in the existing organizations and what can be done to minister more effectively to them?
3. If a teenager attended a meeting of any church program organization, would they be provided with an opportunity to become a Christian?
4. How is evangelism viewed by organizational leadership?

As you answer these and many other questions you will begin to see a common direction for the church program organizations. When all the questions have some answer, proceed to condensing these answers into one statement. You may want to consult your church constitution for an example.

When the function has been defined, make several copies and place in prominent places in every area where an organization meets. This will bring about a new awareness of the evangelistic intentions in each group. Once you have defined the function, then you should discover the possibilities.

Discover Evangelistic Possibilities

One way to discover the possibilities is to meet with the leadership of all the youth church program organizations. Make this an informal but meaningful meeting. Design a chart that lists all the high schools and middle schools within the ministry area of your church. For this project, you could estimate the enrollment of each school. Should you desire the exact number of students, simply call the school. Many times they will give the enrollment by grade and gender.

When you have completed the enrollment count and divide that number by the number of churches near you. This, theoretically, will give you the potential number of youth to which each church should effectively minister. Usually, this will be more youth per church than any one given church could logically handle. This experience will help youth leaders to visualize the big picture of your potential and the need to depend on God for resources.

The best place to begin a youth ministries evangelistic emphasis is to check the rolls of the existing organizations for unsaved youth listed. This is the first step because these youth are already related to your church. Many of them just need an opportunity to invite Christ into their hearts. Leadership will want to take the initiative to approach each of these youth and talk with them about their spiritual condition.

Next, conduct an in-house survey. Many church members have unsaved teenage relatives. Obtain all the necessary information about these youth and file it for immediate use.

A neighborhood survey is also an excellent way to discover many unchurched and unsaved youth. People today are very transient. Youth may have moved into your community without your knowledge. A survey will help to locate these new prospects. Surveys should be constantly reviewed to add and subtract names of potential prospects for the kingdom of God.

It is important for us not to be limited to existing methods. Youth leadership needs to have some creative thinking about how to minister and evangelize youth through each of the existing organizations within the church. As the function is defined, ask each organizational leader to describe ways that their particular group could reach out to other youth in the surrounding area. Once you start at home and in the community, you can begin to impact the middle and high schools in your ministry field. Dare to dream. God will not give you a vision for which He will not provide equal resources to turn that vision into reality.

Determine Directions

Once you have completed defining the function and discovering the possibilities, move on to determine the directions and goals for the future. This step deals with the strategy plans of reaching a desired point in youth evangelism. It may consume more time but the old adage "If it's worth doing, it's worth doing well," certainly is true in this case.

Always be careful to include organizational leadership in the decision-making process related to any action you hope to take. Have each leader list all the evangelistic activities or events that were conducted by their particular organization last year. Divide these into at least two different categories, *evangelism training* and *evangelism experiences.* As you place them on a wall chart, you can see an obvious balance or overbalance in one or two areas. As you see the area of greatest need, you can then begin to rank these needs into a priority list.

After completing the priority list, begin to formulate a strategy of training and projects that will alleviate the deficiency in a given area. Place these on the church calendar to ensure they are carried out. The projects should include areas such as discipleship training, witness training, mission training, or projects that will ultimately end with a witness being shared. Every event or project should include a opportunity for youth not to only respond to the gospel but to share with others what God is doing in their lives. These events and project must also fulfill the overall statement of purpose determined earlier.

For example, Sunday School might promote a high-attendance Sunday at the beginning of a scheduled revival. On that Sunday teachers should give an evangelistic Sunday School lesson with testimonies from Christian youth and time for unsaved youth to receive Him as personal Lord and Savior. If the missions organizations are planning a summer-mission project then include a training event with an actual witnessing experience. Then, as part of the project, plan a time of street witnessing or mall visitation.

Every season of the year should include training or projects that will assist you in fulfilling the priority needs one by one. Obviously, you cannot meet every need within a one-year time span. Therefore, you must look at a two- or three-year calendar. This would serve only to create more excitement for the entire group and a longer tenure for most youth workers.

Using existing organizations is an effective vehicle for evangelizing youth. However, each organization must have a definite, deliberate strategy. That strategy must be witness training, witness experience, and witness action.

If a youth ministry has defined the function, discovered possibilities, and determined the directions of the church program organizations, then you are ready to deploy your resources. There are vast numbers of people available to assist you in completing the task of using church organizations in evangelism.

Deploying Resources

The primary resource is people and in every denomination there are qualified people who can consult with the leadership in each church organization. These persons will be extremely valuable to you as you seek to fulfill your purpose. A youth worker told me that he had invited an experienced denominational youth leader to come to his church for a conference and, to the surprise of the youth worker, he came! Think about using the team approach of solving problems and use other youth leaders in your denomination to assist you.

Generally, churches in a geographical location associate together in some way. These associations with other churches provides a resource for interaction with experienced leadership (that is, Sunday School director and/or teams of people with expertise in Sunday School leadership). If a team of people exist they often can provide specialized training in each particular age group. They will assist you in developing a strategy for making Sunday School evangelistic and growing.

Sometimes churches have organized an associational youth committee. This committee is responsible for associational youth events and special training events for youth and youth workers. These resource people will promote and conduct special evangelism training events and processes.

Knowing and using your resources can be the most important part of directing evangelism within the churches' organizations. Someone has said, "All of us are smarter than one of us." It will pay real dividends to spend time with other youth leaders and ask them for ideas to improve the evangelistic fervor of your church's program organizations.

Other youth leaders are the primary resource for sharpening your youth ministry. However, there is an abundance of other resources, books, periodicals, and video aids available to give greater impact to the overall evangelism ministry. Look at the literature order forms from different publishers or contact your local book store for an in-depth list of possible resource items. Some of these resources are listed at the end of this chapter. You will also find a similar list of resources at the end of each chapter in this book.

Ideas

1. Have periodic meetings with all youth leadership to encourage participation and to offer assistance. Invite them to your home for a meal or refreshments. An informal setting is more conducive to openness to new ideas.
2. Visit individual program leaders and ask their advice or response to any new idea you may wish to share with them.
3. Conduct an Evangelism Awareness Seminar. Invite all related Sunday School, Church Training, discipleship leaders, church music, missions leadership like Pioneers, High School Baptist Young Men, and Acteen leaders. Be sure to include outreach leaders and class officers.
4. Do a visitation blitz in a subdivision of homes or a section of the community. Hand out tracts and church information and set a goal of how many times you will verbally share the gospel.
5. Conduct a "Training Sunday School Workers in Evangelism seminar". Include all Sunday School teachers and officers.
6. Do a study of all events, activities, or special training done within the past year. Did these meet any great need? Be honest. Anything can be justified, but did it really meet a specific need?
7. Lead in a Youth Evangelism Showcase. Have each organization

create a booth or display describing some ministry event or activity and how it is evangelistic in its thrust. Key on the evangelism emphasis more than the event or activity itself.

8. Have Pioneers and Acteens join a service at an inner-city rescue mission or halfway house. Let them distribute tracts and share their faith in Christ.

9. Assign each organization a function (that is, pack-a-pew, bring-a-friend, and so forth) on a particular night of a revival meeting.

10. See who can create the best poster advertisement campaign. Have judges and give prizes to the best.

Resources

The following items have been coded and can be ordered from the respective printer or publisher.

WMU Woman's Missionary Union, Highway 280 East, 100 Missionary Ridge, Birmingham, Alabama 35243-2798

BBS Baptist Book Stores are located throughout the United States

HMB Home Mission Board, Orders Processing, 1350 Spring Street, N.W., Atlanta, Georgia, 30367

C.Lit. Church Literature can be ordered from the Baptist Sunday School Board, 127 Ninth Ave North, Nashville, Tennessee 37234

BTN Baptist TeleCommunications Network videotapes can be ordered from the Baptist Sunday School Board at the above address

BHC Brotherhood Commission, 1548 Poplar Avenue, Memphis, Tennessee 38104

Evangelism Resources—Missions/Ministry Organizations

HMB 222-02P *Journey Packet* is an envelope of resources that will guide youth leaders through the relational evangelism developmental steps. This packet includes three books *Journey into Life, Journey into Small Groups,* and *Journey into Discipleship.*

HMB 222-16F *N.E.S.T.* National Evangelism Support Team catalog with information on creative ministries

BBS 6334-12 *Training Youth to Witness Kit* is a packet of materials designed to train youth in witnessing.

BBS 6210-17 *Friends Are for Helping* is a book on peer ministry as an avenue for evangelism.

WMU *Accent* magazine a monthly magazine with regular articles on witnessing and evangelism.

BBS 6338-94 *Studiact: Acteens Individual Achievement Plan,* (Revised) is a book of evangelism ideas for high-school girls.

BBS 6332-32 *Guiding Acteens in Studiact* is the leaders' guidance for the book listed above.

BHC *Mission Activities for Pioneers* is a book of ministry ideas for evangelism.

BHC *Probe* magazine a magazine published for High-School Baptist Young Men with ideas for ministry and evangelism.

C.Lit. 1803-8 *Living with Teenagers* is a magazine for the parents of teens. This magazine will help parents in relating to and understanding their teenager.

HMB *As You Go: A Manual for Mission Youth Groups* is a manual containing idea and suggestions for mission trips.

C.Lit. 7268-7 *Mission Trip Training Pack* a box of materials that will help a youth group get ready for a mission trip.

C.Lit. 7780-2 *Parent-Teen Relationships* is a study module for parents and teens (eight sessions).

C.Lit. 9145-5 *Youth are Ministers, Too!* is a resource for YouthPlus Care Sunday School Strategy that will help youth in ministry to their peers.

BBS 6335-99 *Missions Challenge* is a study guide for missions action and witnessing for High-School Baptist Young Men.

HMB 202-01P *Prayer for Spiritual Awakening Seminar Instructor's Manual* gives guidance to leading the seminar.

HMB 202-03P *Prayer for Spiritual Awakening Seminar Overhead Transparencies* for use in seminar

HMB 202-06P *The Youth Edition: of the Prayer for Spiritual Awakening Manual* was designed to be used alongside the regular *Prayer for Spiritual Awakening Manual.* The Youth Edition has the same identical blanks as the other edition, some illustrations have been added and the copy has been rearranged to a 8½-by-5½ copy size. The Youth Edition was redesigned and three-hole punched to fit into the *DiscipleYouth I* and *II Notebooks.*

C.Lit. 7624-2 *How to Pray for Others module* is a ten-session study that teaches the practice of intercessory prayer.

C.Lit. 7214-1 *DiscipleYouth II Retreat Booklet* contains exercises in prayer and spiritual awakening for a weekend in home retreat.

Evangelism Resources—Discipleship Organizations

C.Lit. 7278-6 *DiscipleYouth I: The Beginning,* retreat booklet by John Hendrix is an individual study booklet to be used on a retreat. It provides a study of John 1:29-51 and introduces all youth to the DiscipleYouth process.

BBS 5133-21 *My Salvation: Secure and Sure* is a four-session book which helps youth study the doctrine of salvation.

BBS 5133-91 *Youth Affirm: The Doctrine of the Holy Spirit* is written by Herschel Hobbs and helps youth to understand the place of the Holy Spirit in witnessing.

C.Lit. 7277-8 *DiscipleYouth I Leader's Guide* compiled by R. Clyde Hall and Joe L. Ford. Contains administrative materials, procedures for retreats, and small-group studies. Also, contains guidance for conducting discipleship/evangelism training, using all the materials in the *DiscipleYouth I Kit.*

C.Lit. 7276-0 *DiscipleYouth I Kit,* compiled by R. Clyde Hall, Jr. and Joe L. Ford, contains a copy of *DiscipleYouth I Notebook, DiscipleYouth I Leader's Guide, DiscipleYouth I: The Beginning, Keep Giving Away the Faith, Meaningful Moments with God, Deepening Discipleship, Decision Counseling Guide, Survival Kit for New Christians,* Youth Edition, and teaching aids.

C.Lit. 7279-4 *DiscipleYouth I Notebook* compiled by R. Clyde Hall, Jr. and Joe L. Ford contains activities to guide youth in discipleship and environmental witnessing.

C.Lit. 7201-8 *DiscipleYouth II Kit* compiled by R. Clyde Hall, Jr. and Joe L. Ford provides a leader with all the items needed to conduct DiscipleYouth II. Contains a leader's guide, a retreat booklet, teaching and promotional aids, brochures on *DiscipleYouth Songs, DiscipleYouth Bibles,* and more

C.Lit. 7214-1 *DiscipleYouth II Retreat Booklet* by John Hendrix contains exercises in spiritual awakening that will be a spiritual renewal tool for youth. Also, provides a spiritual development tool for introducing DiscipleYouth II.

C.Lit. 7216-6 *DiscipleYouth II Notebook* compiled by R. Clyde Hall, Jr. and Joe L. Ford contains content and work sheets focused on witness experience and disciple making.

BBS 4501-03 *DiscipleYouth Songs* compiled by Mark Blankenship. More than thirty songs and choruses included (Broadman).

BBS 4589-77 *DiscipleYouth Songs*, split-track cassette (Broadman).

BBS 4611-04 *DiscipleYouth Bible* designed especially for youth of today. Contemporary English text, *New American Standard Bible* (Holman).

BBS 4437-79 *DiscipleYouth I Filmstrip*, a 75-frame color filmstrip with 16-page manual. Interprets *DiscipleYouth I* (Broadman)

C.Lit. 0262-7 *YouthSearch: A DiscipleYouth Witnessing Plan* by Bill Falkner and Betty Wilfong. Contains specific suggestions for enlisting youth in training. Includes a guidebook, promotional aids, and a copy of the book *Keep Giving Away the Faith*.

C.Lit. 7222-4 *The Roman Road, A Witnessing Training Tool* compiled by Dean Finley. Guides adults and youth in a study of the Scripture passages in Romans that describe God's plan for a person's salvation. Booklet blends Bible study, Scripture memory, and singing the Scripture texts set to music. A leader's guide and skit also are contained in this booklet.

C.Lit. 9254-5 *Commitment Counseling Manual* compiled by members of the National Task force for Counselor Training. Provides information and procedures to use in counseling individuals responding in a decision service.

BBS 5130-69 *Dare to Share* by Roy Fish. Examines reasons for witnessing. Youth will be challenged to incorporate witnessing in their lifestyle.

BBS 5131-71 *Deepening Discipleship* by W. L. Hendricks. A training tool for youth, leading them to develop discipling skills needed to nurture new converts, as well as one another.

C.Lit. 7217-4 *DiscipleHelps: A Daily Quiet Time Guide and Journal* compiled by R. Clyde Hall, Jr. Helps youth develop a regular quiet time and provides tools for daily Bible study, Scripture memory, and prayer.

BBS 5130-53 *Keep Giving Away the Faith* by Dave Bennett. Provides youth with information for witnessing, methods, skills need and way to develop skills.

BBS 5131-28 *Meaningful Moments with God* by George E. Worrell. Leads youth to have meaningful times alone with God and encourages memorization of Scripture passages.

C.Lit. 7213-3 *Youth Learning to Witness* by Joe L. Ford. Leads youth to develop skills for witnessing. Scripture Memory Cards are included.

C.Lit. 7730-7 *Learning and Serving: Workbook for Youth*. A workbook designed for a four-session study. Contains material to help youth new church members (a) understand their relationship to the Lord and to their church and (b) participate meaningfully in the church's program of work. Suitable for individual or group study.

C.Lit. 7732-3 *Learning and Serving: Small Group Leader's Guide.* A booklet that helps leaders train new church members of all ages.

C.Lit. 7295-0 *Belonging* (Youth Edition) Thirteen sessions covering such areas as the meaning of conversion and church membership, church history, church organization, and sharing faith with others.

C.Lit. 7296-8 *Belonging* Teaching Guide. Guides the teacher in presenting the thirteen sessions to youth.

C.Lit. 7286-9 *Survival Kit for New Christians, Youth Edition.* Provides youth with a step-by-step plan for prayer, Bible study, and Scripture memory.

C.Lit. 7287-7 *Survival Kit—Leader's Guide for Adults, Youth, and Children.* Provides teaching plans and administrative suggestions for using each of the Survival Kit workbooks. Includes plans for group study and one-to-one counseling of new Christians.

C.Lit. 7282-8 *A Guide for the Journey: Survival Kit 3, Youth Edition* by Thomas D. Lea. This eleven-week study continues the Survival Kit format of daily study and exercises. Youth will learn principles of biblical interpretation, tools of serious Bible study, and Bible study methods.

C.Lit. 7288-5 *The Journey Continues: Survival Kit 2, Youth Edition* by Ralph W. Neighbor, Jr. An eleven-week study for all Christian youth that helps them know how to apply biblical principles to every area of life. Youth will get guidance on how to form a Christian life-style that avoids the dual dangers of legalism and libertinism.

BBS 4340-99 *DiscipleYouth "Life" Patch:* A rainbow patch with the word *Life* on the front it may be sewn on any jacket or hat. It is to be used as a witnessing tool using the word *Life* as an acrostic for presenting the gospel.

BBS 4341-85 *DiscipleYouth "Life" Pin:* A lapel rainbow pin with the word "Life" on the front. It is to be used as a witnessing tool using the word *life* as an accrostic for presenting the gospel. Also, used to recognize youth who have completed DiscipleYouth I and II.

BBS 4341-80 *DiscipleYouth Prayer Pendant:* A pendant for youth to be worn around the neck. It is a symbol based on the Circle Your World with Prayer Retreat. It serves as a prayer reminder for the wearer to pray for the lost in the world.

BBS 9218-01 *Welcome to God's Family* booklet: A follow-up tract to use after a person accepts Christ as Lord and Savior.

C.Lit. 1239-4 *equipping youth* a magazine that provides suggestions for leaders in leading DiscipleYouth groups and other discipleship helps.

C.Lit. 1201-4 *Church Training* magazine provides helps in all areas of discipleship and contains support for DiscipleYouth materials in a section titled "DiscipleYouth Developer."

C.Lit. 1220-4 *Baptist Youth* is a weekly periodical for youth of all ages. This magazine is used to train youth in evangelism and discipleship.

C.Lit. 1224-6 *The Youth Disciple* is a magazine for older youth issued quarterly to train youth in discipleship and related issues.

C.Lit. 1226-1 *Youth Alive* is the magazine for younger youth that covers the same material in *The Youth Disciple*.

BBS 5130-58 *The New Connection: A Resource for Street Evangelism* is a training piece for youth. This study trains youth how to do evangelism in public areas (that is, beach, malls, shopping centers, and parks).

BTN 3267-BTN 3278 *Getting Ready for DiscipleYouth* is a discussion and demonstration of approaches and activities used in DiscipleYouth I and II, along with other related resources. These are monthly programs hosted by Curt Bradford and Dean Finley.

EVANGELISM RESOURCES—BIBLE-STUDY ORGANIZATION

HMB 212-19F *TELL Witness Training* Brochure describes the Tell Witness Training process. This is a self-contained witness training program complete with cartridges and projector.

HMB 212-22P *Lay Evangelism School Student Handbook* is used by the participants of the Lay Evangelism School. This training has three phases which span twenty-six weeks. This training will help in conducting prospect survey, giving a testimony and sharing a witnessing booklet.

HMB 212-04P *Lay Evangelism School Teachers Manual* is for the leader of a Lay Evangelism School. It contains suggestions for using these materials to train youth in personal evangelism.

HMB 212- 15P *The WOW Event Leaders' Guide* gives complete guidance for conducting a WOW Event weekend. This event trains the youth how to present an evangelism tract in an evangelistic home visit. This weekend is planned and promoted by the outreach leaders of the youth Sunday School departments. The event should be led by an experienced teacher, but anyone with a good understanding of evangelism is qualified to serve as the WOW teacher. In order to conduct the WOW Event a church needs to obtain a copy of the *WOW Event Leaders' Guide* and enough evangelistic tracts for each youth participant to have five. This guide provides all of the instructions for preparation and conducting the weekend. It also contains work sheets to be used by the youth during the training. Permission is given to duplicate these work sheets.

HMB 212-08P *The Real Life* tract is designed to be used with The WOW Event and Advance Training.

HMB 212-37P *Continuing Witness Training Equipper Manual* guides the equipper in training two apprentices for thirteen weeks. This process has been used to train order and more mature youth. It requires a significant amount of commitment for youth to finish the training. (These materials may only be ordered by a certified equipper)

HMB 212-38P *Continuing Witness Training Apprentice Manual* is used by the apprentice for thirteen weeks. (These materials may only be ordered by a certified equipper)

HMB 212-60P *The WOW Advance Leaders' Guide* is for equippers who lead the WOW Advance Training. The WOW Advance Training is a thirteen-week course in personal evangelism training. It is similar in its process to the Continuing Witness Training (CWT) offered for the entire church. However, it is designed to fit the developmental level of youth ages thirteen to seventeen. A church must send someone to a WOW Advance Training Workshop before ordering these materials. The thirteen-week training process requires that an adult be a certified equipper. This adult and two youth meet together each week for a time of prayer, study, and witnessing. (These materials may only be ordered by a certified equipper)

C.Lit. 7220-8 *How to Witness* module. This course equips Christians to witness in today's world. The learning approaches include small group and one-to-one, spread over six sessions.

C.Lit. 7139-0 *Invitation to Youth Bible Study* is the youth study piece for conducting outreach Bible studies for youth in their homes.

C.Lit. 7140-8 *Invitation to Youth Bible Study: Teacher* is the leaders guidance for youth outreach Bible studies.

C.Lit. 9103-4 *Youth Are Witnesses, Too! Revised* is a box of materials for training youth to be involved in outreach and evangelism.

BBS 5163-22 *The Youth Challenge: Sunday School Outreach* is a book that gives suggestions for youth outreach.

BBS 5193-38 *The Youth Challenge Resource Kit:* supports the teaching of the book.

C.Lit. 8108-4 Cultivative Witnessing *Leaflets for Youth.* A set of leaflets to be used by youth in witnessing to their friends.

BBS 5270-78 *Pack 3: Developing Reaching and Ministering Skills* a notebook of resources and guidance for outreach.

C.Lit. 1142-0 *Youth Leadership* magazine contains regular articles with suggestions for support of outreach and YouthPlus.

C.Lit. 1150-3 *Youth in Action* is the weekly evangelistic Bible study guide for grades 10-12 in youth Sunday School.

C.Lit. 1158-6 *Youth in Discovery* is the parallel study guide to *Youth in Action* for younger youth, grades seven through nine.

C.Lit. 1161-0 *Bible Book Study for Youth* a uniquely designed quarterly that leads youth of all ages to study the Bible one book at a time.

BTN 0816 *Training Sunday School Workers in Evangelism* is a twenty-minute videotape by Bill Latham, Harry Piland, and Roy Edgemon discussing the Equipping Center Module available by the same title.

BTN 0146 *Helps for the Youth Sunday School Outreach Leader/Secretary* is a seventy-five-minute videotape that outlines the job responsibilities of this position.

BTN 0215 *Ideas for Reaching Youth Through Sunday School* is a forty-five minute videotape on biblical principles for outreach with youth and guidelines for planning youth outreach

BTN 0053 *Making Effective Visits to Youth* is a one-hour videotape that trains youth leaders in how to visit youth in their homes.

BTN 0149 *Outreach Ideas for Youth Sunday School Workers* is a forty-five-minute video for choosing and conducting outreach projects.

BTN 1615 *YouthPlus: Planning a Year of Youth Sunday School Work* is a sixty-minute video giving guidance to the whys and hows of starting a new Sunday School for youth.

BTN 0426 *How to Build an Evangelistic Sunday School* is a thirty-minute video that describes basic approaches and actions needed to develop a strong evangelism emphasis in Sunday School.

BTN 0083 *How to Have an Effective Visitation program* is a thirty-minute video giving practical suggestion on how to establish and maintain a Sunday School Visitation Program.

BTN 0170 *How to Make a Faith Sharing Visit* is a thirty-minute training video for home visitation.

BTN 0135A *Making an Evangelistic Visit* is a sixty-minute video that gives practical help on presenting the gospel in a home.

BTN 0167 *The Sunday School Outreach Worker:* Thirty-minute video that tells how important is the outreach worker and how they function.

Evangelism Resources—Youth Choir/Recreation

BTN 1772 *Recreation Reaching Out* is a thirty-minute videotape that gives ideas and resources for evangelism through recreation.

BBS *52 Complete Retreat Programs* is a resource with retreat ideas. Two key retreats are teaching youth to share their faith one to one and teaching youth to share their faith from a platform.

HMB 211-17P *Promise of Life: Youth/ Adult Partnership Revival Planbook.* Previously these were usually called youth-led revivals which was a misnomer. These revivals were never led typically by youth. They were led by college students. The term youth-led revival today is misleading. The assumption by the church is it is for youth only. However, the name should reflect that the revival is for the whole church. The Promise of Life Revival combines the enthusiasm of youth and the wisdom of adults. The committees in the *Promise of Life Planbook* include nine adults and seven youth. Adults and youth are paired to form committees. Each committee is assigned approximately fifteen tasks in preparation for the revival. This Revival Planbook is divided into three sections. Section One is the committee structure. Section two gives guidance to the revival team coordinator. Section three includes suggestions for the revival team.

BTN 0199B *Church Ministries to Students* April, 1985, a thirty-minute videotape that focuses on church revivals that are usually led by college students.

BBS *A New Connection: An Evangelistic Youth Musical* is a musical made up of short one-act vignettes. The musical is designed to be presented on beaches, parks, and other public arenas.

BTN 0256 *Planning for and Presenting a Musical* is a thirty-minute video that describes the steps required to successfully plan and present a youth musical.

BTN 1974 *What's Happening with Youth Choirs* is a thirty-minute video that features a panel discussion of the current status of youth choir ministry across our nation.

C.Lit. 1601-6 *Church Recreation* magazine contains ideas for retreats, camps, drama, puppetry, as avenues for evangelism.

C.Lit. 1320-2 *Opus Two* a medium difficulty contemporary choral music magazine published quarterly. It contains Scripture songs based on the Scriptures youth are asked to memorize in DiscipleYouth I, II, and WOW Advance Training.

C.Lit. 1325-1 *Opus One* is also a contemporary choral magazine for easy limited vocal ranges.

C.Lit. 7748-9 *Preparing Your Church for Revival* module. Through this study leaders can plan and conduct the kind of revival their church need. The study includes four sessions.

BTN 0018 *Reaching People with Tracts* is a ten-minute videotape which introduces the innovative use of tracts and instructions for ordering and storing them.

BTN 0354 *Tracts Alive* is a seventy-minute videotape that deals with how tracts are used in witnessing

Resources for Administrating an Evangelistic Youth Ministry

BTN 0366 *A Balanced Youth Ministry* is a fifteen-minute videotape that gives practical advice on balancing all the parts of Youth ministry. It also gives techniques for balancing time spent in behalf of youth, youth parents, and youth workers.

BTN 1563 *Youth Ministry: A Shared Ministry with Parents* this thirty-minute video contains ideas for programing concepts and ideas for youth leaders to use in an expanded ministry with parents of youth.

BTN 1562 *Youth Ministry Teleconference* is a sixty-minute videotape of a teleconference conducted with Merton Strommen in discussing future trends affecting youth ministry.

BTN 1774 *The Role of Recreation in Youth Ministry* is a thirty-minute videotape that suggests how to use events in the church to reach young people and to strengthen organizations through retreats, socials, and sports activities.

BBS 5160-21 *Understanding Today's Youth* is a book by Dan Aleshire that equips church leaders of youth to understand and relate to youth.

BBS 5161-21 *How to Guide Youth* is a book that enables church youth leaders to develop a basic understanding to the church educational process.

BBS 5290-99 *Youth Ministry Planbook 3* a workbook that helps youth leader administrate an effective youth ministry.

BBS 5610-07 *Summer Youth Ministry Ideas* a book containing a host of ideas for not only the summer but year-round youth programing. One chapter spells out ideas for youth evangelism.

BBS 5280-15 *Youth Leadership Training Pak* provides leaders of youth with a study of youth and how they learn.

BBS 5280-05 *Youth Ministry and Church Programs* is a book with an overview of youth ministry and the work of each program organization. This book is contained in the *Youth Leadership Training Pak.*

· BSB 5290-42 Ross, Richard, *31 Truths to Shape Your Ministry,* is a book with general guidelines for youth ministry.

BBS 529023 Taylor, Bob R., Compiler, *The Work of the Minister of Youth* is a book providing hints and suggestions for youth ministry.

Riley, Lonnie, *Youth Awareness Manual,* State Convention of Baptists in Ohio, 1984, a manual workbook to be used in planning an evangelistic youth ministry.

5290-99 Ross, Richard, *Youth Ministry Planbook 3,* is a general workbook that gives aid and suggestions for planning, directing, administrating, coordinating, and implementing an overall youth ministry strategy.

HMB 223-98F National Youth Evangelism Resources is a booklet that provides information about youth evangelism conferences and training for youth leaders in evangelism.

6
Discipleship and Evangelism
Clyde Hall

Introduction

Evangelizing and discipling youth should be one of a church's greatest priorities. The youth who are evangelized and discipled today will be leaders in AD 2000. They will be making decisions that will affect our churches, schools, and communities on local, state, national, and worldwide levels. Introducing them to Jesus Christ and discipling them before they graduate from high school is vital to them personally and to the future of humanity. There is an urgency to our call to evangelize and disciple youth—an urgent *now!* Evangelism and discipling go hand in hand. You cannot have one without the other.

What are evangelism and discipleship? There have been many attempts at defining them. The definitions I like best are: "Evangelism is being, doing, and telling the gospel of the kingdom of God, in order that by the power of the Holy Spirit persons and structures may be converted to the lordship of Jesus Christ."[1] "Discipleship is the Christian's lifelong commitment to the person, teaching, and spirit of Jesus Christ. Life under Jesus' Lordship involves progressive learning, growth in Christlikeness, application of biblical truth, responsibility for sharing the Christian faith, and responsible church membership."[2]

Biblical Basis

The Great Commission says, "Go therefore and make disciples of all the nations" (Matt. 28:19). Making disciples includes both evan gelism and discipleship. It is winning people to Christ and nurturing them in the faith. Jesus made disciples and He intended the church to continue this practice. After Jesus' resurrection from the grave and before His ascension, he commanded His disciples to make disciples of all nations. That command has never been rescinded. It is still our mandate. Delos Miles comments, "That is the reason many think of evangelism as making disciples. I seriously doubt that one can arrive at a solid foundation for understanding the meaning of evangelism apart from discipleship."[3] The central goal of the Great Commission is to make disciples.

Jesus Christ is the only truly mature person who has lived. He is our model for evangelism and discipleship. He "kept increasing in wisdom and stature, and in favor with God and men" (Luke 2:52). Christ is the source of life. "When Christ, who is our life, is revealed, then you also will be revealed with Him in glory" (Col. 3:4). He is the Vine and we are the branches. We grow and bear fruit only as we abide in Him,

> I am the true vine, and My Father is the vinedresser. Every branch in Me that does not bear fruit, He prunes it, that it may bear more fruit. You are already clean because of the word which I have spoken to you. Abide in Me, and I in you. As the branch cannot bear fruit of itself, unless it abides in the vine, so neither can you, unless you abide in Me. I am the vine; you are the branches; he who abides in Me, and I in him, he bears much fruit; for apart from Me you can do nothing (John 15:1-5).

Therefore, we must walk in vital union with Him, "As you therefore have received Christ Jesus the Lord, so walk in Him" (Col. 2:6). Our roots "having been firmly rooted and now being built up in Him and established in your faith, just as you were instructed, and overflowing with gratitude" (v. 7). The maturing process requires not only the uprooting of the old nature but also the cultivation of the new nature until Christ's life is in us, "My children, with whom I am again in labor until Christ is formed in you" (Gal. 4:19).[4]

Another form of the Great Commission is Acts 1:8 "but you shall receive power when the Holy Spirit has come upon you; and you shall be My witnesses both in Jerusalem, and in all Judea and Samaria, and even to the remotest part of the earth." This verse "lifts up five basic truths which dominate the book:

• The Holy Spirit is the divine Agent to initiate, supervise, energize, and accomplish the purpose of God in the church-building program referred to in Matthew 16:18.
• The apostles of Jesus Christ are the representatives of the church of Jesus Christ and the initial agents of the Holy Spirit through whom the divine purpose is to be initiated and directed.
• Witnessing is to be the major means of accomplishing the divine purpose.
• Jesus Christ Himself is the content of the Christian message.
• The total inhabited world is to become the sphere of God's gracious operations and gospel witnessing.
   While the words and phrases may differ, whichever Gospel version you choose has at its heart the making of disciples.[5]

The Bible is very clear: All persons including youth without Jesus Christ are eternally lost. We are all sinners (Rom. 3:23). The penalty for sin is death (Rom. 6:23). The payment God made for our sin—Christ died for us (Rom. 5:8). If we confess Jesus as Lord and ask God to save us, He will. (Rom. 10:9-10, 13). Rejoice, you are now one of God's children (John 5:24) and do four things:

(1) Read your Bible each day (1 Pet. 2:2-3).
(2) Pray every day (1 John 1:9).
(3) Be baptized and join a church (Acts 2:41-47).
(4) Share your faith with other people (Matt. 28:18-20).[6]

Youth Culture

Youth workers who minister effectively in the youth culture must be closely acquainted with the youth world and related to it. However, a major danger exists. It is tempting for them to begin to focus on the temporary and forget the eternal. They must live among youth without acting like youth themselves. Youth vocabulary, interests, and fads are constantly changing. However, the deeper, basic needs of youth remain the same. The expression of those needs will vary.

It is these unchangeable factors that a youth leader must give priority to.

Youth and youth leaders who have made a commitment to grow spiritually and are involved in evangelizing and discipling youth have learned to set priorities in their lives. If this is not their commitment then contact with the youth culture will compromise their ministry.

Peter Drucker maintains efficiency is the ability to do things in the right way; effectiveness is the ability to do the right things. Many leaders are efficient, but are not effective. It is useless to be efficient with the trivial.

The heart of Drucker's voluminous writings is found in five practical guidelines for effective leadership. Study the guidelines which follow . . .

1. Manage your time.
   a. Conduct a time inventory. Keep a record to determine how your time is actually used.
   b. Identify the "time wasters."
      (1) What do you do that does not need to be done at all?
      (2) What do you do that wastes the time of others?
      (3) What do others do that wastes your time?
2. Focus on results, not activities.
   a. Be goal-oriented in your approach.
   b. A focus on results builds teamwork and encourages others.
3. Build on strengths, not weaknesses.
   a. Build on your own strengths.
   b. Build on the strengths of those with whom you work.
4. Set priorities in your life and work.
   a. Recognize the importance of concentration.
   b. Set priorities and stick with them.
5. Make effective decisions.
   a. Define and analyze the problem.
   b. Develop alternate solutions.
   c. Select the best solution.
   d. Convert the decision into action.
   e. Check to see how the decision worked.[7]

Today's youth culture continues to make excessive demands on youth. Priorities determine the way youth and youth leaders spend their time. The first step in building an evangelistic-discipleship lifestyle is to establish priorities for your life and work. Using the five guidelines shown, evaluate your own life-style and lead youth and other youth leaders to do the same. What is priority in your life and the lives of your youth and youth leaders? Is evangelizing and discipling youth among your priorities?

Implementation

Evangelism and discipleship are best expressed through a local church. Each has been, and in many instances continues to be, implemented separate and apart from a local congregation of believers. However, the most effective evangelism and discipleship programs are those that focus believers on a local church. The real test of any discipleship or evangelism program is the relationship they maintain to other believers (that is, the church).

The first step in implementing any discipleship/evangelism emphasis in the church is developing a complete strategy. This strategy will need to be balanced. The strategy is so important because it will guide the entire process. Foundational to any strategy is peer support for youth. Again, this must be provided through the church program organizations of a New Testament local church.

Youth Evangelism Strategy

First, let's look at five approaches to evangelizing youth and then some guidelines for discipling youth. Dean Finley has suggested there are five approaches to evangelism based on the life-style of Jesus. Each of these needs to be included in a strategy of youth evangelism and discipleship. (For further explanation see the chapter "Building an Evangelistic Youth Ministry.)

1. *Prayer for Spiritual Awakening.* Jesus was a person of prayer (Matt. 6:5-15; 11:25-26; 14:19).

2. *Relational Evangelism.* Jesus related to many specific individuals. (Matt. 8:5,14; 9:23).

3. *Environmental Evangelism.* Jesus made a regular practice of sharing the gospel "as he went about" (Matt. 13:24-32).

4. *Presentational Evangelism.* Jesus not only shared the gospel "as he went about," but also went out of His way to present the gospel to individuals on a regular basis. (Matt. 8:1,28; 9:1,20,27)

5. *Informational Evangelism.* Jesus sought to redeem all who would come to Him. He was continually attempting to reach the masses (Luke 23:27; Matt. 5:1; Mark 6:34; 7:14; 8:1).

Finley suggests that a youth ministry should include, simultaneously, a balanced trust of all five approaches to youth evangelism. He refers to this as *Christstyle Evangelism.* Each approach is implemented through a church's existing church program organizations.[8]

Furthermore, two basic truths should be basic to any strategy:

1. Non-Christian youth are interested in the gospel.
2. Christian youth can lead their peers to Christ.

Youth of today are looking for meaning to their lives. Many are seeking answers to deep questions about God and life, and are, therefore, responsive to the gospel.

Several things to keep in mind as you develop a strategy for evangelizing youth:

(1) Youth need to know a plan of salvation. The Roman Road to Salvation is an excellent plan (Rom. 3:23; 5:8; 6:23, 10:9-10,13) for youth to learn to use. These Scriptures are contained in a tract "Have a Good Life" by Dean Finley.

(2) Youth need good models in their adult leaders and peers. One of the greatest means of winning non-Christian youth to Christ is to live the Christlike life before them. Many a youth's spiritual appetite has been whetted by seeing a Christian adult and/or children/youth follow Christ's commands in their daily lives.

(3) A church's youth ministry needs to include evangelistic efforts to reach parents of youth and train parents of youth to share the gospel with their youth. One of the greatest experiences a parent can have is presenting the plan of salvation to one of his/her children and leading him/her to accept Christ as personal Savior and Lord.

(4) A church's youth ministry should include evangelistic training

and opportunities to share the gospel through its church program organizations: Bible-teaching program, discipleship program, missions program, music program, weekly worship services, weekday activities, camps, and retreats.

All that a church does should be geared for evangelism and discipleship.

Basics Youth Face in Witnessing

Why don't youth witness? What problems do they face when it comes to sharing the plan of salvation among their peers. Larry Richards has cited four reasons why youth do not witness:

> The reason most often mentioned was fear. There was a deep concern for what other kids would think. Potential ridicule, fear of making a fool of oneself, uncertainty about acceptance if they should speak of Jesus Christ in personal relationship terms, all loomed large in youth's decisions to remain silent. Knowing the power of peer group . . . and youth's need to belong, we can be sympathetic with such doubt and fears.
>
> A second reason youth advanced was lack of "know-how," "I wouldn't know how to begin," or "I wouldn't know what to do if someone asked a question," or "I don't know enough Bible verses," appeared on the majority of the papers. While teens could point to training classes in the church, to role-play experiences in youth groups, and even to Sunday School units on "how to witness," they felt totally inadequate for the task. The concept of witness as a simple sharing of what Christ means to them as persons, of an introduction of one friend to another, seemed foreign.
>
> A third problem that loomed large was a lack of relationship with non-Christians. Few teens who responded spoke of non-Christian friends. Many explicitly said they "didn't know any unsaved kids well enough to speak to them" about Christ. Like their elders, the associations of Christian young people were often circumscribed by the church crowd. Knowing others than these as friends—the kind of friends who come over to your home or who you hang around with when you have free time—was unusual.
>
> A final problem was a sense of aloneness. Nearly all the teens expressed a belief that other Christian young people ought to witness,

too—but nearly all said also, "If I were to witness I'd be the only one around doing it." The obligation of involvement in personal evangelism is something all give lip service to. And something most do not carry over in action.[9]

Provision needs to be made to help youth overcome their fear of witnessing. "On the job" is the primary way to help youth with their fears. On-the-job training allows them to watch someone else model witnessing. This will help youth in providing content and a witness experience from their presence. Gradually, they will become bolder in their witness.

A Youth Discipleship Strategy

There are three basic ingredients in a good youth discipleship strategy. These ingredients will meet the multitude of need in any youth's life. The three strategies are a discipleship celebration, discipleship labs, and discipleship centers.

The discipleship celebration combines music, fun, fellowship, study groups, and involvement in churchwide worship into a complete package. Three important factors in the celebration is:

1. It is a weekly event. Youth must have regular contact with other youth and adults who are growing in their faith.

2. Discipleship celebration is for all youth, even non-Christians. The celebration is a time for exploration and interaction with the Scriptures and their application for life.

3. An overall plan for guiding youth in study of all of the major doctrines of the Christian faith over six years. This plan helps youth leadership to avoid the pitfalls of always dealing with surface issues. The plan must include study of ethics, church history, church polity, and doctrines (that is, God, mankind, salvation, sin, justification, second coming, relationships, and so forth).

The second ingredient of a good youth discipleship strategy is discipleship labs. These labs are not content-oriented study times. Discipleship labs are events, experiences, and activities that provided youth an opportunity to experiment with Christian skills. For example, many churches provide an opportunity for youth to lead a church worship service at least once a year. This activity gives youth an opportunity to try out their skills in a safe supportive environment. Discipleship labs require more commitment and maturity from teens than discipleship celebration.

The third ingredient in a good discipleship strategy is discipleship centers. Discipleship centers are several short studies or activities that can be grouped together around one theme or doctrine. A discipleship center strategy on evangelism might include a youth retreat study of the Roman Road witnessing plan, along with a follow-up study on six consecutive Wednesday nights of a book that teaches youth to share their faith. A discipleship center of ethics might include a one-day seminar based on youth case studies of dating, abortion, parents, and so forth. Youth could spend the day role-playing these situations and discussing possible solutions. This one-day seminar could be followed by a week-long camping experience that leads youth to study a book on determining ethical values.

Basics Youth Face in Discipleship

Dan Holcomb in his book *Costly Commitment* has suggested twelve guidelines to help youth mature in the faith. These guidelines are for personal growth and are appropriate for adults and youth alike. They are also elements to use as a checklist as you ask yourself the question, Are the youth in my youth ministry program being challenged, provided with tools and instruction for evangelism and discipleship development which is needed to cause these things to happen in their lives? If not, then give consideration to scheduling and selecting resources which will disciple youth in these areas. Here are the basic instructions for discipling youth:

1. *At the beginning of each day, youth need to make a fresh commitment of their life to Jesus Christ.* Thank God for the new day and its opportunities for growth and service. Ask Him to help you be sensitive to His presence and obedient to His will throughout the day.

2. *Become a serious student of the Bible.* The Bible is God's Word to you. Study it daily. Bring your life under its authority. Concentrate on its major passages and themes. Involve yourself in the drama of redemption. Memorize key verses, such as John 14:6, 13-14, Romans 8:28;

10:9-10; 1 Corinthians 10:13; Ephesians 2:8-9; Philippians 4:6, 19; 1 John 1:8-9; Psalm 27:1; 37:4-5.

3. *Cultivate a balanced and disciplined prayer life.*

Sound all the keynotes of prayer: (1) Adore, or praise, God (Ps. 103:1; 145:1-3). (2) Thank Him for what He is, for His mighty works, and many blessings (Ps. 75:1; 106:1-2). (3) Confess your sins to Him (Ps. 32:5). (4) Ask Him to supply your needs (Luke 11:9-10; Phil. 4:6,19). (5) Pray for others (Eph. 6:18; 1 Tim. 2:1-2).

4. *Deal swiftly and honestly with sin in your life.* Do not allow sin to flourish and control you. Confess and get rid of any attitude or behavior that corrupts your life and compromises your relationship with Christ. Adopt 1 John 1:8-9 as a life principle:

> If we say that we have no sin, we are deceiving ourselves, and the truth is not in us. If we confess our sins, He is faithful and righteous to forgive us our sins and to cleanse us from all unrighteousness.

5. *Take time each day to unwind and be silent.* God declared, "In repentance and rest you shall be saved, In quietness and trust is your strength" (Isa. 30:15). Be alone with God. Be quiet. Relax. Listen. Be still and know God (Ps. 46:10). Get in touch with yourself by getting in touch with Him. Take time for creative brooding. Turn loose of your imagination to wonder, to dream, to hope. Become sensitive to the wonders and beauties of God's creation. Learn to see Him in surprising places and among unlikely people.

6. *Be satisfied with nothing less than the fullness of God's Spirit in your life.* The Bible commands us to "be filled with the Spirit" (Eph. 5:18).

7. *Become involved in the ministry of the church.* Do not waste your time looking for a perfect church. Get out of the balcony and into the action with a real-live-flesh-and-blood fellowship of believers, who, like you, are being saved, warts and all, by the grace and power of God. In the process or worshiping, rejoicing, weeping, hoping, failing, succeeding, confessing, witnessing, studying, playing, and growing with other Christians you will take a giant stride toward maturity.

8. *Cultivate vital and meaningful friendships.* Life is relational. We grow in relationships with others and in accordance with the quality of our

relationship. Enlarge your circle of friends. Keep your relationships with them on a constructive and wholesome level. If you cannot do this, find new friends.

9. *Keep alert mentally.* God wants your mind to be clear as well as clean. Eliminate fuzzy thinking and sloppy study habits, as well as negative, destructive, and lustful thoughts. Do not let television program your thinking. Activate your mind. Cultivate your capacity to read. Make friends with good literature. Discipline yourself to think, to make critical and responsible judgments.

10. *Nurture and discipline your body.* "Your body is a temple of the Holy Spirit who is in you." You must "glorify God in your body" (1 Cor. 6:19-20). Your body must be servant, not master. Bring its appetites and impulses under the control of Christ. Get sufficient exercise and sleep. Eat nourishing food. Smoking, alcoholic beverages, and drugs are out! God deserves the strongest and healthiest body you can give Him.

11. *Magnify your role as witness.* By the quality of your life, tell the world that you are a Christian. Be sensitive to opportunities to share your faith with those who need Christ. Your Christian identity and commitment will be strengthened as you communicate your faith to others.

12. *Do not let discouragement defeat you.* Sometimes you may appear to be growing rapidly toward maturity. At other times you will feel that you are making no progress at all or even taking two steps backward for every step forward. Certainly, you will get discouraged. But don't let bad experiences overwhelm you! Be patient! The season is young. You will lose some games on the way to the pennant, but stay with the game plan outlined in these guidelines. Forget past defeats and "press on toward the goal for the prize of the upward call of God in Christ Jesus: (Phil. 3:14). Remember God loves you. He is with you, and He is able to see you to maturity.[10]

Youth Discipleship and Evangelism Strategy

Youth leaders need to look first at objectives for evangelism and discipleship. What do they want accomplished in the lives of their youth and youth leaders in the areas of evangelism and discipleship?

There must be a blending of the two strategies. Is it possible for teenagers to attend a regular weekly discipleship meeting and have opportunities to accept Jesus as their Savior? Furthermore, are youth who accept Jesus as Savior being provided opportunities for growth? All discipleship and evangelism strategies must pass the test of balance and blend. Consider the following youth discipleship-evangelism strategy for your church. It provides a basis for evaluating the strength of discipleship and evangelism in your youth ministry. There are four levels to the strategy, each level with learning objectives. Here is the strategy:

Personal Preparation
At this level, youth will . . .
1. Examine the meaning of discipleship.
2. Realize that all areas of their lives—physical, mental, social, emotional, and spiritual—belong to God.
3. Study the total life as a witnessing tool and commit themselves to God's service.
4. Begin a regular quiet time with God, including systematic Bible devotions and daily prayer.
5. Learn to memorize Scripture purposefully.
6. Study the Bible.
7. Fellowship regularly with other believers.

Witness Training
At this level youth will . . .
1. Study the Bible's message of salvation.
2. Learn how to give a personal Christian testimony.
3. Understand the meaning of salvation and how to share it with others.
4. Understand what it means to "win the right to be heard."
5. Learn how to use the Bible and Scripture memorization in sharing of their faith.
6. Train in some advanced witnessing techniques and in apologetics.

Witness Experience
At this level, youth will . . .

1. Develop a prayer concern for non-Christians.
2. Develop or refine witnessing skills with other Christian youth.
3. See witnessing in action by observing another Christian.
4. Pray for and share Christ with several non-Christian friends.
5. Develop a plan for person-to-person evangelism.
6. Share witnessing challenges and victories with church leaders.

Spiritual Development
1. At this level, youth will . . .
1. Review the basics of Christian growth—prayer, Word of God, doctrine, churchmanship, and witness.
2. Share the basics of Christian growth with new Christians.[11]

The Youth Leader as a Model
   When youth leaders model an evangelism and discipleship life-style they are showing youth real-life applications of the Christian life. Youth follow the examples of people they like and admire. The persons they like who live alongside of them become a powerful influence in their lives. Youth will learn effective evangelistic methods by going with a youth leader and observing a youth leader make a gospel presentation. Youth are challenged to develop the basic disciplines of the Christian life as they observe their youth leaders memorizing Scripture, studying God's Word, and praying fervently for lost youth. Actions do speak louder than words.
   Larry Richards summarizes what needs to take place in a modeling relationship:
1. Youth need frequent, long-term contact with their leaders (their models).
2. Youth need a warm, loving relationship with their youth leaders.
3. Youth need exposure to the inner states of their leaders.
4. Youth need to observe their leaders in a variety of life settings and situations.
5. Youth leaders need to exhibit consistency and clarity in behaviors, values, and so forth.
6. There needs to be a correspondence between the behavior of the youth leaders and the beliefs of the community.

7. There needs to be an explanation of life-style of the youth leaders conceptually, with instruction accompanying shared experiences.[12]

"These factors help us see that instruction and modeling are not contradictory or mutually exclusive. Instead, they point us to a situation in which truth is taught, explained, and expressed in words. They also point us to other dimensions of the teaching/learning situation which make it more likely that the concepts will be perceived as realities to be experienced rather than simply as ideas to be believed."[13]

Summary

God's Word commands that a church evangelize and disciple its youth and that youth commit to this life-style. It is not optional. Youth are living in a culture that demands much from them. To respond to God's command, youth must determine priorities in their lives. They must be led to choose an evangelism and discipleship life-style as a top priority. A church's youth ministry must include a strategy for evangelism and discipleship which includes the five approaches to evangelism and guidelines for discipleship development. Youth will most readily respond when church leaders are modeling New Testament evangelism and discipleship disciplines before them. The religious sensitivity of adolescence and their interest in spiritual things should be a challenge to youth leaders to be faithful in the presentation of the plan of salvation and discipleship development.

Ideas

1. Youth leaders wanting to keep current on the youth culture might consider some of the following: read school newspapers; attend school events (plays, concerts, and athletic events); become acquainted with magazines youth are reading, check the newsstands; listen to youth and be sensitive to their vocabulary, interests, and fads.

2. Train a nucleus of teens in evangelism and discipleship. Begin, even if it is only with one or two youth. Multiply yourself!

3. Plan a regular time of dialogue with the parents of youth. They can teach you much!

4. List prayer requests in a journal. Pray and review requests periodically. You will be encouraged to see God at work in the lives of your youth and youth leaders.

5. Go where the youth are. Find out where they gather: school-bus stops; local hamburger or pizza places; and just "hang around." Let them know you are genuinely interested in them. Work at establishing a trust relationship. Shared experienced develops mutual trust. The more experiences, the more trust. The more trust, the more shared experiences.

Resources

Each of the following resources are coded for your ordering convenience.

(BBS) Available at Baptist Book Stores

(CMD) Available from Church Materials Department, 127 9th Avenue, North, Nashville, TN 37234

(HMB) Available from the Home Mission Board, 1350 Spring Street, N.W., Atlanta, GA 30367

Discipleship/Evangelism

(CMD) *DiscipleYouth I: The Beginning* by John Hendrix.

(CMD) *DiscipleYouth I Kit,* compiled by R. Clyde Hall, Jr. and Joe L. Ford.

(CMD) *DiscipleYouth I Notebook,* compiled by R. Clyde Hall, Jr. and Joe L. Ford

(CMD) *DiscipleYouth II Kit,* compiled by R. Clyde Hall, Jr. and Joe L. Ford

(CMD) *DiscipleYouth II Retreat Booklet* by John Hendrix.

(CMD) *DiscipleYouth II Notebook,* compiled by R. Clyde Hall, Jr. and Joe L. Ford

(BBS) *DiscipleYouth Bible*

(BBS) *The New Connection: A Resource for Street Evangelism* by Terry McIlvain

(CMD) *The Roman Road, A Witness Training Tool,* compiled by Dean Finley

(CMD) *"Have a Good Life!"* by Dean Finley (tract)

(CMD) *Commitment Counseling Manual,* compiled by members of the National Task Force for Counselor Training.

(BBS) *Costly Commitment* by Daniel Holcomb.

(BBS) *Dare to Share* by Roy Fish.

(BBS) *Deepening Discipleship* by W. L. Hendricks.

(CMD) *DiscipleHelps: A Daily Quiet Time Guide and Journal,* compiled by R. Clyde Hall, Jr.

(CMD) *DiscipleNow Manual,* compiled by R. Clyde Hall, Jr. and Wesley Black

(BBS) *Keep Giving Away the Faith* by Dave Bennett

(BBS) *Meaningful Moments with God* by George E. Worrell

(HMB) *The WOW Event Leaders Guide*

(CMD) *Cultivative Witnessing Leaflets for Youth*

(HMB) *Promise of Life: Youth/Adult Partnership Revival Plan Book*

(BBS) *My Salvation: Secure and Sure!* by Lavonn D. Brown

(BBS) *Truths That Make a Difference* by Lavonn D. Brown

(BBS) *Choose the Best!* by Lee Davis

New Church Member Training Materials

(CMD) *Learning and Serving: Workbook for Youth*

(BBS) *The Journey Continues: Survival Kit 2, Youth Edition* by Ralph W. Neighbour, Jr.

(BBS) *Survival Kit for New Christians, Youth Edition* by Ralph W. Neighbour, Jr.

(BBS) *A Guide for the Journey: Survival Kit 3, Youth Edition* by Thomas D. Lea

Ethical Issues

(BBS) *Determining My Values* by Clyde Lee Herring

(BBS) *The Great Adventure, Building Christian Relationships* by Clyde Lee Herring

(BBS) *God's Will, A Dynamic Discovery* by T. B. Maston

(BBS) *Youth Ministry Planbook 3*

(BBS) *Summer Youth Ministry Ideas,* Bob Taylor, compiler.

General Training for Youth Leaders

(BBS) *Youth Leadership Training Pak,* Compiled by R. Clyde Hall, Jr.

(BBS) *Understanding Today's Youth* by Dan Aleshire

(BBS) *Youth Ministry and Church Programs* compiled by R. Clyde Hall, Jr.

(CMD) *Mission Trip Training Pak* compiled by R. Clyde Hall, Jr. and Valerie Hardy

(BBS) *We Have These Treasures: A Profile of Youth Leadership Gifts* by John Hendrix

(BBS) *Youth Becoming Leaders* by Art Criscoe

Notes

1. Delos Miles, *Introduction to Evangelism* (Nashville, TN: Broadman Press, 1983), p. 47
2. Church Base Design, Southern Baptist Convention.
3. Miles, p. 22
4. Dan Holcomb, *Costly Commitment* (Nashville, TN: Convention Press, Revised 1987), pp. 30-31
5. Miles, pp. 123-124. This is an adaptation from George W. Peters, *A Theology of Church Growth* (Grand Rapids, MI.: Zondervan Publishing House, 1981), pp. 16-19.
6. *DiscipleYouth Bible* (Nashville, TN, Holman, 1985), pp. 5a-8a.
7. Arthur Criscoe, *Youth Becoming Leaders* (Nashville, TN, Convention Press, 1984), p. 36
8. Dean Finley, *Building an Evangelistic Youth Ministry* (Atlanta, GA, Home Mission Board, 1987) p. 78.
9. Lawrence O. Richards, *Youth Ministry* (Grand Rapids, MI: Zondervan, 1972), p. 280.
10. Holcomb, pp. 31-32.
11. *Church Training,* April 1986, The Sunday School Board of the Southern Baptist Convention, p. 38.
12. Lawrence O. Richards, *A Theology of Christian Education,* (Grand Rapids, MI: Zondervan, 1975), p. 84.
13. Richards, p. 85.

7
Creative Evangelism
Bill Cox

Introduction

The seven last words of the church may very well be "We have never done it that way!" There is no way of knowing how many great new ideas for reaching youth with the good news of Jesus Christ have been cast aside with the same phrase. The rejection of good ideas often stops the ideas from coming altogether.

Our society is changing rapidly, and the youth culture is becoming increasingly diverse. Traditional ideas may work well in reaching people with traditional backgrounds. But we need fresh, creative ideas to touch many who are in great need of Jesus, but who may not relate to "the way we've always done it."

This chapter does not just pass on some of the newest ideas for reaching youth with the gospel. There are volumes of books full of ideas. Instead, the intent is to stimulate all of us to use our own God-given creativity in ways that will communicate the gospel. Too often we waste the precious gifts and talents God has given us by burying them. God didn't give us brains just to keep our ears apart.

You won't find a Scripture reference for "But we've never done it that way." In fact, throughout the Scriptures we can see God working in unique and creative ways to reach people in many different manners. A creative idea is not good, or of God, just because it is creative. However, often instructions from God are new and creative. After all, God is the Creator and He did not stop creating with the creation of the universe. "Therefore, if any man be in Christ, he is a new creature; the old things have passed away, behold, new things have come" (2 Cor. 5:17).

Biblical Basis

"What's that you say you're building, Noah? An ark? But we've never needed one before. My daddy and granddad and their grand-dad before them never had an ark, so what makes you think we need one now? You're just always trying to stir up trouble, Noah."

"Joshua, some of our older soldiers don't like trumpet music. Why don't we just use our harps?"

"Davey, you don't have the experience, equipment, or training to get through to a Goliath. Besides, no one's ever been able to do it."

"Hey you guys. Yeah, Paul and Silas. Knock off all that praying and singing. Don't you know this is a prison? Next you will want to be singing 'Jailhouse Rock'!"

"Mr. Stephen, don't you realize that you're the one on trial here today? Why must you bring in all these stories about other people from the Scriptures? Our minds are made up."

"Did you hear that Peter and John were downtown preaching again today? Yeah, they upset the Sadducees because they wouldn't quit saying Jesus was raised from the dead. How many became believers? I think I heard someone say it was around five thousand."

New ideas and different ways of doing things are not always well received. All through the Bible those used by God were often misunderstood, criticized, scorned, mocked, and persecuted. Yet, their devotion to God and concern for His work kept them going in spite of the opposition. Jesus promised similar blessings in Matthew 5:10-16 for those who accepted the challenge of living for Him and being salt and light for the world.

Scan the Bible to see what creative methods God used to get His message across. Ask Balaam if God ever worked in creative, unusual ways. Ask Jonah if God's creativity with a fish was effective. Reminisce with Moses and Pharaoh about God's methods. Burning bushes? Frogs? Gnats? Locusts? Now that's creative! Ask Moses if God always brings water from a rock in the same way? Ask him what happens if we do not do it God's way and try to do it like we did before?

Without a doubt, the ultimate example of creative evangelism is Jesus. The Gospels are a textbook in how to reach people in fresh and unique ways.

Jesus invested His ministry in some rather unlikely people. Before Jesus changed their lives, most of the twelve disciples were obviously not the religious leaders of their day. Yet Jesus recognized something in them and, over a period of time, they became a strong force in advancing the kingdom of God. They were from a variety of backgrounds. This gave them opportunities to identify with men and women from some similar backgrounds. In our youth evangelism work, we don't need all of our leaders from the same mold. We need leaders of varying types and with different experiences to help us reach a broader spectrum of youth. The background and associations of various disciples opened chances for Jesus to minister to those who greatly needed Him. For example, in Matthew 9:9-13 we read:

> As Jesus passed on from there, He saw a man, called Matthew sitting in the tax office; and He said to him, "Follow me!" And he rose, and followed Him. And it happened that as He was reclining at the table in the house, behold many tax-gathers and sinners came and were dining with Jesus and His disciples. And when the Pharisees saw this, they said to His disciples, "Why is your Teacher eating with the tax-gathers and sinners?" But when He heard this, He said, "It is not those who are healthy who need a physician, but those who are sick. But go and learn what this means, 'I DESIRE COMPASSION, AND NOT SACRIFICE,' for I did not come to call the righteous, but sinners.

Since the Pharisees questioned the idea of Jesus eating with "sinners" it apparently was not the norm for ministers to do such a thing. Jesus didn't mind stepping beyond "But we've never done it that way."

The biblical account of Jesus' encounter with a Samaritan woman at a well as recorded in John 4:4-26 gives a classic further insight into His commitment to touch people where they were. In this situation He crossed at least three manmade barriers to share God's love and truth. The woman was shocked that a Jew would have anything to do with a Samaritan. She marveled that a man would engage in such a conversation with a woman in that culture. If she had known Jesus was a priest, she would have been speechless.

In this same passage we can note the clever way that Jesus used what they had in common to steer the conversation toward her recognition of Him as Messiah. Their common need for water was all it took to launch Jesus into a message geared to meet her other needs.

The creativity of Jesus perhaps shines forth most brilliantly in the parables He told. He taught from the Old Testament scrolls but drew heavily from contemporary culture to illustrate and elaborate on God's truth.

Jesus was a master at taking the common ground or the material or subject at hand and building a message on it. He could talk about being the "living water" or the "bread of life." When He was with farmers, He drew heavily on illustrations they could understand. When with fishermen, He didn't talk about plowing, harvesting, and seeds as much as He talked about things related to the sea and the fishing industry. Jesus told Peter and Andrew, two fishermen, "Follow Me, and I will make you fishers of men" (Matt. 4:19). They responded to that invitation, but Jesus was creative enough not to use the same invitation with everybody else, especially since not everyone is interested in fishing, regardless of the type.

When the disciples were about to chase away a group of children, Jesus not only corrected the situation, but also used it as an opportunity to teach about the importance of being childlike in His kingdom. Jesus recognized "teachable moments."

The everyday elements of bread and wine were creatively used by Jesus to teach deep truths that we will always remember. The disciples never forgot the time Jesus washed their feet to convey His message about servanthood and humility. Words alone wouldn't have had nearly the same impact.

We would do well to remember that Jesus didn't limit Himself and His ministry to one way of doing things. Sometimes we see Him preaching on a hillside surrounded by thousands. At other times we see Him taking the time to minister to individuals, giving us a great model for creative personal evangelism. He also spent a lot of time equipping and training a small group of disciples who would be able to help carry the message of His good news. Some of His ministry was in formal synagogue settings, while much of it was under the trees, on the mountain, in a boat, in homes, along the roadside, and even at parties. He didn't put all His eggs in one basket or even all His files on one floppy disk (for those not accustomed to carrying baskets of eggs).

If we are serious about penetrating our contemporary youth culture, we'd best follow the example of Jesus. It's going to take more than one way of doing things.

Youth Culture

It is misleading to talk about "the youth culture" in a way that suggests there is one life-style for all youth. In the United States alone there is tremendous diversity in youth culture. It is influenced by geographic location—rural, urban, or suburban—financial factors, and local history. A world view increases the diversity even more.

The best we can do is to recognize some general trends that affect different youth in varying degrees, keeping in mind the wide variety of backgrounds and experiences from which youth come. Consider the following trends and their effect on youth in our culture.

Technology

Youth are influenced by the rapidly increasing technology pervading almost every area of their lives. They are more at home in front of a television, video game, or computer keyboard and monitor than in front of a pulpit. As a result, this generation is very visually oriented. Their parents were content to listen to music, but youth today watch their music as well as listen to it. Many of the visuals are very abstract in nature. There is a lot of symbolic imagery. Is media the language of today's youth? How can they hear the gospel unless we speak their language? What will we have to create to get our message across?

Attention span is decreasing. Music videos tell a whole story in three minutes. The thousands of commercials that bombard television viewers present their message in thirty seconds or less. Life's major issues are presented and solved in one-hour TV dramas or, at least, two-hour movies. Computer technology puts answers literally at our fingertips. If you need answers, press the right buttons and a wealth of information is yours in lightning-fast time. How many teens are going to sit still for a hour-long worship service? Is it time for us to create a thirty-second gospel message?

Music plays a major role in the life of most youth. There is no longer the need for an electrical outlet. Portable "jam boxes" and even smaller players and headphones make it easy to take music along for almost nonstop listening. In some situations music and those making it even achieve a godlike status among devout listeners. Much of the praise is worship of violence, sexual immorality, drugs, alcohol, and rebellion, while tearing down parents, teachers, and other traditional authority. Life itself is even cheapened in some popular music. The life-style and influence of many music idols is quite contrary to scriptural teaching, to put it mildly. How will the gospel be heard? Do we need "Jam Boxes for Jesus?"

The mass media have contributed to a value system no longer limited to the influence of a local region. Grandpa's wise old stories have been replaced.

Culture

Speaking of Grandpa, another very important cultural consideration is the abundance of nontraditional home situations. With the divorce rate around one in every two marriages, family is no longer the originally issued Mom, Dad, brother, sister, cat, and dog. Single-parent homes and blended families resulting from remarriage are now the norm rather than the exception. Greater mobility has taken many youth away from grandparents and other family, who not long ago had a big influence on growing up. We must not limit our thinking about family life to the way it used to be.

Poverty is, of course, still a big problem for many young people today, but affluence isn't necessarily the answer. The American dream can turn into a nightmare. I live in a suburb that has been dubbed "The Golden Ghetto" by some recent secular sociological studies. Young people there are surrounded by so much success and materialism that they are blind to some very real needs. The inner poverty is a definite reality. Success is usually short-lived and accompanied by stress to achieve despite the tremendous competition. "Failure" is common and devastating. Youth are taught to pursue fortune, fame, and power, only to find that they are not satisfying. Life can, even if one has a high IQ, become seemingly shallow and not worth living, adding even more possibility to the chance of suicide.

Thoughts of death are not uncommon among teenagers. Suicides, drug overdoses, and alcohol-related accidents claim the lives of classmates with some degree of regularity, particularly in larger high schools. The threat of nuclear annihilation helps pose the thought in some young minds that a long life is a long shot.

Diversity

Various studies have suggested the middle class is shrinking while the rich get richer and the poor get poorer. Some have time on their hands and little chance or motivation to learn responsibility. On the other side are youth holding down jobs to help the family and who have very little free time. It may take different strategies to reach those in different situations.

Because of the great diversity and rapidly changing society, the generation gap is very real for many people. Some, but by no means all, in older generations have grown frustrated in trying to understand teenagers and have even written them off. That attitude is a big mistake.

Even though much of the view of youth culture can appear negative, a closer look reveals great opportunities for effective evangelism. Lack of stable home lives, uncertainty about the future, disillusionment with material possessions, and other insecurities can result in many youth desiring something that is real and lasting. They desire someone to care about them and offer some special attention. Obviously the drug, alcohol, and sex abuse is a strong indication of a desperate search. Youth will respond to the gospel when they are confronted with it in a way they can understand. God wants all to know Him, and He is busy creating ways to get His message across.

Implementation

Creativity: The In's and Out's

Before considering any specific suggestions for moving toward more creative evangelism, we need to work on developing the proper frame of mind. You have heard people say, "I'm just not creative." Sometimes, I want to lovingly shake people who say such things. All of us have creative gold mines within us. We just have not tapped them. After all, we're created in the image of the ultimate Creator—God. As Christians we have the Spirit of the wonderfully inventive Jesus living within us. To claim no creativity is to insult our Creator.

Such claims also serve as self-fulfilling prophecy. We'll never become creative as long as we are convinced we're not. We usually tend to live up to our own expectations. It helps greatly to be around people who think positively and encourage fresh ideas.

As Christians we are taught the importance of humility, but that should not extend to denouncing God-given ability that He wants us to use in serving Him and reaching others. When we remember the source, it should help keep us humble, yet also excited about the unlimited resources that are ours.

If we apply Jesus' parable of the talents to our concept of talents, we must admit we don't all begin with five talents in the creativity department. The beauty of the parable is that we have the chance to invest whatever we have and watch it increase. Maybe you only consider yourself a number one when it comes to creativity. Bury your talent and lose it, or use it and have the potential to move right on past some lazy folks with five talents.

A poster in my studio at home suggests "The best way to have a good idea is to have a lot of ideas." For every good one there may be plenty of rotten ones. That's part of the price you must pay to be creative. Creativity is not for the fainthearted.

The power to change lives does not lie within our methods or ideas. That power belongs to God alone and is available to us through His

Spirit. Whether we are fresh and creative or traditional, we are only the extension cords which join God and those we want to reach. Creativity is no substitute for genuine love and compassion. Our creativity should be an expression of our love in action.

Even though our methods may change, our message doesn't. "Being creative" doesn't give us license to get sloppy with the gospel. We must present the good news about Jesus Christ clearly and accurately in order to be valid in our evangelistic efforts. We must also take great care to not compromise biblical principles whatever the methods.

Being creative also doesn't mean throwing out everything that's not new or original. Some things should be done the same old way. Not because it would be a sin to make a change, but because many old ideas and traditions are still quite effective. Some old programs need creative life breathed into them.

Being creative goes far beyond imitating "the world" by simply Christianizing secular ideas and practices. We do need to understand secular trends as we try to touch youth where they are. It is important to offer positive alternatives to some of the negative messages coming through popular media. Creative ministry can do this, and more. Sometimes we are heard by keeping up with the trends. Other times we need to be fresh and different by going against the norm.

We've already seen from a biblical perspective that new ideas aren't always met with unanimous approval. Don't take that to mean we've always got to be controversial. As much as possible, we need to be sensitive not to offend our brothers and sisters. With a little more thought and creativity, we just might be able to accomplish the same objectives without being offensive. Examine your attitudes and motivations as a part of getting into the right frame of mind.

If you're convinced you can be creative without getting run out of your church, we are ready to think about ideas that will help you be creative.

Guidelines for Creativity

There is a place for fully developed evangelistic plans, procedures, methods, and instruction. This is not going to be one of those places. To make it such would help perpetuate our frequent practice of just borrowing programs from each other. As someone once said, "Give a man a fish and you've fed him for a day. Teach him how to fish and you've fed him for a lifetime." The greater concern here is improving our lifetime fishing skills. The following guidelines will help you in creating your own youth evangelism methods, strategies, and ideas.

Involve People

Jesus invested His ministry in a variety of other people, including some unlikely characters. As your thoughts are triggered, bear in mind others around you who can be involved in youth evangelism. Look for people with varying skills, personalities, and opportunities and train them to be a part of a team effort.

Go to Them

In general, the church has moved towards a come-and-see-our-program approach. Jesus, on the other hand, took His message to the people. Where are the teenagers in your area? Probably more than anywhere else, they are at school. There is a tendency to think that we can't touch them there, but there really is much we can do within the system. I know people who become substitute teachers for no other reason than to build relationships with non-Christian kids. They don't preach during class, but are available and ready to share Christ when opportunities arise. Consider the possibilities of becoming a chaplain for a school team or a sponsor of a club desiring special expertise. School social events and trips often need additional chaperons. Make your availability known. Here, again, is a chance to get other appropriate people involved.

Many youth have jobs, which more and more are keeping them away from church. Patronize the places they work and build relationships with youthful waitresses, grocery sackers, salesclerks, and fast-food servers. Look for a good opportunity to talk with them about their relationship with Christ. Be careful not to infringe on their work responsibilities. You may need to schedule a time to talk further or follow up a conversation with a personal letter.

Most teams would like to play all their games at home. But we've got to be willing to play on their court. Once we've done that, it may be easier to get them to play where we have the home-court advantage.

Give serious thought also to a third possibility. "Neutral" sites such as civic auditoriums, gyms, and stadiums are less intimidating to nonchurch youth, but still allow us to control the program.

Speak Their Language

Ever since the Day of Pentecost the Holy Spirit has been getting the gospel into the language of the listeners. Part of going where youth are is also learning to communicate in their own language. When we send missionaries to foreign cultures we don't ask them to learn our language before we tell them about Jesus. We study the native language and culture and try to identify with them. We can't lift youth out of their culture and ask them to learn our traditions and languages before we agree to share Christ. Paul said, "To the weak I became weak that I might win the weak; I have become all things to all men, that I may by all means save some. And I do all things for the sake of the gospel, that I may become a fellow partaker of it" (1 Cor. 9:22-23). Paul wasn't afraid to get to know those he wanted to reach. He didn't insist they play by his rules. He understood Jesus' challenge to be in the world but not of the world.

Practice Stewardship of Existing Resources

The home-court advantage is only an advantage if we use it. Many churches let opportunities for evangelism slip by because of some strange idea that a worship service is the only place someone can or should get saved. Who says you can't present an evangelistic message and give an invitation in Sunday School, during church-league basketball practice, or at the church picnic? We need to shift our thinking to the belief that evangelism can happen anytime and anyplace if we plan, prepare, and present.

Some of us have grown pretty accustomed to the hours on our schedule of ministry, but society isn't nearly as concerned about our schedule as in the past. Many youth have jobs that keep them from church, even on Sunday mornings. School activities very often crowd out church youth activities. It's nearly impossible to avoid all conflicts in programming, but we may need to investigate the need to offer ministries with an evangelistic thrust at other than traditional times. An increasing number of churches are turning to Saturday evening worship services and Bible study for those who have to work on Sunday mornings. In light of crowded after-school schedules, some youth groups are scheduling meetings early in the morning before school begins. In some churches it may be necessary to repeat the same ministry several times and even in several places to reach the target group.

Update Old Ideas

Be creative in getting kids to church to hear the gospel. Come up with new variations on the old "bring 'em back alive" or "kidnapping" ideas. Some churches have trips and activities in which church youth can only go if they bring a guest. A variation is to sell to church youth two-for-one tickets for a Christian concert with the second ticket good only for a guest. I know of churches that sponsored "air band" contests and "wrestling nights" to bring in large numbers of nonchurched youth. Once there, they also heard the gospel and had opportunity to respond. Even those who didn't respond became prospects for follow up.

Consistently attracting non-Christians to church takes more than just one gimmick after another. Remember Jesus said, "And I, if I be lifted up from the earth, will draw all men to Myself" (John 12:32). You can gain attention in a lot of ways, but the best attraction is still twofold. You need people who genuinely care about leading others to Christ, and you need interesting, helpful content.

Regardless of whether we are home or away, we need to be finding that common denominator and those teachable moments, just as Jesus did. Keep your eyes open for the everyday occurrences in life that lend themselves to being illustrations for important biblical truths. Keep up with current events in the world, school activities, and local interests. Work them into evangelistic messages and personal evangelism conversations. It is not that hard to find contemporary parables because Jesus Christ really is relevant in today's society.

Consider the Audience

How we present that message is important. We can't compete with multimillion-dollar productions that secular communicators use, but we can do so much more than most of us are doing. We are a visually-oriented society. How can we visually portray the gospel, remembering the typical short attention span? The possibilities are unlimited.

Clown ministry, mime, and drama are very powerful tools of evangelism. Many people who are not particularly gifted speakers have great potential in these visually expressive areas. Sometimes more can be said in a three-minute skit than in a forty-five-minute sermon.

Use these creative means of ministry at church meetings, but also look for other opportunities outside the church at places like shopping malls, grand openings, parks, campgrounds, hospitals, and club meetings. Christmas, Easter, and other special times of the year are often the best times to approach such a possibility. Always make sure to work through proper channels, and don't settle for anything less than your best effort when carrying the good news into the marketplace.

Use Multimedia Approaches

Why not another step? Moving into the area of homemade video productions opens up great possibilities for the many people with video cameras and camcorders. Let youth write and help produce videos designed to speak to their own generation. If you have a lot of youth, let different teams complete in a contest with awards such as best message, best use of music, best production value, most original, most creative, and so forth. Is it possible a local pizza place or other restaurant might help sponsor such a contest and have a video night showing the productions on a large-screen television at the restaurant?

The same things can be done with slides and audio tape. Make pictures at a ball game or other school event and have a fellowship afterwards showing the pictures that were just made. With the right approach, plenty of nonchurch kids will show up to see themselves.

Plan to help them see not only themselves, but Jesus Christ as well. Provide the opportunity for response.

Relate to Needs

Jesus was on a mission of calling people to repentance and into the kingdom of God. How He did this varied as He encountered different needs. At least some of our implementation should begin at the point of what needs we encounter in youth around us. For example, what can we do to reach youth from single parent or blended homes? Could you provide a support group or enlist a Christian counselor to be ready to help out? Consider the possibilities of matching up praying, evangelistic grandparents whose own grandchildren live in another town with youth who live apart from their grandparents.

It's sad to say, but the church has too long relied on some of the least effective means of communicating. From almost every standpoint, preaching is one of the weakest means of lasting communication with youth. Yes, God does use simple preaching, as well as dynamic preaching, to reach many people. We reaffirm it is the Holy Spirit more than methods that makes a difference. But why not allow the Holy Spirit to work through as effective communication means as possible?

Much of my personal work has included three-screen multi-image presentations and special-effects chalk drawings. It's been amazing how much people pick up in such presentations and how long they remember even small details years later. People of all ages are very open and excited about different and creative means of sharing Christ. Some youth who won't even listen to preaching can be captivated and won simply by communicating in a different way.

There will always be those whose rallying cry is "just preach the Bible." I say a hearty amen! To that I would add, be biblical in your evangelism by following the example of Jesus and other great leaders in the Scriptures. They didn't excuse themselves with "but-we've-never-done-it-that-way" thinking. Honor the Lord with your creativity!

Ideas

Since one of the definitions of *creative* is "original," it is impossible to give you creative ideas. By the time it gets to you, it is no longer original and, therefore, no longer creative. Think about it. Therefore, unlike the other chapters in this book the ideas are not supplied for you. You will want to use the suggestions in this writing to help stimulate your thinking toward your own original ideas.

Invite several youth and leaders together for a brainstorming session. Explain to them the rules of brainstorming.

1. If an idea comes to your mind no matter how silly it seems you must vocalize it.
2. We will only take three minutes to brainstorm a topic.
3. *No one* may comment on any idea that is mentioned. Any comment will kill the flow of ideas.
4. All talking for the three minutes should be in the form of suggested ideas.

All ideas that are mentioned will be written on a blackboard or overhead projector. After the three minutes are over the ideas can be reworked.

Here are some areas that your group will want to brainstorm:

1. Where can we find youth to tell them about the gospel?
2. How can we use our existing resources for evangelism?
3. How can we make our church program organizations more evangelistic?
4. What individuals in our church have gifts and talents that could be used in creative evangelism?
5. How can we involve adults in evangelizing youth?
6. What other people in our community could help us minister and evangelize youth?
7. What could we do to get the gospel to every teen in our community?
8. What community events are there for us to be a part of, and how can we use these as an avenue for evangelism?
9. How can media be used to tell youth about Jesus?

10. What recreational activities can we conduct that would provide an opportunity for witnessing?

11. What can we do to tell schoolteachers and administrators about Jesus?

If creative juices are still not perking, or you need some additional ideas to help stimulate your own, consider some of the following resources.

Resources

Ideas, Volumes 1-40 (Youth Specialties, San Diego, CA).

Ross, Richard. *Summer Youth Ministry Ideas* (Convention Press, Nashville, TN, 1986).

Price, Nelson L., *I've Got to Play on Their Court,* (Broadman Press, Nashville, TN), (out of print)

McCloskey, Mark. *Tell it Often - Tell it Well* (Here's Life Publishers, Arrowhead Springs, CA).

Dale, Robert D. and Delos Miles, *Evangelizing the Hard-To-Reach* (Broadman Press, Nashville, TN).

Miles, Delos, *Evangelism and Social Involvement* (Broadman Press, Nashville, TN, 1986).

Stone, J. David, ed., *The Complete Youth Ministries Handbook* (Creative Youth Ministries Models, Ltd.).

Dunn, David, *Try Giving Yourself Away* (Prentice-Hall Inc.,).

Pate, Billie, *Ideas for Youth Outreach,* Volume I, (Convention Press, Nashville, TN).

Phillips, Elgene *Ideas for Youth Outreach,* Volumes II and III (Convention Press, Nashville, TN.).

Thompson, W. Oscar, Jr. *Concentric Circles of Concern* (Broadman Press, Nashville, TN, 1981).

Ford, Leighton, *Good News is for Sharing* (David C. Cook Publishing Company, Elgin, IL, n.d.).

Robertson, Everett, *The Ministry of Clowning* (Broadman Press, Nashville, TN, 1983).

McIlvain, Terry, *The New Connection: A Resource for Street Evangelism* (Convention Press, Nashville, TN, 1988).

8
Recreation and Evangelism
Don Mattingly

Introduction

Young people need a growing personal faith tested and forged in the crucible of daily living. Faith cannot be forced on a young person, it must be nurtured and grown through the personal support of caring adults. It must be a faith that follows the role modeling of significant leaders. Youth's faith is tested in the laboratories of teenage existence whether they are riding the bus to school or hanging out in a mall with a group of friends. Youth need faith to deal with making the school baseball team or getting cut on the final day. Youth's faith must be able to withstand the perils of growing up in a decade when teenagers' parents divorce as frequently as newlyweds and suicide among young teenagers between the ages of twelve and eighteen has become the number-two killer of these teens.

To have this personal faith a young person must be told about Jesus. Youth need to meet and get to know Christian youth leaders and young people so they can be told about Jesus. Many times words of witness are spoken but are not heard by teenagers today because the lives of Christians do not bear out the witness. More frequently, the young people who need to hear the witness are never present because they feel the church has nothing to offer them.

How can they hear without a witness? How can they accept unless they hear? How can they hear if the church does not touch their lives?

Biblical Basis

Young people today are looking for purpose, meaning, and an excitement about life. The world offers temporary thrills, but the world's cheap thrills have a high price tag, and, in the end, the quest to satisfy self is never complete. The Bible shares life's purpose, and meaning must be outwardly directed in serving others and Jesus Christ.

Christ is our example in choosing a purpose for life. "The thief comes only to steal, and kill, and destroy; I have come that they might have life, and might have it abundantly" (John 10:10). When a life is full, there can be nothing more added to it. When a life is full, the results are blessings and happiness. When a life is full, there is always a resource of strength to draw upon when hard times come.

The world has worked so hard to pull itself up by its own bootstraps for so long it has an overinflated impression of being able to solve any problem it encounters. The world sets its own standards of success and then restructures each time the economy finds a way to stimulate spending and to take advantage of human greed and desire for more things. Dr. Gordon Dahl says that searching and working for success have even infected the lives of Christians and are present in every congregation throughout the country. He summarizes our predicament thusly: we have our priorities so misplaced we tend to "worship our work, work at our play, and play at our worship."[1]

Youth often get caught up in this stressful life-style. Many rush from school to work to buy expensive clothes or cars. Many athletes don't even try out for high-school teams because they were burned-out in children's leagues. The push to compete and win is a growing American work ethic. Few youth or adults experience the true refreshment of body and spirit that comes from leisure.

Dahl believes the inability to have the right perspective on worship is closely related to wrong views of work and play. All three, he suggests, are closely related.[2] Jesus' example for us was a balance in life. "And Jesus kept increasing in wisdom and stature, and in favor with God and men" (Luke 2:52).

Youth ministry in the church must take into consideration these four basic areas of youth needs. Jesus grew intellectually, physically, spiritually, and socially. Youth need to experience some success in each of these areas to be accepted in society and to be able to gain maturity as a young adult.

The problem of relating recreation and youth ministry in most churches today is not planning, but events planned with little purpose and for the wrong reasons. In some churches, recreation is equated with youth ministry. Frequently, two softball teams, a fall retreat, winter snow skiing, and a spring banquet are thought to be a great youth ministry. While there is nothing wrong with these, without a purpose they can become walls keeping out people who do not like athletics or who do not have a great deal of money.

Effective recreation includes all types of activities that will interest young people who have different talents, interests, and abilities. Youth leaders must use these events to help other things to happen such as building individual self-esteem, supporting the Bible study and discipleship programs of the church, and reaching young people who do not have a church home and an active growing faith in Christ.

Recreation can be an effective tool. Church-sponsored activities can build relationships and communication. Recreation events can be the first point of contact, and provide opportunities for later evangelistic witness and follow-up. Retreats or backpacking trips can offer opportunities for a personal witness. If events are planned with evangelism in mind, then touching lives will be the result.

Youth Culture

Youth are striving to find a life. Many feel parties, outings, and activities are a definite part of that full life. The church must offer creative Christian social events where young people can grow together in a wholesome atmosphere. Youth have friends who are striving to find meaning, purpose, and a foundation upon which they can base their life. The church must use recreation as an evangelistic tool for touching lives with the message of Jesus Christ. "Whether, then, you eat or drink or whatever you do, do all to the glory of God" (1 Cor. 10:31). The need for a well-balanced ministry to youth today is quite clear. Let's get on with it for the glory of the Lord.

Recreation is so important to evangelizing youth because it is a part of their life. Ask anyone to list the top ten characteristics of youth. In that list you will find something implying youth are active, on the go. They have energy to burn. Secondly, you will find in the list the need to socialize. These two elements are keys to any good recreation. Thus, recreation must be a part of a good youth evangelism strategy.

Implementation

It is Sunday morning and the youth Sunday School department director catches the eye of the youth minister as she quietly enters the room. Yes, she has an announcement to make about the coming youth activities for the week. Tuesday night will be an All-Youth Visitation, and all youth and teachers need to be at the church by 6:30 P.M. Most of the eyes in the group stay glued to the floor as only a few of the young people seem to be paying attention. The youth minister continues. "On Friday night we have something really great; a lock-in." The eyes begin to come up as the youth seem to catch the excitement in her voice. She says that there will be pizza, skating, a movie, and a new game called Crab Scoccer in the fellowship hall. *Hey, now, that sounds like fun!*

Which event will have the greatest attendance?

Which event would you have wanted to go to when you were in junior high or middle school?

Evangelism/visitation often gets the "short end of the straw" because we feel young people like the other types of activities more. We don't promote evangelism in an interesting manner because we don't think youth will want to attend. Youth don't come because it is not presented as a priority. It is a vicious cycle. However, recreation can support youth outreach events and can help build an enthusiasm for reaching other young people. It can provide the opportunity for youth to share a word of personal witness about their church's youth ministry and Jesus. Here are three suggestions guaranteed to help your youth evangelism efforts improve in quality of visits and in quantity of persons out visiting. Each one is as easy as P.I.E.

Combine Recreation and Evangelism

Suggestion Number One—Increase the quantity of evangelism events by combining a recreation event with it. Youth will have a desire to participate and will participate with enthusiasm. Put the dates on the calendar for a full quarter, a year, or as far ahead as you plan your youth ministry calendar. So often, evangelism activities are the last thing planned before a youth ministry calendar is printed. Make evangelism a priority and stick to the plan.

Increase the number of evangelism events and decrease the other types of fellowships or parties each month. In the modern world of color, sight, and sound, our social events need to be well planned and interesting.

Evangelism events should be planned on Saturday and Sunday afternoons during the school months. This ensures there will not be a conflict with athletic events, school club activities, or study time. Every young person seems to be very busy these days and we cannot expect them to come when conflicts arise in their schedules. Weekends offer a bit more flexibility to choose to come to evangelism events.

How about visitation/evangelism during the summer months? Anything goes during summer and evangelism should be a high priority for every event especially softball games, miniature golf, and volleyball. Also, remember to add such items as watermelon, homemade ice cream, and hot-fudge sundaes to your visitation/evangelism agenda.

Evangelism events can be planned on week nights, weekends, or just about any time of the week during the summer. Remember they should be creative, well publicized, and spaced throughout the summer.

Improve Quality of Evangelism/Visitation

Suggestion Number Two—Improve the quality of visitation/evangelism time spent in the homes of youth by assigning each young person a part of the visit. When I was a youth minister in Texas it was frustrating to hear youth comment they were really lucky that night because no one was home where they went so they did not have to make a visit. They were there for the visitation/recreation/ evangelism event, but their hearts really weren't in it. They were relieved when they couldn't find an apartment number or when no one was at home.

Finally, I decided to give every young person in the car a part to say at each visit. There were different parts for a visit to an absentee's home than to a new person who had just moved to the city. We also had a different plan if we were visiting a young person whom we knew had never accepted Christ as his personal Savior. Of course we must always seek to be sensitive to the Holy Spirit in each visit for the opportunity to share personal witness.

Preparation is the key. Pray for each visit before driving to the assigned address. This time of prayer will add a note of spiritual depth to each event. Pray for the Holy Spirit to prepare the way in the heart of the young person. Pray for courage to speak clearly. Pray for discernment to sense why the young person has not been coming to church. Pray for God's glory to come from that visit.

Involve each young person in the car by assigning a part of the visit. Practice these parts in the car on the way to the house or apartment. Here are some parts of a visit and a word of explanation about each.

A Visit to a Sunday School Absentee

Greeting—Assign one young person to speak when a person opens the front door. This person should introduce herself and, depending on how well the group knows the family, make other introductions. If the group is not immediately invited in, this person should ask if the group could come in for a few moments.

Introduction—After being seated inside the home, another young person introduces the reason for the group's visit—that the absentee has been missed in the youth group. Try to find out is if there is a problem that can be alleviated.

Promotion or publicity—Every visit should have a time when an up-coming youth event can be highlighted. The visitors should extend a special invitation to the coming event. If a special recreation time is planned later, then extend an invitation to be a part (see suggestion three).

Presentation—Another young person can begin to close the visit by presenting the absentee with something from the church. If the absentee has not attended since the beginning of a new quarter, take a copy of the new Sunday School quarterly or leaflet for the next week. Other good ideas are copies of devotional magazines or the youth calendar for the upcoming months. The psychology of leaving a small gift makes the absentee feel important and can help motivate the person to be at Sunday School next Sunday.

Prayer—Another youth should immediately express appreciation for a chance to visit. The request to close in prayer is always greeted with appreciation and adds a note of spiritual depth to the visit. It also is an appropriate way to end a visit and to give each person a time to stand up and to prepare to leave. If the young person has accepted the invitation to go with the group to bowl or to play miniature golf, a prayer may not be appropriate.

A Visit to a Prospect Who Is New in Town

Greeting—If the family has had little contact with your church, the greeting should include the name of the church, its location, and the name of the adult with the group. Other introductions might be appropriate while standing outside on the porch.

Introduction—The introduction in the home of a new prospect should include some or all of the following:

a. Where did the young person live previously?
b. What school does he or she attend?
c. What classes are they taking?
d. What hobbies do they enjoy?
e. Where does the father and/or mother work?

Promotion and Publicity—Sharing about the youth ministry at your church is very important in the home of a new prospect. Some suggestions would include:

a. Times and days of the week for Bible study, discipleship, missions, music, and recreation events.

b. Information about the youth minister or youth leaders who coordinate youth activities.

c. What are some of the upcoming events?

d. What type of events did the young person enjoy at past churches?

Presentation—Giving a small gift is just as appropriate in the home of a prospect as in the home of an absentee.

Prayer—Closing in prayer is a signal to the parents of this young prospect that your youth ministry is more than just "fun and games" and it brings a fine closure to a visit.

A Visit to a Youth Who Has Never Accepted Christ

As was previously stated, every visit is a possible opportunity to share a witness for Jesus Christ. However, evangelistic visits should always be a definite part.

Greeting—Since your young people usually know the young person at least on a casual basis, the greeting should be short and genuine.

Introduction—This should include an expression of concern for the young person and a personal testimony. There are many effective pamphlets that can be used to lead a young person through the Scriptures and to share God's plan of salvation. A marked New Testament is also a good tool. In any event, the young person should be given the opportunity to pray to receive Christ. All other young people present should be praying during this time of sharing for both the presenter and for the youth to whom the witness is being shared.

Future Plans—If the young person does pray to receive Christ, encourage that person to make a public confession of faith and be baptized. If the young person does not accept Christ, assurances of continued support should be pledged.

Presentation—The presenter will want to leave the tract or a copy of a devotional reading magazine with the young person.

Prayer—Praising God for His blessings for life in Christ Jesus is entirely in keeping with this visit either as a time of celebration or as an opportunity of continued witness.

Adult Drivers Are Not Optional

Enlist adult leaders from Sunday School, Church Training, and missions and music organizations to provide transportation. Effective youth evangelism events must have adults to drive cars and to coordinate the assignment of parts for each visit. Too often visitation/evangelism is thought of as a task for only the Sunday School teachers. If evangelism events are to be a focal part of a total youth ministry, then sponsors should represent all the youth church program organizations.

Another important reason for this concept is the safety factor. Youth often get excited with their friends in the car and tragic accidents can occur. Accidents happen when adults are driving also, but parents are much more apt to support youth evangelism and to urge their teenager to attend if they know an adult is going to be present in each car. Even if an accident does happen, parents are much less suspicious of the causes.

Include Those Visited in the Activity

Suggestion Number Three—Increase the effectiveness of youth evangelism activities by inviting absentees and prospects to go with your youth group to the recreation event that follows.

Prospects need to feel like they are making new friends and are a part of the group. Parents like to feel their children are making Christian friends in their new city or new church. They will often give their consent for their teen to go with your youth group and even encourage their participation.

Individuals who have been absent from Sunday School need the fellowship of the youth group to feel comfortable in returning to Bible study. When a young person has been absent from Sunday School for six weeks or for six months, there is a barrier between them and the Sunday School class. The barrier is the unknown of what's been going on since they have been absent for an extended time.

Most of that barrier can be destroyed by one volleyball game on the church lawn. During the game the absentee can be encouraged to come back to Sunday School the next morning. When the youth walks in the door the next morning for Bible study, he is no longer someone who hasn't been seen for six months, but is someone who made a great save the afternoon before or the person who helped the youth minister up when he dived for a ball. Recreation draws the young person back into the fellowship of the group and now the Sunday School class has the opportunity to nurture the individual.

Almost everybody likes to bowl, go on picnics, or throw frisbees. Combining recreation and evangelism enables youth to have fun and to reach out into the community with a personal witness of love and acceptance. Look for creative party and fellowship ideas and adapt them to an evangelism activity. Be creative. The young people will be able to tell the difference in this new emphasis on evangelism and will support it with their presence and their prayers.

Ideas

Banana Outreach

The biggest interest in a night of visitation/evangelism that I have ever witnessed involved everyone being told to bring a banana. In fact, the statement was actually made "No one would be admitted to go visiting unless they had a banana." No exceptions.

The youth began arriving and immediately began to ask what they were going to do with the bananas. No answers were given and they were quickly divided into groups and sent out to visit. When they arrived back at the church, the bananas, ice cream, and all types of fruit toppings were waiting for them to make a twenty-foot-long banana split. The banana splits were made in a new rain gutter that had been carefully washed and wrapped with tin foil. After everyone had fixed their banana split, separate bowls were given to each young person.

Kidnap Breakfast

When is the best time to find teenagers at home when you go visiting? Why, 8 AM on Saturday morning! So plan to drop by the homes of a few absentees or prospects for your youth group and watch their surprised faces. Here are a few clues for the success of this event:

1. Always call ahead and let the young person's parents know in advance you are coming. This way they will be up and they will help you pull off the surprise on their own teenager.

2. Boys should go to boys' houses and girls only into girls' homes. If you really do plan to go in and wake up a young person who is sleeping late, common sense makes this guideline a necessity. To make this more fun, don't give the young person much time to get ready and hustle them out the door to the prescribed recreation event.

3. Have a super recreation activity planned that everyone would like to attend later in the morning. The object of a kidnap breakfast is to take the young person out to eat and to go roller skating, hiking, or water skiing at the lake.

4. Be gracious if the young person feels awkward and doesn't want to go with you. Thank them for being such a good sport and tell them you are looking forward to seeing them in a better condition at Sunday School next Sunday.

Bike Hike

What could twenty-five young people on bicycles have in mind on a Saturday morning as they converge on the church parking lot? They just might be planning to visit the homes of area teenagers who are prospects for their church youth ministry. Twenty-five young people and adults riding up on bicycles into anybody's yard will get some attention, and every church youth group should be constantly looking for ways to influence the world in a positive manner.

If the young person has a bicycle and enjoys riding, invite him or her to come to a neighborhood park for brunch and a game of blind volleyball. If they don't enjoy riding, offer them a seat in the support vehicle traveling with the bike riders. Always have a pickup truck or a van available in case of a bicycle breakdown or fatigue.

Take Me Out to the Ball Game

One of the sad realities of church sports team in the present decade is that they frequently play in front of almost empty bleachers. One time I played in a men's basketball game when there were only twelve people in the whole gym. There were five players on each team, one scorekeeper, and only one referee. The other referee didn't even care enough to show up.

So this summer when the girls' or boys' softball teams have a game, use this opportunity to go visiting first and then to collect a big bunch of supporters for your team. Afterwards, the whole group can go out for an ice-cream sundae or drop by a youth worker's home for refreshments. This drop-in should be prearranged, of course.

Agape Feast

Youth who care about the needs of others can share the message of Jesus Christ and their love and support by participating in an *agape* feast. Publicize that youth visitation this month will feature an *agape* feast. After a time of visitation/evangelism bring all of the absentees and prospects back to the church fellowship hall. When youth return, have tables ready with shoe boxes, construction paper, felt-tip markers, and brightly colored ribbon. Have the kitchen crew ready with cookie dough, brownie mix, and other good things to eat.

An *agape* feast is an evening of sending fresh baked goods to friends of your church in brightly decorated boxes. Each box should contain notes of love and expressions of care and support. Boxes can be hand delivered to shut-ins or to people in the local hospital. Also, mail them to church members in the Armed Forces, college students, or to missionaries. This is an evangelism event that enables youth to reach out thousands of miles.

Fifth Quarter

One of the best evangelism events is for a church to invite the whole football crowd to a fifth quarter, an after-game fellowship at the church following a football or basketball game. Each fellowship is planned around a theme with free refreshments. The most popular fifth quarter each year is always a Halloween movie that begins at midnight on the Friday night closest to October 31. Other popular events are a bluegrass concert on the church parking lot and a magic show by a professional Christian magician.

There is a big difference between feeding a large group of young people for free and having an opportunity for evangelism. Youth workers must be prepared to meet the guests and find out if they are active in a local church. One way to get the names and addresses of everyone in attendance is to offer door prizes. Ask everyone to register on a slip of paper as they come in the door. The registration slips can then be used in visitation/evangelism the next week.

One sharp youth minister thought of a creative way to publicize a fifth quarter. He had school-spirit placards printed in official colors. He gave one to each student who entered the stadium one Friday night. On one side it probably read, "Go Broncos." On the other side was printed an invitation to the fifth quarter and to other youth ministry activities at the sponsoring church. Guess what was right in front of the eyes of each student as they raised their "Go Broncos" placard during the game?

Think evangelism and the creative ideas will begin to flow.

Resources

Morrow, Gregg and Morrow, Steve, *Recreation: Reaching Out, Reaching In, Reaching Up* (Nashville, TN, Convention Press, (5169-37).

Mattingly, Don, *Recreation for Youth* (Nashville, TN, Convention Press, 5200-02).

Wadley, Rick, *Recreation for the Small Church,* (Nashville, TN, Convention Press, 5200-19).

Smith, Winifred Tabb and Smith, Frank Hart, *52 Complete Retreat Programs,* (Nashville, TN, Convention Press 5200-23).

Smith, Frank Hart (comp.), *Fellowships, Plenty of Fun for All* (Nashville, TN, Convention Press, 5200-08)

Smith, Frank Hart (compiler). *52 Complete After Game Fellowships* (Nashville, TN, Convention Press, 5200-18).

Notes

1. Gordon Dahl, *Work, Play, Worship in a Leisure-Oriented Society* (Minneapolis: Augusburg Publishing House, 1972), pp. 12-19.
2. Dahl, p. 20.

9
Youth Evangelism Schools
Jim Lagrone

Introduction

Youth evangelism schools are proving to be one of the best ways to train youth in the areas of evangelism and discipleship. It could be that this is the finest type of evangelism/discipleship training ever condensed into one week. A basic premise of these schools is that evangelism and discipleship are best learned together. There must be a healthy tension and a beautiful blending of the two concepts.

The basic philosophy commits youth and youth leaders grounded in their faith to become active in evangelism. They learn how to live and grow in their faith. As a result of this intensive evangelism school, the young person and their leader will live a different life-style. They will become the type of person God wants them to be, a dynamic, Spirit-filled Christian who is clearly different from the culture by his/her radical commitment to Jesus Christ.

The youth evangelism school is a week-long event that challenges, disciplines, exhorts, and moves youth to walk with Christ. How that is done is answered in this chapter. The youth evangelism school is not a replacement for youth camp. It is a highly intensified, one-week school experience that trains and motivates youth to do evangelism. Its intensity level is that of college prep courses and it has all the dynamics of an encounter group. These schools, which are already being conducted in a number of states have several names, including SuperSummer Schools, Advanced SuperWOW, and Key Leadership Weeks. A key concept in these schools as they were being developed was to limit attendance to just a few committed youth and their leaders. These youth would then return to their churches and be models for the other youth in the church.

Even since the 1960s the youth subculture has gone through a tremendous struggle caused by rapid change. It is even harder to imagine what teenagers will be like and the choices they will have twenty years from now. These struggles demand some intensive teaching and spiritual preparation. We have moved past the day of laid-back classes and spoon-fed Bible studies. These methods will not provide teens with the help they need for growth in Christ.

Teenagers are being forced to deal with extended adolescence. Christian teaching must be more critical and demand more of them. Music, leisure, television, and movies are major influences in teenagers' lives. These are influencing the life-style decisions of youth today. Too often we get little spiritual maturity from youth because we do not demand anything of them.

Biblical Basis

The youth evangelism school demands something of a young person! This is biblical because the Bible demands something from us. It costs to be a Christian. We are not going to be saved by works, but belief and faith are not developed without effort.

The Bible tells us, "Train up a child in the way he should go, Even when he is old he will not depart from it" (Prov. 22:6). This is a basic promise in Scripture. We need to honor that promise, respect it, and act upon it.

The apostle Paul reminded us that much of his ministry was teaching. He said, "And the things which you have heard from me in the presence of many witnesses, these entrust to faithful men, who will be able to teach others also" (2 Tim. 2:2). Therefore, our goal as leadership and as Christian teachers and counselors should be to train and entrust the tools of the faith to youth.

We must remind young people not to hold back. They need to be witnesses today. They need to be growing. They need to be maturing right now to minister effectively in their community. We are preparing them to be of service whatever their vocation.

Jesus was the world's greatest Evangelist, Discipler, and Teacher. Some of His greatest teachings are found in the Sermon on the Mount. "For He was teaching them as one having authority, and not as their scribes" (Matt. 7:29). He taught them, He shared, he poured out His life into them so they, in turn, would multiply His witness and His teaching. The Sermon on the Mount shares how a person who is rightly related to God should act and conduct his/her life in a secular society. Jesus' teachings are in contrast to the thought of His day.

Today's youth culture needs the same powerful teaching. It needs to hear Jesus' life-transforming instruction. A youth must make a choice to be Christian, to be different, to live as God wants. Youth must be trained in making right choices.

When was the last time youth in your church were challenged to be peacemakers, to be pure in heart, to extend mercy, to hunger after what is righteous and good? When was the last time we encouraged our young people in our churches to integrate these qualities into their life-styles?

Jesus warned His listeners to take His words in the Beatitudes to heart,

> You are the salt of the earth; but if the salt has become tasteless, how will it be made salty again? It is good for nothing anymore, except to be thrown out and trampled under foot by men. You are the light of the world, a city that is set on a hill cannot be hidden (Matt. 5:13-14).

This has obvious evangelistic connotations. Jesus then spoke on honesty and how it affects our relationship with Him and how it would affect our evangelistic testimony if we could not be trusted. He spoke of giving, self-sacrifice, and actually loving the people in the world in which we live. Young people are crying out for love, not cheap love that has been perpetuated upon our society, but deep, unconditional love.

Jesus taught that righteousness is not just a matter between a person and others, but between a person and God. Youth evangelism schools help youth learn that righteousness is not being good in the eyes of their peers. Righteousness involves comparing their lives to God's standard.

Jesus also taught how to pray. The necessary conclusion: and effective evangelistic school is going to teach youth to have a praying life-style. Sometimes the words, *personal quiet time, time alone with God,* are used so much they have lost their meaning. It is a daily necessity for us to make contact with our Savior. We must communicate with God, not only to get us through the day, but to prepare us for the day. We will not evangelize unless we are spiritualized and empowered from time alone with God.

A youth evangelism school must deal with a youth's life-style if the young person is going to become effective in evangelism. If a youth cannot live a clean, moral, and pure life-style, then how can they convince others that Jesus makes a difference?

Jesus ended His Sermon on the Mount with instruction about judgment and how to find the straight gate. Likewise, the evangelism school has to deal with judgment and holiness.

Training for an evangelistic life-style is a biblical necessity. Training for evangelism is not some hit-or-miss proposition. It is possible to go through a memorized gospel presentation and not care about the soul for the person. A fake religion, a shallow faith, and life that does not back up what one is saying will not be accepted in the skeptical world we live in.

A youth evangelism school biblically prepares the students for today's world. It gives them a reason to go back and share. It gives them the tools to better share and the methods to continue to grow as dynamic Christians.

Youth Culture

Youth evangelism schools have a strong success rate because they are designed with the youth culture in mind. The prime ingredient is the call for genuine commitment to Jesus Christ as Lord and Savior. Many in today's world have a belief in a "Him" or a belief in some nebulous being in the sky. Young people must be taught not to accept the secular view of Christianity. They must be challenged to have a commitment to Jesus and have a genuine desire to grow in their commitment, to mature in their faith, and share themselves with other people. Youth are looking for something to commit their lives to in the midst of a shifting, fast-paced society.

Second, a youth evangelism school teaches absolute guidelines and principles for living. An effective evangelist must have an effective life-style to back up his message. In these days, the Christian must be solid and committed to the moral principles God gave us. Otherwise, there would be no difference in our life-styles and our witness would be ineffective. Today youth are hearing the culture say, "Do your own thing!" or "It doesn't matter what you believe!" America's society has fostered a generation in search of values.

Consider a typical teenager with little or no communication with his/her parents. They are unable to discuss strong contemporary issues and the pressures faced in school and life at church because they are considered taboo. They are primarily influenced by the Hollywood version of morality. They spend forty hours a week being taught television's morality. They read secular morality and guidelines for life in school textbooks. They hear athletes and rock musicians' versions of morality. One wonders if the church's version of morality can be heard.

One only needs to read the statistics of divorce, violent crimes, teenage suicide, the amount of alcohol consumed, and look at the rampant, uncontrolled drug abuse in our country to realize that somewhere along the line something is not working. Whatever approaches to teaching doctrine we have used in our churches in the past, youth need to internalize these teachings. The youth evangelism school represents a new and exciting approach to motivate youth to live in the light of God's Word and to share that light with others.

Third, the youth evangelism school also calls for learning. The major part of a youth's time is spent in school during the year. Youth are students. Their life's task is to learn how to do life. The youth evangelism school capitalizes on this major youth culture activity. The curriculum and daily schedule are designed to maximize the effect of God's Word in a youth's life for a week. Most of the youth evangelism schools involve a minimum of six hours in classroom and worship services daily. Even the recreation is designed to build relationships.

Environment is an important factor in any educational process. Therefore, the best youth evangelism schools are being conducted on college campuses. The college dorms and cafeteria serve as accommodations during the week. Most colleges operate at a limited capacity during the summer and are glad to host groups. Both secular and denominational colleges are available for this purpose. The college campus has an academic atmosphere and, therefore, is conducive to intense instruction. Depending on the college facilities youth may have access to a wide range of activities including tennis, bowling, game rooms, and so forth. The use of the college campus for training prepares youth to go on to college. In many cases youth will attend the college where the youth evangelism school is conducted. Many have heard about or even experienced the shock of being a freshman on a college campus. Conducting a week of evangelism training on the college campus sets a precedent for youth who will latter attend college.

Fourth, the youth evangelism school calls for action. If any one word describes youth and their culture it is *action*. Youth are always on the move. The youth evangelism school calls for action during the week and when youth get home. We all are familiar with on-the-job training and practice teaching for those learning new skills. It is important for youth to have an opportunity to practice what they have been learning. Many youth evangelism schools include an afternoon or evening in which youth make witnessing visits to non-Christians in the community.

The youth evangelism school is a first step, a building block, and a lifetime experience. Youth must go back home and exercise what has been learned, not to just rejoice over the learning, but to keep on learning.

Situations during a class in school, between classes, during recess, lunch break, ball games, outings, even during church activities can provide witnessing opportunities for youth. These opportunities are there and if the young person is effectively growing and trained to share his faith, youth evangelism schools give them a tool, show how to use the tool, and tell when to use the tool.

Implementation

The success of a youth evangelism school depends on several key factors. Since the intensity of the youth evangelism school is high, teaching plans and teaching methods are different. To accomplish the goals of equipping youth for evangelism in a short time, methods and content are very precise and invariable.

Age Grouping

The first factor is the separation of junior-high and senior-high students from each other and from the younger age groups. We are told the world's knowledge is doubling between every four and six years. Our world is turning so fast and things are going so quickly that we are in the midst of a technological boom. Sometimes twelfth graders have little in common with seventh graders. Consider physiological differences and it becomes obvious why public educational systems have strong age-group divisions based on developmental psychology.

Generally, these age-groups divisions are distinguished by color. Various colored T-shirts help to identify the groups during recreation and at other times. T-shirts are usually printed with an original logo designed to depict the theme of the week.

Curriculum Design

Curriculum designed to fit every age level is often so generic it becomes ineffective in today's world. Public schools have insisted that curriculum must be designed for a specific age group with specific needs. This is also a important ingredient for curriculum in a youth evangelism school. A class of eleventh and twelvth graders have much in common as a basis for discussion. However, if the class includes seventh graders the discussion has to be more general in order to include everyone. For example, the topic of dating is much different for twelvth graders than for the seventh graders. There are times when age groups should be mixed. However, the more intense the training the greater the need for specialization provided through age-group grading.

Some youth evangelism schools do not allow seventh and eighth graders to attend. The curriculum is designed to match the maturity level of the youth attending, however this younger group is often omitted because of the intensity of the week.

Most schools have a graduated curriculum. The first year a youth attends the basic school. Each year youth move up to different levels of spiritual growth and curriculum. The person coming for the third year is facing a far more advanced course than the person coming for the first year.

This creates a desire to keep coming back because the student continues to grow as he/she matures as a Christian. Youth are not constantly being fed at the basic level over and over.

Since the different levels provide a graduated level of curriculum, this provides for a variety of subjects. A student is able to progress to a higher level of learning and deal with a more intensive style of material and a wider variety of subject matter.

All of the basic schools deal with practical areas of the Christian life. The quiet time is a basic, essential tool in growth for any age Christian. We have all heard the testimony, "If someone had only shown me how to pray, I would not be in the mess I am in now." These schools offer the opportunity to learn how to pray and to spend time alone with God every day.

The basic school teaches how to read the Scripture with expectancy, to meditate, to systematically read, to have a plan, and to do this each day. The advanced courses remind youth of these basic tools each year but with new insights.

Once a student learns the basics of quiet time, worship notes, and basic discipleship, he can go on to discuss more contemporary matters. These may include building self-esteem, dating, one-parent households, step-brothers/step-sisters, and sexual pitfalls. Other topics include politics, evolution, humanism, contemporary music, decision making, and God's will. The potential curriculum for these schools at the graduate level is unlimited. Practically no subject is too taboo to touch given the college setting.

Usually the curriculum materials are provided in a nine-by-six-inch three-ring notebook. The material is printed in a workbook format with just enough printed content to aid the youth in their note taking. The notebook is also used by youth throughout the following year for recording their Christian growth and spiritual insights.

Also included is training for adults who work with youth. Most youth leaders need fellowship with other leaders. They need an opportunity to hear new ideas, new methods, and discuss speakers and musicians who can help them. The adult schools are designed to deal with problems and difficulties of youth leadership. Youth leaders need fellowship and support to deal with tremendous variance of opinions among the young people and so many different life-styles. The adult schools help train youth by training their leaders.

Family Groups

Without a doubt, the prime ingredient of a youth evangelism school is the family group. The family group consists of ten to fifteen youth of the same gender. It is also made up of youth from different churches. It may be that two youth from the same church are in the family, however, youth are challenged to learn to build relationships. The key to this cell group is the leader. Different terms are used for these leaders: Lab Leader, Mom and Pop, Family Group Leader, but all the terms mean essentially the same. The use of the terms "Mom and Pop" is folksy yet builds immediate expectation within the relationship. The leader must be a committed dynamic Christian who is excited about young people.

They minister to a group of ten to fifteen all week. They eat, sleep, and work with them twenty-four hours a day. These leaders are the "disciplers." They pour themselves into the youth and help the group realize their potential.

As youth arrive for the school they are assigned to a family group and meet their Mom and Pop. The small-group leader is assigned in advance. He/she helps them check in and begin the relationship and building process. Everyone attending the school wears a name tag all week for everything. This promotes instant name identification. Name tags are color coded with a school and have the individual names printed in large letters. Obviously, this group's leader has to be a growing Christian, understand basic evangelism, basic discipleship, relationships, and how to help all from the boisterous young person to the shy introvert. They have the most challenging assignment of the week, but they also have the most rewarding.

Effective small-group leaders are trained. They cannot be expected to perform and to share what they are not trained to do. These Moms and Pops are trained for their task during a retreat, sometimes conducted several months before the school starts. In some cases these leaders are trained on Friday, Saturday, and Sunday before the school starts on Monday. Some schools take their staff many months ahead of time for a weekend retreat. Still others train their staff on a two-day workshop period just before the week begins. Whatever method is used, training has to take place for the staff to be effective. The staff examines the study material and the overall process of evangelism. The staff will know what is expected and will be more responsive to the needs of the young person.

If the small-group leaders are not excited, gung ho, knowledgeable Christians, then the rest of the week will not work. This is the cornerstone of the school! Don't give up on this! You must find enough staff to allow for proper teaching and small-group interaction to succeed. The small-group leader is a catalyst for the large-group process. After the large-group meeting has taken place and material is given to the student, the small-group leader goes over the material one more time, and helps the student to understand and digest it. This person also has to answer questions and lead open discussions about the content.

The small-group leader also acts as recreation coordinator for his group. Often a family group is teamed with another family group in their school of the opposite sex. This team will strive together on the learning/recreation activities.

Many of the young people who come have not been able to open up to their parents, pastor, or other adults. However, because of the closeness that develops during the week and the anonymity of a person who does not live in the community with the youth, they eventually open up to the small-group leader. The family-group leader is the central cog in the evangelism-school concept. Without the successful small-group leader, 90 percent of the teaching would probably not take place.

Basic, Advanced, and Leadership Schools

These schools are made up of six to twenty family groups. The color-coded schools have all the excitement of a local school. The school is usually led by a dean, assistant dean, and a music leader. These three work together to build a group loyalty by all members of their school. This identity is developed be the school color, school song, and school cheer. The schools are also the basic unit for competition. Familites do not compete against each other. Families cooperate together to gain points for their school throughout the week. Schools are usually age-group graded and led by a teaching dean. Youth are expected to sit together as a family group during the school teaching time.

The Teaching Dean

The deans of the large groups are another major factor in the youth evangelism school. The premise is to find a dynamic youth leader or a pastor who relates well to youth and let them deliver curriculum material through well-prepared lectures. Then the smaller group dynamic is implemented in family discussions. The large-group dean presents the Bible study, the principles, and curriculum to be learned for each session.

The dean of this large-group setting is, of course, extremely important. He/she needs to be a person who can communicate effectively with enthusiasm to the young person. If a young person is sitting in class and feels like he is missing something, he is more likely to take notes. If someone bores them and does not share with them what they need to be learning, they will likely reject the person and the message.

Discipline and Challenge

It is a wrong assumption that youth do not want to do any Bible study, pray, or worship. Some youth leaders have tried to play and recreate the majority of the time and then throw in a Bible study to "Christianize" the recreation. As a result, young people were not challenged. They did not want to come back. Leadership ended by trying to throw a bigger party or event to get youth's attention. The philosophy of the youth-evangelism school is that you will get their interest by giving them a challenge.

Relationship Building Through Recreation

Good, solid enthusiastic group-building recreation can also teach and build relationships. The family group participates with another family group in competition and recreational events deemphasizing athletic ability with an emphasis on teamwork and enthusiasm. Family groups earn points for their school.

In Arkansas we award points at the end of each competition based more on enthusiasm than the one who actually won the event. This allows for the nonathletic young person to participate on equal grounds. In general, the recreational activities are noncompetitive. The key is the excitement and the dependency on each other and group dynamic involved.

The recreation does not become something to just let the kids blow off steam. It becomes something to let them learn principles and dynamics involved in the Christian life. It involves the helping of each other, the stroking of the other person's ego, the assistance of struggling together to accomplish the same goal. All of this leads toward the realization we do love each other, need each other, and are different. Jesus loves us all for what we are. The entire philosophy is to recreate with a purpose, not just play.

College Environment

The college setting is by far the best for this type learning experience. It does something psychologically when you sit behind a desk in a college classroom while the teacher or dean of your school presents the materials in lecture format. The cafeteria food, the air conditioning, all the essentials of the college setting blend in to emphasize to the older young person what lies ahead of them. This is a place of learning, not just a summer recreation experience.

Praise Worship Services

The final factor of the success of these youth evangelism schools in a high-energy, high-excitement, inspired worship service involving all of the schools. Many of our young people have not yet learned worship services can be fun, exciting, and challenging. Most of the youth evangelism schools have long worship services. They are not bound by time and are not set in the traditional one-hour mold.

The music is centered around choruses, solos, ensembles, and the aim is communal worship. It is music with meaning and prepares everyone for a tremendous message. Worship time will include testimonies, school cheers, and recognition of the day's victories. The worship is the highlight of the day. It is a time for youth to express the joy they have in Jesus. They should also once again receive the proclamation of God's Word and an evangelistic appeal.

It is pleasant to see all across the country where youth communicators and people who specialize in sharing with young people are in the forefront as speakers at this worship time. Many speakers are nationally known. The key is to find someone who can communicate to the teenager in the eighties, and more toward the nineties. God has uniquely gifted individuals in this area.

The speaker should be well schooled and versed in the art of giving an invitation. It is wrong to preach the gospel and then not to allow time for a decision. A young person should have an opportunity to recommit his/her life to the Lord or make other decisions. Generally, decisions are made in the family group times following the worship service.

Find a speaker who can communicate and speak to young people. If the speaker goes over the head of his audience, he still missed even if he sounded good doing it. We don't need misses, we need some direct hits.

Those you put on the platform to lead are a reflection of the steering committee's leadership. If they are quality people, the committee will be seen as a quality organization trying to do a quality event. If they are ineffective, unresponsive, and cannot relate to the young person, then the committee will be seen in a negative light.

Youth evangelism schools are unique and demanding upon the sponsoring individuals. Great blessings come with great responsibilities. To accomplish greater goals for Jesus Christ involves greater discipline, preparation, and commitment. The evangelism schools demand a commitment not only from young people, but from deans, family leaders, and everyone involved.

Beginning a Youth Evangelism School

Just how does one start a summer evangelism school? Either one person or a group can do it. The dream begins in one heart and quickly spreads to several others. If you have the desire to involve your youth in a youth evangelism school, then surely there are others in your state who have the same dream, desire, and goal for their own youth programs.

The need is to find one person or committee to act as a focal point for all the decisions to be channeled through. It is best to work through a state denominational office. Others who would like to have one on a smaller scale could work through a country, association, or group of churches.

Perhaps the key is involving youth leaders. It is their program. They should make the decisions. A steering committee of selected youth leaders who are excited and committed to the project can make the decisions on most details of your evangelism school. Therefore, it is their project. If people are involved, they tend to give complete support and invest themselves. Find that group of leaders who are of like mind and have the same goal and make your plans to get there. The philosophy is: we can all do together what no one of us can do alone.

Several steps will help you implement your youth evangelism school in an easy cohesive manner. First of all, pray. This is not a token prayer. If we are seeking to do God's will, if we are seeking to grow young people in the Lord, we need to have God's direction for it. If we don't have God's direction, it will be a manmade plan and have manmade results. We need God to empower every step of the way, every class, every idea, every thought, every movement involved in the school. Prayer is the essential element of seeking the mind and heart of God on what he would have you do in this particular area.

Second, in organizing your evangelism school, meet with other youth leadership of like mind and faith. Begin to pray, talk, and dream about the potential of the school. You cannot overlook involvement from other key individuals. For any type school to succeed, it has to have various amounts of support from a wide variety of church sizes and geographic boundaries.

Third, have a clearly stated purpose. If the purpose is clearly defined then participants will better understand the use of methods and rules. The main purpose is to provide training, inspiration, confidence, and tools for youth and youth leaders to become life-style evangelists. The purpose should include all the things you hope to accomplish through your school.

The next step would be to decide for quality over quantity. There is no need to start off with a thousand participants. Start off with a basic foundation for a good work and it will grow. If the school is built on basic biblical understanding, it will grow.

The only person usually worried about the quantity is the leadership involved. Your leadership can handle a smaller group at first and this will help to produce a quality experience. When your peers hear about how great your school was, then their interest will be raised. Besides, the smaller group probably is the most effective teaching tool and can actually win more people and influence more people. We need to get over this youth leader's hangup about having to get all the numbers we can before we are successful. If you provide a quality program, the numbers will take care of themselves. Quality comes first over quantity.

Fifth, determine to keep the evangelism training and evangelism emphasis a priority. Obviously, this ties into the purpose, but it is easy to have a stated purpose and then water it down to where evangelism is not the priority. The desire of the evangelism schools is to create a life-style evangelist. We need more experiences for our young people where they will learn something and then put it into action. The successful evangelism school helps youth get serious about evangelism, take it back home with them, put it into action, win some young people to the Lord, be different on their campus, and be alive in their church service.

Sixth, effective promotion is another foundation step in organizing and beginning your youth evangelism school. Persons need to know what you are doing. They need to feel they have all the information at their fingertips. They need to understand the purpose, dates, and times. They need to have posters and see advertisements in papers and magazines read by youth and youth leaders. Direct communication by letter and by telephone is unbeatable for getting the ideas across. Effective promotion will allow your experience to be richer and more people will be aware of what is going on.

Once it is all said and done there is not substitute for *work!* We can have the greatest dreams, the greatest goals, the greatest aspirations, the greatest wisdom, the greatest facilities, the greatest teachers, and all the other greatest things possible, but, if we don't work and don't get out and get after it, it won't get done. It's simple. If we come up with an idea, expect it to just be laid out together, expect the idea to be good, and take care of itself, we are sowing our own seeds of destruction. We must work to get the message across, to get the staff trained, to get all the promotion done, to get the facility and get it priced correctly to have a quality program, to get other youth leaders involved, to get the young people there.

The final step is to evaluate. There must be a system designed to allow both the student, the adult leadership, and the staff to evaluate the process. After evaluation, take some of the suggestions and use them. There is nothing wrong with using someone else's ideas and suggestions. The young person who is going through the experience may be better equipped to make suggestions than the leadership who is working in the office. The youth are in the middle of it. They know what they need much of the time. They need to have an opportunity and basis on which to evaluate.

Evaluation is essential for the ongoing program to keep it current in the youth arena. If we don't stay current, our first-year program will be out of date in three years. We must stay on the cutting edge to make the evangelism school all it can be.

Be Brave Enough to Evaluate It

The youth evangelism school is one of the brightest new events for young people that has come on the scene in recent years. It is a dynamic Spirit-filled week with the Lord, emphasizing sharing the evangelistic life-style with other people. It is quite obvious to most Christians today unless we involve the laity, unless we involve our young people in sharing their faith one-on-one, we are not going to change the course of our world. God gives the increase, but we have to be useful and usable tools to spread the gospel in our schools, where we work, and in every aspect of our society.

Evangelism training once a year is not enough to develop the evangelistic life-style. The evangelistic life-style encompasses the whole being. We are Christians. We are different. We should be able to share why we are different.

We live in an exciting and challenging day, therefore, we need to meet our day with unique methods of teaching the Christian faith. Meet that challenge! The youth leader serves on the most fertile field of evangelism in our country! The youth evangelism school helps the youth to make the right choices. As a youth worker, get involved and develop or attend a youth evangelism school. Youth are too valuable to the kingdom of God to let them go untrained and unnurtured in the life-style to which all Christians are called.

Ideas

1. Contact six other churches in your area and see if they are interested in planning a youth evangelism school with you. Supply them with a copy of this book and ask them to read this chapter and give you their opinion.

2. Conduct a week-long summer youth evangelism school just before youth start back to school. This will encourage them to begin witnessing as the new year starts.

3. Conduct a minievangelism school on a weekend during the school year.

4. Write existing youth evangelism schools for information about registration and promote this among the youth.

5. Begin to apply some of the youth evangelism school principles to your annual summer youth camp.

6. Begin a prayer group of youth leaders. The specific direction of the prayer group should be to seek the Lord's wisdom in providing evangelism training for youth.

7. Call the director of an existing youth evangelism school and ask him/her to help you start one in your area. The director may have available video footage of past schools.

8. Make plans to attend an adult school during an existing youth evangelism school. Enlist several other youth leaders from your church and/or other churches to attend with you. The adult school is designed to train you in various youth evangelism approaches which can be implemented the rest of the year. This will also allow you firsthand experience in observing the operations of a school.

9. Contact the administration of a local denominational college and inquire if they would be interested in hosting a youth evangelism school.

10. Conduct a Bible study with other youth leaders. Focus the Bible study on a search of the Scriptures for how Jesus trained His disciples in evangelism.

Resources

If you would like more information or would like for your youth to attend a youth evangelism school then contact one of the following:

SuperSummer: Youth Evangelism School
Evangelism Department
Arkansas Baptist Convention
P.O. Box 552
Little Rock, Arkansas
Phone: (501) 376-4791
Comment: One week each year; approximately eight-hundred attendance.

Florida Baptist Convention
1230 Hendricks Avenue

Jacksonville, Florida 32207
Phone: (904) 396-2351
Comment: One week a year; approximately three-hundred attendance.

Advanced SuperWOW: Youth Evangelism School
Evangelism Department
Georgia Baptist Convention
2930 Flowers Road
Atlanta, Georgia 30341
Phone: (404) 455-0404
Comment: One to five weeks a year, up to seven-hundred per week.

Kansas-Nebraska Convention of Southern Baptists
5410 West Seventh Street
Topeka, Kansas 66606
Phone: (913) 273-4880
Comment: One week a year with approximately four-hundred attendance.

SuperSummer: Youth Evangelism School
Evangelism Department
Louisiana Baptist Convention
Box 311
Alexandria, Louisiana 71309
Phone: (318) 488-3402
Comment: One week a year with approximately two-hundred attendance.

SuperSummer: Youth Evangelism School
Evangelism Department
Mississippi Baptist Convention Board
Box 530
Jackson, Mississippi 39205
Phone: (601) 968-3800
Comment: One week a year with approximately two-hundred attendance.

SuperSummer: Youth Evangelism School
Evangelism Department
Missouri Baptist Convention
400 East High Street
Jefferson City, Missouri 65101
Phone: (314) 635-7931
Comment: Two or three weeks a year with six-hundred each week.

SuperSummer: Youth Evangelism School
Evangelism Department
Baptist State Convention of North Carolina
P.O. Box 1107
Cary, North Carolina 27511-1107
Phone: (919) 467-5100
Comment: One week annually with approximately six-hundred attendance.

Youth Evangelism School
Evangelism Department
South Carolina Baptist Convention
907 Richland Street
Columbia, South Carolina 29201-2398
Phone: (803) 765-0030
Comment: One to three weeks a year with four-hundred each week.

SuperSummer: Youth Evangelism School
Evangelism Department
Baptist General Convention of Texas
Suite 1211, Baptist Building
Dallas, Texas 75201-3355
Phone: (214) 720-0550
Comment: Three weeks a year with six-hundred to a thousand each week.

10
Vocational Musicians and Evangelists

Larry Wood

Introduction

Having served as a vocational evangelist for nine years, I have discovered exciting opportunities open to the local church through evangelists. As an evangelist, I have traveled much of America and have found a lack of vision among many churches in reaching lost youth for Christ. Through trial, error, and the wisdom of others in evangelism, I have come to see the positive impact that can be made on youth.

Today, youth are discovering that life in the fast lane has no real hope, purpose, or direction. Suicides among teens are up drastically. Teen pregnancies and abortions; use of alcohol and drugs; the disenchantment of youth today with friends, family, and society are all on the increase. With this backdrop of need the evangelist and local church together can make a great impact for Christ.

The vocational evangelist and musician have a positive message of hope and encouragement to share with young people. They are gifted by God to share this message. They are capable people who are able to share this good news.

Biblical Basis

The Scripture gives us some revealing passages and insights into the evangelist and his role. There are three passages in the New Testament that speak specifically of the term "evangelist." A study of these passages helps define the role and nature of the evangelist. The three passages are Acts 21:8; 2 Timothy 4:5; and Ephesians

4:11-13. A look at Acts 21:8 reveals Paul and his friends lodged with "Philip the evangelist." Paul was on a missionary journey and spent time with Philip in his home. Although the New Testament refers to Philip as the only evangelist by name, the reference is seen in the lives of many biblical characters. A study of Philip the evangelist shows a man called and gifted to be evangelist, one who declares the good news.

When first mentioned, we see Philip as an encourager of the Christians (Acts 6:5). He was chosen as one of seven disciples to minister the Word. The Scripture then declares that the Word of God spread and the church grew rapidly. Philip was a proclaimer of the good news. He is later seen following God's direction. While in Samaria in a great spiritual awakening, God called him into a desert (Acts 8:1-40). Philip had the exciting opportunity through obedience to share the "good news" with an Ethiopian eunuch. The eunuch was searching for real life. Empowered by God's Spirit, Philip the evangelist shared the "good news" of Jesus (V. 35). The eunuch then placed his faith in Jesus as the Son of God. This passage gives us insights into the work of an evangelist. The evangelist is obedient, sensitive to God's voice, patient, prepared, and a bold witness for Jesus.

Look at 2 Timothy 4:5. Here Timothy was encouraged by Paul. "But you, be sober in all things, endure hardship, do the work of an evangelist, fulfill your ministry." The work of an evangelist is to declare the good news of Christ to lost people. Everyone can do the work of the evangelist. We must understand that telling the good news is God's desire for all believers. This must be the priority of any youth ministry.

How can an evangelist help your youth ministry? "And He gave some as apostles; and some as prophets; and some as evangelists; and some as pastors and teachers; for the equipping of the saints for the work of service, to the building up of the body of Christ [the church]" (Eph. 4:12-13). The Scripture says these gifted men are given to the church to equip the saints for the work of ministry. The term "equip" literally means to "mend the nets." These gifted men are to mend the body of Christ. They are to shape up the saints. The evangelist is a good-news bearer who is to build up the body by adding new converts to the church and by helping Christians grow.

The New Testament evangelist was one who forthrightly declared the evangel, the good news to a lost world. He called people to faith in Jesus Christ. Like Philip, today's evangelist takes the message of Jesus to persons who don't know Him. Today, we see a man like Billy Graham, who concentrates on telling the good news. He does not waver from this mandate. To fulfill the biblical role of a God-called evangelist one must take the message outside the walls of the church. We are to be fishers of men like those powerful examples of the past and present.

Today we must go to lost people. History has revealed that through the ages God has used the itinerant minister, both preacher and musician, to effectively reach the masses. God's same gifts, power, and purpose are evident today. God's Word encourages Christians to do the work of an evangelist. It also encourages us to use the God-called evangelists to reach the lost. Today, some may question the role of the evangelist, yet God still honors the office. We must not let misuses keep us from seeing God's real purpose in the use of the evangelist. God sees the church as the *base* of ministry, not the *place* of ministry. Matthew 28:18-20 gives us God's strategy for reaching the world with the good news. We are to share Jesus with all people as we go. The evangelist is uniquely gifted to help churches reach out to the lost.

Youth Culture

The whole church must be concerned about reaching lost youth. We understand the message of Christ gives freedom and liberty. Today's youth are barricaded by an antivalue culture. They must hear the good news of Christ. A look at the current youth culture helps us understand the plight of today's youth. The itinerant minister has a unique opportunity to observe youth in many situations. This helps them bring a multidimensional approach in their ministry.

"The 1980s find youth with four big issues facing them. They are identity, relationships, finding answers (communication) and absolutes."[1] Our present society is constantly changing.

In past decades youth were militant and aggressive. However, today's youth can be described as apathetic and passive. They are concerned about themselves more than others. The National Institute of Mental Health indicates there are five major societal influences on teenagers today that make it difficult for teens to cope. The influences are a soaring divorce rate, greater academic pressures, more working mothers, family mobility, and affluence. Consequences from this pressure today are:

1. Mental illness and depression—15 percent of the 65.2 million youth under age eighteen are suffering from depression;
2. Teen runaways (1.5 million in 1986);
3. The prediction for 1987 was that one in ten or 1.3 million teenage girls would become pregnant;
4. Four million girls and seven million boys will be sexually active;
5. Drinking—there are 3.3 million problem drinkers between the ages of Fourteen and Seventeen
6. And, most tragically, an increase in suicide. Suicides among teens rose 300 percent between 1955 and 1975. Suicide is the number-two killer of teens today.[2]

The youth scene is alarming! However, there is hope. We know that hope to be Jesus. While youth today are passive, they are looking for answers. Much of their entertainment revolves around music. This can be a way the church, evangelist, and musicians can work together. Generally, the vocational music evangelist has a particular style that they prefer. If that style is contemporary Christian music then they usually communicate well to today's youth.

The appeal of a guest youth communicator and guest musicians can make a positive impact in the lives of teens. There is an excitement and appeal of having outside persons come into the local church and community. The itinerant ministers join hands with and complements the local church's efforts. We have all cringed at the rock concerts being held in our cities. Many times these concerts are produced by individuals with a perverted life-style. Their songs are designed to promote this life-style among the listeners. These concerts appeal to the herd instincts of youth. Youth like and need to be with other youth. A church must find a way to meet this need. It can be met by inviting an evangelist or musicians to minister in your church.

This great dilemma in the lives of youth today must compel the church to renew and intensify its efforts to reach youth for Christ. These itinerant ministers can be used to help bridge the gap in the youth culture.

Implementation

Youth ministers and church leadership must understand and implement a thorough approach to the evangelization of today's youth. For too long we have not maximized the effectiveness of both the local church and the itinerant minister. Let us consider an approach in reaching youth that seeks to use the best gifts of the local church and the God-called itinerant minister. The emptiness and despair of teens today gives us a great opportunity to speak the "good news."

An approach that must be considered is the use of the itinerant minister. How can you plan an evangelistic meeting that will impact your community for Jesus? How can you use the itinerant minister effectively? How do you start? Who would you invite to help you? How would you determine the successfulness of your efforts? Is there a mystical maze in working with itinerant ministers or are there steps that can be clearly defined? The following are answers to these questions. We will deal with each step in the process. We will give you specific ideas and resources, also.

In order to use a vocational evangelist, musician, or any other itinerant minister, you must plan ahead. Some of these individuals and groups must be scheduled at least a year before they come to your church. Allow enough time for enlistment of the teens. You also need to prepare your church and community prior to the itinerant minister's coming.

Enlist Leadership

Begin by meeting with your pastor and staff and agree on a date for the meeting. It is understood that you and your leadership already see the need for a strong evangelistic outreach. It is suggested that you schedule the meeting at least six months to a year in advance. Longer will be needed if you invite some of the leading youth communicators of our day.

Once the itinerant minister has been invited you should confirm by letter. This will enable you and the itinerant minister to have a definite commitment. Both parties should follow through with this commitment.

Plan Preparation

God will use a gifted itinerant minister, but He also uses a prepared people. Preparation is a must! Make sure the church works hard at preparing. An example of an iceberg gives us a glimpse at the importance of preparation.

> Approximately 10 percent of an iceberg appears above the surface of the water, and the 90 percent below is unseen. The visible part compares to the period when the Crusade meetings take place and publicity and advertising about the event pervades the community. Many people erroneously assume that this is all there is to an evangelistic Crusade. So often people are not aware of the tremendous amount of effort that goes into the preparation and the preservation which is essential to reaching the goal of "making disciples." Some have the mistaken notion that "a prayer, a poster, a preacher, and a place to meet" are all that is needed. Evangelists who have been involved in a single-church or city-wide meetings preceded by limited preparations tell us the results are also very limited. There are not short cuts to preparing. That is why efforts are begun months in advance of the actual Crusade meetings in order to ensure a harvest.[3]

The pastor, minister of youth, or youth leader needs to inquire about preparation materials from the itinerant minister. Many itinerant ministers have their own suggestions and preparation materials. If an itinerant minister doesn't have his own materials you may contact the Mass Evangelism Department, Evangelism Section, of the Southern Baptist Home Mission Board for excellent preparation materials. Other suggestions are listed in the resource section of this chapter.

Preparation Principles

Here are a few basic principles for having an effective meeting with an itinerant minister. Understanding and applying the following principles are essential for effective evangelism effort.

1. Evangelism is a work of the Holy Spirit. Earnest prayer for the working of God's Spirit is the highest priority.
2. The goal of evangelism is making disciples. Planning and preparation should be undertaken in light of this goal.
3. Reaping requires sowing. This is true of the spiritual harvest, and it is true of the organizational preparations.
4. Evangelism is built on relationships. Every Christian has a part in evangelism by his loving outreach to those who surround his life.
5. Involvement produces commitment. The larger the circle of involved people, the greater will be the surrounding circle of lives that are touched for evangelism. Involve every member of the congregation in some aspect of the event.
7. Evangelism involves action and prayer. Crusade preparation requires a balance between the human and spiritual sides of involvement and prayer.[4]

Witness Training Preparation

The youth worker should involve a lot of youth and adults in this preparation phase. An effective event must have adults involved. The more adults are involved the more teenagers will be involved. The youth worker should deal with the motivation of reaching the lost during this preparation phase. Specific helps on how to invite your lost friends to the service, how to witness to them personally, and how to share one's personal testimony are a must. Today most adults and youth have some fear of rejection and don't know how to cultivate, witness to, and bring the lost into a church revival or crusade. Spiritual preparation, as well as physical preparation, are important. Once young people are motivated to witness and try it, you can't stop them.

Publicity

The method of publicity used is also vital.

> We live in a highly modernized age. Yesterday's methods will not suffice for promoting today's products. The days of mimeographed handbills in filling stations are gone. The twentieth century demands twentieth-century methods. Let it be clearly understood that we are still promoting the oldest product in the world. It does not change, but our means of attracting people to it must. We must ever be geared to the times, but anchored to the rock when it comes to revival publicity.[5]

The secular world is bombarding youth today with slick messages through radio, television, printed media, and music. In this day of heightened visual publicity, we must be more effective in publicity for the cause of Christ. A flyer that says "Revival," is not enough to get the attention of today's youth or adults. We must be creative and make this an inviting opportunity for youth and adults. A personal invitation and printed publicity go hand in hand.

The most effective kind of publicity is to use quality printed material and then put it into the hands of persons who will not only invite but also bring lost friends to the scheduled event. The preparation phase of the meeting must include practical teaching on inviting lost friends to the crusade. The most capable itinerant minister can't reach those who aren't present.

Finances

Another important item in the preparation phase is finances. The youth minister or pastor needs to communicate early with the itinerant minister concerning financial arrangements. The tendency is to neglect these needs until the meeting is almost over. That's too late. Put yourself, the church, and the visiting minister at ease by discussing finances early on. Agree on the method of paying for preparation costs for publicity. These preparation costs and expenses should be placed in the church budget. Make sure that all concerned parties knows the differences between the cost of the expenses and a love offering. Clearly state your arrangements for the love offering to the itinerant minister and to your people during the nightly meetings.

When you discuss the forthcoming revival with your evangelist, discuss the manner of the receiving and dividing of the love offering frankly. Don't embarrass him by expecting him to bring up the subject. Tell him your church's usual policy and ask him his desires. When you accepted the call to the pastorate of the church, you probably discussed the salary with the pulpit committee. You should do the same with the men you invite. This is good sense and good business. Don't pretend that it isn't important and that just anything will do. It is important and just anything *won't* do. The care of our family, education of our children, and payment of our bills are important to all of us. Have a clear understanding and do the best you can in the offering. I have never had to apologize for an offering I gave a man, or for any cause. It is with a great deal of pride that I hand a good-sized offering check to every man that preaches from my pulpit. God blesses a cheerful giver. He likewise blesses a church that expects to do big in the matter of the love offering.[6]

Consider the following as you work with the full-time itinerant minister;

Some pastors say, "I make $150 a week, so $150 for the itinerant minister is enough." But considering the fact that you also have house allowance, retirement, gasoline expenses, convention expenses, free secretarial help, free stationery and stamps, outside income from weddings, revivals, and funerals, $150 a week could actually total $250 a week with benefits.

A visiting evangelist, to the contrary, often must pay his own travel expenses, convention expenses, buy his own envelopes, and pay for his own retirement, health insurance, utilities, secretarial help, pictures, stationery, and so on. In the event of a prolonged sickness, he has no income. All of this should add up to an additional $50.00 a week, or $300. Multiply this by the fact that to be with you one full week means two weeks of the evangelist's time, and the result of simple arithmetic is that to live as well as the pastor, the evangelist would have to receive around $600 before any real love offering, over and above basic expenses, was given. All of these and other factors should be considered in receiving a love offering. This must be explained, publicly, to the people. Too often the people are never told that the evangelist is a full-time worker without a guaranteed income.[7]

The church who gives generously will be blessed. Treat the God-called itinerant minister fairly and honestly. Never make the mistake of sending the offering later. When the event is over, payday for the itinerant minister has arrived. Make arrangements to have the money counted and have a check ready. The itinerant minister probably needs it then, not next week.

Satan often will try and use finances to undermine the blessings of God. Stop this before it happens! The Lord will receive praise for a job well done! When the minister of youth or pastor communicates well here with the itinerant minister and his people, there will be a greater excitement in the overall meeting. Remember, the itinerant minister is a gift to the church. Take good care of him.

The Communicator

In short, a good evangelistic event will involve three things:

1. The preparation of the people and the preacher by much time alone with God;
2. The creation of a warm service—a genuine, friendly, happy setting created by the atmosphere of musician and preacher; and
3. The delivery of an evangelistic message.[8]

God has gifted the itinerant ministers in delivering God's Word. Let us use them well! In planning an evangelistic youth event, special attention must be given to securing an itinerant minister who communicates to youth. However, don't make the mistake of advertising the meeting as only for youth or a youth-led event. The effectiveness of the meeting in evangelizing youth will be in direct proportion to how many adults are involved. If you advertise your event as a youth event adults often will not participate. Advertise it to your people as a churchwide revival. Then the itinerant minister can gear his content to both youth and adults. Special emphasis can be given to youth activities before and after the services.

Remember that there are a large number of itinerant ministers today. Not all are skilled in either evangelism or in communicating to youth. The itinerant minister you use must be a communicator to youth! He must proclaim the "good news" in the language of the

Vocational Musicians and Evangelists

179

young people or they will "turn him off." He must also be more than just entertainment. He must have a clear understanding that you have invited him to your church to proclaim the gospel, not just to sing or speak.

A youth communicator does not and cannot compromise belief or the content of the gospel. He must understand and relate to the thought patterns, attitudes, and needs of youth culture in presenting his message. Look for this kind of man when inviting an itinerant minister. The itinerant minister, when relating to youth today, needs to proclaim the message of Christ with authority and urgency.

> Urgency is another ingredient of this aspect of the evangelist's ministry. Of course, whenever we preach, there is a sense of urgency in the message, but this comes to a climax at the moment of invitation. The urgency I feel at that time is compelling. I know there could be many who, if they leave without making their commitment to Christ, may never have another opportunity like this again. When the call for a decision has been made and many are responding, I still feel a continuing sense of urgency for those who are holding back. I've felt the same urgency as I've shared Christ with an individual on a plane, or in an office. Urgency is an indispensable part of the work of an evangelist.[9]

If we could really see the plight of youth and adults from eternity's point of view, it would rekindle our urgency and desire for reaching youth and adults with the good news.

Event Location

Now that we have looked at the messenger God uses, let's turn our attention to the place of ministry. Itinerant ministers today work through two basic roles. One works through church revivals or area-wide crusades. The other works through open-air evangelism. Some do street ministry and go where the lost youth are. You would do well to determine the kind of approach you need. The number of itinerant ministers who do open-air evangelism are limited. A number of youth ministers and pastors prefer a church setting. Fix the

location of the event at a neutral site or in the church building. Get
your itinerant minister's opinion.

A neutral meeting site like a football stadium, outdoors in a park,
a high-school gymnasium, or convention center are possibilities. This
setting breaks down barriers of lost youth and adults. By using a
neutral site, you will most likely reach larger numbers of lost persons.
If this approach is taken, make sure you have a good follow-up
process to get those persons involved in the local church.

You may choose to meet in the church auditorium. The strength
of this approach lies in the setting. You may not reach as many youth
as you would in a neutral setting. It will be easier to familiarize them
with the purpose of the church once they make decisions. With either
approach your goal is to make disciples, not just converts.

Work hard on determining your location for the meeting. With
both options you need to major on the specific methods for reaching
youth. The high school campuses offer some of the best possibilities
for reaching lost students today. Work with your school in helping
minister to the needs of students. Get to know your school administration and you will have opportunities to impact youth for Christ
through the schools. Then, when you use a guest evangelist and
musicians, they may have the possibility of scheduling assemblies
with schools. The invitation to conduct assemblies will be enhanced
by the youth director's previous involvement in the school.

The itinerant minister who is able to communicate through assemblies is a gifted person. Most itinerant ministers who do school assemblies have publicity information about the content of their
assemblies. A tape of the assembly program given to the administration will help in the decision to let the itinerant minister speak.
Letters of recommendation from other school administrators are
beneficial. The local church staff should work with the school administrators to secure these assembly programs.

Make sure that the itinerant minister is aware of his limitations in
that setting. Realizing there are many different positions represented,
the itinerant minister needs to major on the young people's needs in
facing drugs, sex, parents, and life. He must state clearly there is an
answer but he doesn't need to present the gospel there. He does need

to let the youth know there is hope. Then they would be invited to come to the meeting that night. This approach is not offensive to other beliefs but it does present an alternative. When the youth attend the service that night they will see that the alternative is Jesus.

When a church is using an evangelist or speaker the message can be enhanced by the use of special music geared to young people. Music is the heartbeat of many of today's youth. We need to be creative in our use of music. We can use good Christian contemporary music to help reach youth. The youth minister or pastor would do well to work with the itinerant minister in getting a person and/or groups to do music for the week. When done properly this can reach lost youth for Christ, and it can make the outreach of your meeting much more effective. There are limitless possibilities in using these groups or persons in neutral settings during the daytime. Through schools, clubs, shopping centers, parks, recreation areas, and more, the good news can be proclaimed. The reality of death, heaven, hell, and the assurance of salvation mandates a positive proclamation to the youth of our day. Use all means possible.

Through thoughtful prayer, preparation, and proclamation the church can have a great experience using the itinerant minister and musicians. The youth of today are open to a straightforward, positive message. The itinerant minister is uniquely gifted to share Jesus in this kind of setting. Use him well!

Ideas

1. The minister of youth can write area churches and make them aware of the special itinerant minister's coming. Be honest with them and let them know that any decisions recorded by their youth will be known to the youth ministers. This honest approach will allow for a better follow-up after the intinerant minister is gone.
2. Encourage the itinerant minister to deal with youth issues in his messages such as parents, self-image, dating and sex, friends, and relationships.
3. Where possible use school assemblies as a means of going to where the youth are. Refer to the chapter on evangelizing youth on campus for specific suggestions.

4. Use specific nights of outreach with a youth emphasis. These ideas will get the attention of youth and encourage them to bring lost friends with them. These could be Pizza Blasts, Children's Night, or parents and Teens' Night.

5. Christian contemporary concerts with a short message and invitation can be used.

6. Make sure you use a good preparation plan with your itinerant minister. Write your itinerant minister and get his suggestions.

7. Use open-air methods of evangelism during the week. Methods could include personal witnessing with both the youth and the itinerant minister at places where youth gather. Witnessing projects, could be at parks, recreation areas, and other youth gathering places.

8. "Bring Them Back Alive," is an emphasis designed to get lost friends into the evening services. Each night prior to the service the itinerant minister meets with the youth at the church. He talks to the Christian youth about the method of getting lost youth to come to that night's service. These youth are then sent out in cars to get other friends to come with them right then. It is important to get the parent's permission. This is a very effective method of reaching lost youth. This method is especially effective in smaller situations and towns.

9. While the itinerant minister is present in the meeting he needs to major on two things; first to motivate Christians to witness to lost people at work, school, and so forth; second, to actually reach lost young people and adults and bring them to the evening services.

10. Use lakes, recreation parks, and resorts in a positive way. Don't look at these places in a negative sense. Use them as points of contact. Have witnessing opportunities at the locations, remembering to work with the authorities.

11. Look at the possibility of three or four churches going together to have an enlarged evangelistic crusade with an itinerant minister who communicates well with youth.

12. Keep the communication open in correspondence between you and the itinerant minister. Write him regularly, asking for his advice and sharing your plans.

13. Design your specific follow-up plan early and train individuals to assist.

14. Capitalize on the strengths of your itinerant minister. Because of his background he may relate especially well in certain areas of youth culture. He may be able to speak in schools and to groups.

Resources

Bisagno, John R., *The Power of Positive Evangelism* (Nashville, TN, Broadman Press, 1968).

Revival Training Seminar Notebook, (Atlanta, GA, Home Mission Board, Southern Baptist Convention).

Graham, Billy. *A Biblical Standard for Evangelists* (Minneapolis, MN, World Wide Publications, 1984).

Huston, Sterling W., *Crusade Evangelism and the Local Church* (Minneapolis, MN, World Wide Publications, 1984).

American Festival of Evangelism, A series of four notebooks, Washington, D.C.

Havlik, John F., *The Evangelistic Church,* (Nashville, TN, Convention Press, 1976).

Evangelism in Southern Baptist History, Baptist History and Heritage, Volume XVII No. 1 (Nashville, TN, Historical Commission, SBC and Southern Baptist Historical Society, 1987).

Ford, Leighton, *The Christian Persuader* (New York, Harper & Row, 1966).

Wood, A. Skevington, *Evangelism—Its Theology and Practice* (Grand Rapids, MI, Zondervan, 1965).

Notes

1. Parenting Teens Seminar, Barry Wood and Emory Gadd, Session #2, Barry Wood Ministries, Lubbock, Texas
2. Ibid, Session #2, "Today's Culture," pp. 1-2.
3. Sterling W. Huston, *Crusade Evangelism and the Local Church,* (Minneapolis, MN, World Wide Publications, 1984), p. 54.
4. Ibid pp. 63-64.
5. John R. Bisango, *The Power of Positive Evangelism* (Nashville, TN, Broadman Press, 1968), p. 56.

6. Ibid, pp. 40-41.
7. Ibid, p. 42.
8. Ibid, p. 8.
9. Billy Graham, *A Biblical Standard for Evangelists* (Minneapolis, MN, World Wide Publications, 1984). pp. 57-58.

11
Evangelizing Youth
on the Campus
Dean Finley

Introduction

Having served as a youth minister in several different churches I had become susceptible to the fallacy it was impossible to do evangelism on the local campus. It was not until I began to travel across America I realized the vast possibilities for evangelism. After interviewing over a thousand youth leaders it became apparent youth leadership should not only consider the possibilities of evangelism but they have an obligation to be involved in the life of the local school campus.

The local junior or senior high campus is one of the most exciting places a youth leader can be. More can be learned about youth and their needs by observing their activities in the school hallways for ten minutes than in a year of teaching youth in Sunday School.

Biblical Basis

The church must have a campus ministry because it has the truths that can help guide youth's life development. The New Testament gives us one verse describing most of Jesus' life. Luke 2:52 tells us about eighteen years of the life of Jesus. This verse describes Jesus' life between the ages of twelve and thirty. The Scriptures tell us a lot about Jesus' birth, ministry, and passion. The Bible tells us about one incident in Jesus' life at the age of twelve while He was visiting in the Temple. Luke 2:52 describes for us what Jesus encountered as a teenager. It tells us Jesus grew in wisdom and stature and in favor with God and man. The next time we hear about Jesus is the beginning of His ministry at age thirty. Luke 2:52 describes the actions of Jesus as He passed through the youth years. Above all, the local school is concerned with the a teenager's intellectual growth. Thus, the church must consider the work of the local school system.

Youth leaders must get involved in the local campus because they have access to the greatest teacher of all time. Jesus is the Master Teacher. The term used to address Jesus during the last three years of His life was Rabbi or Teacher. Jesus said; "You call Me Teacher and Lord; and you are right, for so I am" (John 13:13). Jesus not only taught in word but also through His actions. "For I gave you and example that you should do as I did to you" (v. 15) If you conducted a poll of scholars and asked them to list the ten greatest teachers in the world, Jesus not only would be included in the list, but would be the most often mentioned. Therefore, it is totally illogical for an educational institution to completely ignore the teachings of the greatest Teacher in the world. When a youth leader thinks about conducting a campus ministry the permeating idea is not "How can I get Jesus onto the campus?" but the question is "How can I get the campus turned on to Jesus?" Jesus never left the campus. All of us as youth leaders need to figure out how to join Him. Jesus is a Teacher. You would expect to find a teacher where teaching is going on.

Jesus came "to seek and to save that which was lost" (Luke 19:10). Where are the lost? They are on the local campus. The example of Jesus was to go to those who were in need.

The campus is the place to carry out the ministry of reconciliation that Jesus has given to every Christian.

> Now all these things are from God, who reconciled us to Himself through Christ, and gave us the ministry of reconciliation, namely, that God was in Christ reconciling the world to Himself, not counting their trespasses against them, and He has committed to us the word of reconciliation (2 Cor. 5:18-19).

What was the ministry of Jesus?

> The Spirit of the Lord is upon Me. Because He anointed Me to preach the gospel to the poor. He has sent Me to proclaim release to the

captives, and recovery of sight to the blind, To set free those who are downtrodden, To proclaim the favorable year of the Lord (Luke 4:18-19).

A campus ministry is a necessity because it is a fulfillment of the Great Commission.

And Jesus came up and spoke to them, saying "All authority has been given to Me in heaven and on earth. Go therefore and make disciples of all the nations, baptizing then in the name of the Father and the Son and the Holy Spirit, teaching them to observe all that I commanded you; and lo, I am with you always, even to the end of the age" (Matt. 28:18-20).

Christianity has always had its missionaries who were willing to go wherever God sent them. The local school campus is no less a mission field than Africa or China. As a matter of fact, some of the same principles apply. Consider the following:

1. As we go we must learn the language of the hearers. We cannot speak English to Spanish-speaking people and expect them to understand.
2. One who goes out in the name of Jesus must still learn the culture of the hearers.
3. A missionary must be one willing to minister to those in the mission field.
4. A Christian on mission must be willing to meet the needs of all he encounters including physical, mental, educational, emotional, psychological, and so forth.
5. A Christian leader always depends on the power of God and the leadership of the Holy Spirit to do what cannot be done by them.
6. The Christian on mission does not apologize for going. They are trying to do the best thing one person can do for another person (that is, introduce them to Jesus Christ).

The question for the Christian youth leader is not, Can I minister on the campus? The question is, Am I willing to pay the price to do the ministry? Youth leaders are not going to decide if God wants them on the campus or not; that has already been decided. The campus is a place where there are lost people. God wants to redeem all lost people. "The Lord is not slow about His promise, as some count slowness, but is patient toward you, not wishing for any to perish but for all to come to repentance" (2 Pet. 3:9). As youth leaders we are not going to vote on whether or not it is right for us to move onto the campus. God is already on the campus working even as you read this. The question for us is, Will we go and join in the work God has already set before us?

Youth Culture

Youth culture revolves around local schools. Nine months out of the year youth spend their time in the educational system. Youth are required by law to be in school until they are sixteen. Ask any group of experienced youth leaders what would be the top five influential factors in any young person's life, and without a doubt school is one of those. The school provides a format for friendships and also serves to guide youth in career decisions. Depending on who you speak to it may be that the school is most influential factor outside of the family.

Youth's View of School

To understand youth you must understand their view of school. Of course, there are many reasons teens stay in the school process, social and personal. However, their view of school is different from their reasons. It involves their conception of what the school can do for them. This view molds their attitude about the educational process and institution. It is difficult to generalize feelings because everyone has their own. However, there are some basic ones that can be identified. Youth views can be divided into three groups: the pursuers, the plodders, and the pretenders.

The pursuers are youth who are brought into the school system as a necessity for life. This group includes 30 to 60 percent. These youth usually have very definite goals. They can usually tell you the vocation they hope to pursue. It may be they plan to be an architect, teacher, mechanic, athlete, doctor, and so forth. Generally, they do well in the subjects that prepare them for their chosen field. They view school, or at least classes related to their field, as a means to an end. Therefore, these youth have a future orientation. Often you can find them in an extracurricular activity or club that relates to their interest.

The plodders are youth who attend school because they are required and expected to. This group also includes 30 to 60 percent of the total group. This group lives with few goals. They have a present orientation. Since they have no specific goals when they finish school they see school as a necessary evil.

The third group has no basic interest in school and views it as a waste of time. In many cases they are just attending because of expectation and the law. These students often drop out at the legal age. If they do not, they continue because of peer pressure, adult encouragement, or fear of other options.

Parents' View of School

Another important group that influences the campus environment is parents of teens. Parents are the most powerful influence in a teen's life. The parents' attitude towards the school system will almost always be directly reflected in the life of their teenager. It is obvious that parents have three general views of school: the pusher, the provider, and the passive. These views are found within every social or economic class.

The pusher parents view education as a panacea for the problems youth face. They push their teen to "get a good education so they can get a good job." Grades are often a major discussion for this family. This is true because it is the major form of feedback for the parents to judge if their teen is learning. Also, you may find these parents involved in the PTA or other school volunteer programs.

The providing parent is one who has a somewhat neutral view of the school. They are basically uninvolved in the process. Their only involvement or encouragement is to provide the necessary school equipment and assure the attendance of their teens.

The final group of parents is passive toward the school and the educational process. These parents provide no moral support for the difficulties their teen face in the educational process. They may even have the attitude their teen would be better off getting a job and going to work. They are often critical of the educational process.

Teachers' and Administrators' View of School

The last important group that influences the everyday workings at the local school is the teachers and administrators. This group can usually be divided into two groups; those that view their task as helping youth to learn, and those who teach because it is their way of earning a living.

Those who teach to earn a living are most likely to have the attitude that they teach a subject and not people. Their goal is to accomplish the teaching task, fulfill their job description, and leave. These teachers are like people who are just earning their bread on the job but really their major interest lies somewhere else. It would be hard to support the statement, however, many teachers are teaching for this reason.

Some teachers are teaching because they love students and want to help them. Thank God for Christian teachers who are trying to help youth mature. Not all of these teachers are Christians, however, some teach from a purely humanitarian viewpoint. Nevertheless, they are a group that cares for the students in their classrooms.

All of these views influence the receptivity of evangelism in the local school. It is hard to approach schoolteachers and administrators with how much you can help the teens morally if they do not see that as a part of their task. The problem is never that our message, the gospel, does not fit. The gospel is applicable for all people in all situations. It is our task as youth leaders to communicate it in all situations. Space does not permit a total examination of how evangelism relates to all of the different views of the schooling process. However, each of these provide open doors for evangelism.

Major Ingredients In the School

Consider seven other characteristics of the campus that are integral to youth culture. Each of these provides avenues for ministry. Church leaders will want to brainstorm what ministry actions would provide an opportunity for evangelism.

1. Study—Homework: Youth are responsible for mastery of content.
2. Leadership training: Youth are involved in school government, athletics, and so forth, which allow them to take leadership roles.
3. Process—Cognitive Disciplines: Youth not only have to learn content, but they must learn how to learn. Fifty percent of any study effort is learning how to deal with authority (teachers) and figuring out how to master subject matter.
4. A Class-Structured Society: Technically, we do not have "classes" in our society. However, there are groups based on interest, financial, education, and so forth. Youth must learn how to cross these boundaries in order to be all God intended them to be.
5. Social Reference—Extracurricular Activity: In most cases youth develop their close relationships from the individuals they meet in school.
6. Life's Partner Reference: Youth will marry someone they know. Therefore, the school is a place of introducing individuals to their potential life partner.
7. Vocational Orientation: The school offers both education and counseling related primarily to youth's job preparation.

Each of these seven items are a part of the youth school culture. Each are opportunities for evangelism. For examaple, I once taught a group of teenagers techniques for memorization. During the process they memorized Scripture from the Roman Road gospel presentation. I encouraged them to apply the techniques in whatever they did. After five weeks a youth came into my office with a history test. He had made an A on the test and was so thankful because he had been failing. As you develop a strategy for delivering the gospel to the local campus consider the factors already present. Some ideas related to these factors can be found at the end of this chapter. However, the best ideas will be the ones God gives to you directly as you are sensitive to His Holy Spirit.

Implementation

Youth Leader Responsibility

Youth leadership must know and understand the structure of the local school in implementing a strategy of evangelism for the campus. You may assume it is not possible to do anything on the local campus. However, nothing is further from the truth.

If you listed individuals in the community who are qualified to help young people, the list would have to include the youth leaders in the local church. Sometimes these leaders have more interest in youth than do some teachers or administrators in the school. The church youth leaders are people who volunteer their time. They do not work with youth for material gain. These leaders work with youth because they want to, not because they have to. It can be shown that these leaders not only have the skills and motivation to work with youth but, in many cases, they have a moral obligation to get involved. It is time that youth leaders stop shirking their responsibility and get involved in the local school program.

Youth leaders in the church have a responsibility to both the community and to God. Major emphasis is given every four years to "turn out the vote" for a presidential election. Likewise, every person has been given the right and the obligation to improve the community welfare. Youth leaders in the churches are also a part of the community. Church youth leaders must exercise this right of involvement. If youth leaders avoid contact with the community school system then it will, no doubt, become more secular as the society becomes secularized.

Contextual Strategy

First, understand the structure of the schools. In order to approach the school, a person must consider its whole structure. A strategy must consider staff, teachers, support personnel, and students. Any one who attempts to approach the school must realize than any contact with one of these groups will result in some influence on all of the other groups.

Second, approach schools based on service. Evangelism at the local school campus must be servant evangelism. A great number of schools are in need of funds for services. These funds are generally the last to be allocated in a school budget and the first to be cut. These services touch all parts of the school and profoundly affect the quality of education in the school. No one can resist the ministry of a servant. Jesus set the model for a servant attitude and ministry.

Third, the school is an educational institution. In most cases this means that the school is a provider of information. In some technical sense it is not to teach the students *what* to think, but *how* to think. A strategy of campus evangelism will be effective according to how much it blends with this purpose. If the only or exclusive reason a person is on the campus is to get teens to "buy their product," religious or otherwise, they will find little receptivity.

Fourth, the school is a part of the community as a whole. The local school must be thought of as a part of the community, and not an appendage. It often is not only the center for intellectual training but also is the cultural art center, sports-entertainment complex, and social catalyst for not only youth but the community at large. Therefore, it operates on community principles. Volunteerism is a wonderful process in America, and it provides the lifeblood of any community. Youth and their leaders are not only have a right but a moral obligation to be involved in the local school community and its government. Someone is going to have to make the decisions related to the school community. The school staff will make some but experience proves that those decisions will be influenced by the active voices of the community. I cannot think of anyone more capable of strengthening the educational process than those proclaiming eternal truths based on the gospel of Jesus Christ.

Legal Entanglements

The following information is not intended to be a definitive statement on the legal implications of being involved in the local school system. It should be a starting point for research and dialogue. The attempt is to state some of the implications in laymen's language and not legalese. This information is provided to encourage youth leaders to go ahead and become involved in the school without fear of legal repercussions.

There are at least four major institutions in society: the church, the family, the school, and the government. Each of these has a different societal function. Each institution can be thought of as having a unique personality designed to accomplish a single goal. These goals are all related to every individual of the community and thus sometimes overlap. It is impossible for these institutions to operate totally isolated from each other. The local high school teacher will attend church with his family, and vote for political leaders. Also, the minister may send his children to the public school and be asked to pray at the Fourth of July celebration. The question for the institutions is not how can they operate isolated from the rest; that is impossible. The question for these institutions is how will they work out their relationships because they cannot avoid relating to one another.

A youth leader should first have some understanding of the intentions of legal rulings related to religion in the schools. In recent years much has been said about the entanglement of religious and state institutions. Many have assumed it is not possible for there to be any mention of religion in the public school system. Nothing could be further from the truth. The intention of supreme court rulings is not to eliminate religion from the society. If this were so it would be religious oppression and, thus, unconstitutional. Anyone who hopes to work with the school system must have a basic understanding of the function of the school in the society and how the society views the role of religion. The following points are foundational for America's educational system:

1. The schools are to be a system for the free flow of ideas and concepts. It is an information system and not an indoctrinational institution.

2. The supreme court has ruled limiting only four activities: a. State directed and required on-premises religious training; b. state directed and required prayer; c. state directed Bible reading, d. state supervision of posting the Ten Commandments.

3. Thus the school must not promote religious/philosophical/ideological concepts, nor can it inhibit these.

4. The test of a idea on the school campus must pass the test of not interfering with the process of the school or infringe on the rights of others, including students, teachers, and community.

5. Objections to ideas cannot be based primarily on the content of the concept but must be based on the criterion in the previous statement (no. 4). This means that the state can only restrict those activities that constituted a danger to those interest it is charged with protecting. Some things the school cannot keep the individual pupil from doing:

1. Bringing their Bible to school
2. Praying
3. Witnessing
4. Ministry

Each of these items are the individual's biblical task. It appears that on a personal level there is almost nothing that we cannot do on the local campus. We must be ready to reply, "For which one of these good things are we being accused of doing?" Also, it is important for us to remember that not everything that is lawful is expedient.

School Receptivity

Measure the school system's receptivity to religion as you plan your campus strategy. Take steps to move the receptivity from a one (1) closed school to a five (5) open school.

1. Closed School: This school system is suspicious of any religious person and any religious language. The school authorities are usually anti-religious. Usually this reflects views of particular schoolteachers and administrators. This may not be school-board policy.

2. Community-Service School: This school is open to community service and volunteerism but does not allow "religious activity" within the school building and time. This school is suspicious of motives but will allow monitored actions.

3. Free-Access School: This school will allow the clergy free access to its students at selected times. The clergy and those with religious

agendas are viewed in a positive way and have a right to be available to students.

4. Semiopen School: This school is one that opens classrooms, assemblies, and organizations for religious information. Religious clubs and church activities are not viewed with suspicion. On the contrary, they are encouraged.

5. Open School: the open school is one that has guidelines for religious activities within the school. However, it views school and church as partners in the educational process. This school may even turn to the church for help and assistance.

Rural, Urban, and City Schools

In general, there are some differences in rural, urban, and city schools. Each of these situations demands close examination of the particular school and school systems. However, some of the characteristics of these schools are obvious. The city and rural school tends to be a commuter campus. This means that extracurricular activities may be less than at the urban school. The rural school is probably the closest knit group. The rural community has fewer distractions and persons are usually more aware of what takes place inside the school. Therefore, a single act of ministry in the rural school will have the greatest impact. In contrast, a single act of ministry in an urban school may go unnoticed by both the community and school. Analyze your school system to see how it is affected by the community environment as you plan your campus strategy.

Strategy Is Required

Any campus ministry without a basic strategy or plan is already moving towards failure. The school is a system. It is a highly organized institution with specific goals. The antithesis of school is a student wandering in the hall with no place to go. Therefore, any campus ministry must have a specific purpose, goal, and stated action plan. Without strategy a campus ministry has no hope of survival. The plan is basic to learning to work within the system and not around it.

Implementing Your Strategy

Consider developing the following factors into your campus youth evangelism strategy.

1. Prepare all of those who are going to be involved in the campus ministry in spiritual warfare. This means involving them in prayer, Bible study, and a regular support group.

2. Test your campus ministry strategy to see if it involves youth and adults both inside and outside the school. All of those involved in the campus ministry learn to multiply themselves. They should never work alone on any task. Every action should be done by at least two individuals, preferably three.

3. Your strategy must have more than one approach to the school and may involve more than one school. Are you using many different avenues? Are you attempting to reach every facet? Do not try one approach at a time but choose at least three actions and implement them simultaneously.

4. Prepare every action with a contingent plan. Plan to be flexible.

5. What motivations are within your strategy? What is your motivation? What will be the motivation of adults and youth? What motivations have you offered to non-Christian youth? Why should school teachers and administrators work with you?

6. Identify subgroups of any size and their common ground. Make plans to reach every group within a two-year period.

7. Teach involved youth and adults the biblical doctrine of ministry and service based on the life of Jesus.

8. Enlist several people who will be specialists in the area of conflict resolution. Include in this group a lawyer, a school administrator, and a teacher who all have a positive understanding about ministering to youth in the school.

9. Use the homes of youth near the school as a basis of operation for strategy planning. Also, use these homes for campus meetings.

10. Continue to work at a balanced strategy that is multifaceted.

11. Check to see if your strategy contains multiple evangelism approaches including: mass envangelism, personal evangelism, life-

style evangelism, relational evangelism, and prayer. (See the chapter on "Discipleship and Evangelism" for help.)

12. Simply stated, do the following:

a. Get adults involved who are willing to involve others.

b. Gather information about how the school works and plan to work with the school.

c. Get permission and/or authority from school and church to carry out a plan of action.

d. Get organized and have a plan of action.

e. Involve youth that are related to your local church.

f. Continually revise plans and strategies and originate new approaches.

g. Take bold steps personally.

Conclusion

American has a wonderful educational system. It is the envy of the world and this is proven by so many internationals traveling here to study. The school can not avoid determining its policies and procedures based on ideologies. These will be the ideologies of those who are involved in the leadership of the educational system. *Involvement* is the key word. This involvement is not just limited to those employed by the system. It also includes curriculum writers, teachers, administrators, volunteers, school boards, and other elected officials. It is an obvious fact that church youth leaders will have very little influence on the school if they avoid their responsibility to be involved. The old saying, "Use it, or lose it" applies here. Either church leaders will get busy and be involved in the schools or the schools and their pupils will suffer.

Ideas

1. Many schools are open to outside lecturers who have some expertise in a related subject. I know a Christian college physics professor who regularly lectures at Christmas time about the star that appeared at the birth of Jesus.

2. Many youth leaders have college or academic degrees that would

allow them to substitute teach in the local school. It is a simple process for them to apply for substitute teaching.

3. Groups in the school that are based around a common extracurricular activity are often open to servant ministry. Some of these include sports, drama, vocational interest, academics, government, debate, business, farming, drafting, vocational-technical, woodworking, car repair, computer science, and so forth.

4. Conduct a silent stand-in. Approach the local school administration and ask permission to conduct a silent stand-in of support for the school. The stand-in is to be conducted late at night with every teen enlisting an adult to jointly hold a candle for fifteen minutes as they stand surrounding the school building.

5. Drive your car to the school and park where you can observe students going and coming. The best time to do this is before school starts in the morning. As you watch the students ask God, "Please show me what are You already doing on this campus and how can I be a part of it." Be ready to write these down as the Lord gives them to you.

6. Find out the birthday of everyone you can in the school. Ask a person in your church to be the birthday-cake baker or budget this item. Visit these people at the school with the cake and use the opportunity to build relationships.

7. Begin to get involved in extracurricular activities. Offer to help find resources and provide sponsorship, and so forth.

8. Volunteer for any position open at the school and offer to serve without pay. This includes teaching, coaching, maintenance, and so forth.

10. Counseling is a major need at the school. Offer to help in counseling student vocationally and/or dealing with relationship problems.

11. Very few school systems are designed to deal with emergencies. Offer your help to deal with sick students or family emergencies that arise during the school hours.

12. Offer all of the church's resources to the school including: building, bus, lights, media, grounds, and so forth.

13. Find out what talents the school has to offer and provide an

opportunity for those talents to be used, especially, in the area of music, drama, and so forth.

14. Conduct a one-day vocational introduction with people in your church available for consultations about the vocation in which they serve.

15. Offer the school special-skills training in memorization, religion, car repair, karate, swimming, and so forth.

16. Design yell placards ten-by fourteen inches with the school mascot on one side and information about your church on the other.

17. Plan to feed the masses. The first day of school have a soft-drink giveaway or pizza feed.

Resources

Whitehead, John W., *The Freedom of Religious Expression in Public Universities and High Schools* (Cosway Books, a division of Good News Publishers, IL, 1985).

The Dynamics of High School Evangelism (Campus Crusade for Christ, California, 1974).

Sharing the Abundant Life with High School Students (Campus Crusade for Christ, California, 1974).

Class Room [sic] *Speaking: A Christian Perspective in the High School Classroom* (Campus Crusade for Christ, 1976).

12
Evangelizing Youth Conferences and Rallies

Doug Couch

Introduction

For generations, teenagers have been characterized by rebellion and aloofness, leading some to conclude that teens are unreachable and unteachable. Statistics claim otherwise. In actuality, 60 to 85 percent who accept Christ do so before the age of eighteen. Youth are reachable, and we have a challenging responsibility to reach the lost teen population for Christ. Not only this, but we must also take responsibility for equipping youth to evangelize their lost peers. A youth evangelism conference, whether conducted on an associational, regional, or state level, is an excellent tool for accomplishing both objectives. This chapter on evangelistic youth rallies is designed to help you grasp a practical, working knowledge of how to dream, plan, implement, and follow up a youth evangelism event involving hundreds of adults and youth. A youth evangelism conference may involve as few as a hundred or as many as thirty thousand.

Biblical Basis

The account of Pentecost in Acts 2 sets an example and a basis for the youth evangelism conference or rally. Thousands experienced the thrill of the Holy Spirit moving in their midst, building them up, and preparing them for ministry of their own. Thousands were saved, all those attending were moved by the excitement of the crowd. A crowd gathered to praise and worship our Lord still fosters a natural excitement, built upon with dynamic music and inspirational preaching. These ingredients of the youth evangelism conference create a positive atmosphere conducive to the presence, control, and life-changing power of the Holy Spirit.

Other Scripture texts provide evidence upon which to develop a biblical basis for the youth evangelism conference. In his vision of the many dry bones in a valley in Ezekiel 37:3, the prophet was asked by God, "Son of man, can these bones live?" The text is important in two aspects. First, we must have a vision of the need for youth evangelism. It is the essential first step, for we must recognize and understand the need before we develop a strategy for the solution. Second, we are interested in the spiritual development and well-being of teenagers must ask ourselves, "Can these bones live?" Can our teenagers come to life, rise up, and become champions for Christ in a world of "dry bones" and lost hope? Is it possible for youth to practice a Christian life-style in a non-Christian world of materialism and decaying moral values? Is it possible for Jesus Christ to have personal relevance in the lives of today's teenagers? Just as Ezekiel witnessed the dry bones come to life as God put His Spirit into them, the answer must be an emphatic and resounding *yes*!

While it has been shown that 85 percent of all persons accepting Christ do so before the age of eighteen, it is my opinion that many churches lose close to 90 percent of their youth after the tenth grade. Why? The answer is one word—*relevance*. Someone once said that any information has power only to the extent that the information has personal relevance. There is a marked difference between saying there is a bomb under *a* house and saying there is a bomb under *your* house.

How does this relate to youth? A number of youth involved in the church accepted Christ as children when their understanding of Christianity was limited to the concrete, literal thinking of a child. As that child becomes a teenager, however, his capacity for understanding has embraced the abstract as well. Unless a teenager is led to rededicate his life to Christ, and unless his faith is updated from the concrete to the abstract, the personal relevancy of Jesus Christ is sometimes lost following the junior high years. Jesus Christ is no longer a motivating force in their lives in regard to life-style and witnessing.

Participating in an evangelistic, inspirational event such as a youth evangelism conference helps to challenge youth to a renewed commitment. As youth hear preaching relevant to their needs and see lost friends won to Christ, they can evaluate their own standing with the Lord and His relevance. Thus, the youth evangelism conference also becomes an effective means of building up and strengthening the body of Christ.

Youth Culture

Youth culture is characterized by a distinct set of needs, interests, and motivations. It is essential that we evangelize and minister to youth with this in mind; otherwise, our efforts are lost on an inattentive audience. Advertisers and musicians tailor their messages specifically to youth, to their needs, and at their level. We must do the same in an interesting, motivating, and meaningful fashion.

Some changes are inevitable in the teen years. Once-influential familial ties are now cast aside for peer relationships. Where youth go, what they do, and the decisions they make are now largely determined by what their peers think, say, and do. Thus, a large group gathering such as the youth evangelism conference is an excellent opportunity for youth to find needed fellowship, support, and acceptance. Youth culture's interest in music is recognized with dynamic music and group singing. Inspirational preaching satisfies their shared search for meaning and answers. The whole concept of the youth evangelism conference is directed to the interests of the youth culture. In a time when "bigger is better" the conference can attract large numbers of youth and be a phenomenal, life-changing event.

Another aspect of youth culture is teens' exposure to the glamor of sports, music, and movie entertainment. These things compete for the teen's attention. We must remember an important rule in attempting to reach youth: "Thou shall not be boring!" A quality program with spiritual content that will not elicit snores and boos from the audience is essential. We must be careful to walk a thin line between the two extremes, recognizing both their need for spiritual training and their cultural context.

Specifically, the youth evangelism conference or rally fits into the youth culture by:

1. Providing teens who are always looking for something different to do with an outlet.

2. Provides opportunities for peer interaction.

3. Provides an opportunity for teenagers to identify with and learn from their peers through youth testimonies. Teenagers often feel "no one understands." These testimonies are important, as they affirm the teenagers' sense of normalcy.

4. Provides youth with an exciting alternative in preaching and music to rock concerts and media events.

5. Provides a positive spiritual atmosphere which encourages youth in their faith. The foundations built at these conferences are necessary during the unstable teen years.

Implementation

There are several guidelines to follow in the implementation of a youth evangelism conference. These organizational suggestions are applicable for any level conference, whether associational, regional, or statewide.

Preparation

Planning is an important factor to the success of the youth evangelism rally or conference and encompasses several areas of preparation. First, you must define your target area in which to conduct and promote the conference. It may be within your association, within a region of a sixty-mile radius, or it may involve your entire state. Be confident that the area you select is able to produce a large crowd of youth. Although quality is more important than quantity, a larger attendance stimulates enthusiasm and generates positive approval.

Second, involve others. Contact every church within the target area for a planning meeting to evaluate interest. One way to increase interest is to provide a meal along with the meeting. This will allow volunteer youth leaders to take their lunchtime for the meeting. It will also provide for instant fellowship. At the meeting, discuss the purpose, approach, and planning process of the conference. If it appears that a shared interest exists, proceed to make descriptions of and assignments to various committees. A total of seven committees are necessary to plan and implement the youth evangelism conference. These are publicity, registration, seminars, program, facility arrangements, counseling, and follow-up. Make certain all committee chairpersons and members understand their responsibilities and accountabilities. Attempt to involve as many individuals as possible. Although two to four persons could actually carry about 90 percent of the responsibility, the more you involve, the greater your response will be from their individual areas of influence.

Third, organize a steering committee composed of the committee chairpersons. The primary responsibilities of the committees follow.

Publicity Committee

Without a doubt, the most critical position on the steering committee is that of the publicity chairman. Your youth evangelism conference is sure to succeed with a well-organized, thorough, and excited publicity chairman who is able to generate enthusiasm toward the event. His and his committee's responsibilities include the compilation of information to be included in registration packets. These packets are sent to each church in the designated area of the conference. Mailing lists and labels are usually available from the associational or state office. Each registration packet should include:

1. An introductory letter from the program coordinator announcing the meeting, its purpose, date, time, and location. The letter should also detail registration instructions.

2. A map of the area encompassing the meeting location, marking seminar and rally areas. It is also helpful to highlight restaurants in the area for those groups traveling a distance.

3. A program outline of afternoon seminars and the evening rally.

4. A program poster eleven-by-fourteen inches and fliers to help promote the conference at the local church.

5. Several clip-art pieces carrying the program theme. These are helpful to churches who wish to promote the conference in their newsletter.

6. A list of contacts and phone numbers for persons to call if questions arise. These contacts may receive numerous calls, but it is important to be pleasant and helpful. If a person is turned off to one of the contact people, they could very well be turned off to the program.

7. A registration form with clear, concise instructions for registering and paying fees.

Some may be wary of charging youth to attend church, but when you require a registration fee, you send a message to youth that the rally is worth going to. Teenagers often think things have to cost something to be good. They are accustomed to paying twenty dollars for rock concert tickets and maybe even fifteen dollars for a souvenir T-shirt. Your budget for the conference may also not be large enough to attract top speakers and musicians or secure adequate facilities. The registration fee is an excellent secondary source of finances to help make your program top-notch and have as much of an impact on youth as possible.

Registration Committee

The registration committee is involved in planning and registering all groups who attend the conference. The responsibilities of this committee are:

1. Receive and record preregistration forms and fee payments from the churches,

2. Deposit registration fees,

3. Keep the seminar and arrangements committees informed of the number registered,

4. Prepare a system for late registration, and

5. Handle correspondence with preregistered churches as necessary.

Seminar Committee

If it is at all possible it is best to conduct witness and leadership training seminars at your youth evangelism conference. These sessions can be very helpful to youth and youth workers alike. They provide an alternative to the large-group sessions and provide for more personal interaction. The seminars are generally held in the afternoon, the same day of the evening rally. On the average, 50 percent of those who plan to attend the rally choose to participate in the training seminars. The committee is responsible for selecting the materials for teaching. The committee should be responsible for the following items:

1. Edit the teaching materials and prepare them for youth study with work sheets, booklets, etc.

2. Enlist and train seminar instructors.

3. Organize a strategy for dividing youth into seminar groups.

4. Work with the arrangements committee to secure areas for study.

5. Be available during and oversee the afternoon sessions.

6. Enlist leaders for adult leadership training sessions for those who work with youth.

Program Committee

The program committee is responsible for contacting and securing commitments from those persons selected by the steering committee as the program personnel. In addition, the committee is responsible for meeting the housing, meal, transportation, and other needs of these persons. Many times you will find that your choices for program personnel do not work out due to conflicting schedules or various other reasons. It is wise to have listed a second and third alternative to avoid delay and extra meetings. The program committee will also want to follow up with the following details:

1. Send confirmation letters to program personalities. Plainly state in these letters what is expected of the group or individual. Also, include all arrangements, and details about the handling of expenses, including honorariums or love offerings.

2. Arrange to meet all program personalities at the airport or lodging accommodations.

3. Arrange transportation during the meeting for program personalities, if needed.

4. Arrange for meals of program leadership.

5. Communicate to the facilities/arrangements committee any special needs of speakers and music groups. This may include piano, overhead projector, microphones, platform arrangement, and so forth.

6. Write follow-up letters to program personalities, thanking them for their ministry and sharing the decisions that were made during the conference.

Counseling Committee

The counseling committee chairperson and members should be able to understand the counseling and counselor training process. The decisions that are made during the rally or conference must be recorded and immediate help and encouragement should be available. The committee does not have to perform counseling duties themselves. Prior to the rally, during the afternoon seminars, conduct counselor training sessions for interested adults. A simple announcement from the platform is usually all that is necessary to find a sufficient number of counselors. Instruct them to use the materials, cards, pencils, tracts, and so forth that you have secured and placed in a designated area. Several guidelines to follow during the counseling period are:

1. Every person responding during the invitation should meet with a counselor.

2. Everyone responding should be led in a sincere prayer of repentance.

3. All should be given follow-up material and be encouraged to begin a practice of daily Bible reading.

4. Each person should be encouraged to share with the others in their group the decision they made and share with their local church during the public invitation the first Sunday following the conference.

After the counselors have completed their time with the youth, the committee should collect and tally the decision cards and then pass them along to the follow-up chairman.

Follow-Up Committee

The youth evangelism conference does not end when final prayer has been said or the last light is out. Follow-up is essential. The follow-up committee is responsible for seeing that each teenager who responded at the invitation receives a letter of encouragement in their decision. A letter is also sent to the local church, informing the pastor of the decision made. If a youth has responded but has not indicated affiliation with a local church, contact the pastor of a church near the teenager's home. Inform the pastor of the decision and suggest the youth may be a prospective member or may need follow-up counseling and support.

This committee should also be responsible for gathering evaluations of the conference. The strongest conference becomes a tradition that people look forward to the next year. The best of the conference should be repeated in some way the following year.

Facilities/Arrangements Committee

The arrangements committee is responsible for several rather detailed areas. It is this committee's responsibility to see that the meeting location is prepared for the conference. Heating, cooling, rest room facilities, sound and light equipment, media equipment, banners, decorations, and so forth must be checked according to needs. The committee should coordinate their activities with the program committee to identify potential needs of the program personnel.

Once you have all the committees organized and staffed, let the group decide on the date, place, and program. It is preferable to have a conference in the spring. Be careful to check your date to make sure that it does not conflict with other major youth events such as the prom or spring break. Inform other churches in the target area of the date so that they can make arrangements accordingly and avoid possible conflicts. Not all conflicts will be avoidable, but try not to schedule the conference during competing events.

Make sure the location you choose and the meeting facility you secure is easily accessible to crowds, such as a large church building, arena, or auditorium. Determine the number expected for attendance and select a place large enough to accommodate this group.

You must exercise extreme caution and discretion when organizing the program. Allow the steering committee to have input. Often, their input and insight will be valuable, but maintain control to see that the right type of program personnel are enlisted. These are critical decisions, and you must consider the needs and interests of all youth in the target area. Try to avoid extremes. Make sure the speaker can relate to youth, no matter how good or well known. Keep in mind that the future success of each conference is dependent upon the last year's program. A poor choice of speakers and musicians can break even the most well-planned and attended meeting.

Basic Elements of a Conference

The three basic components of a successful youth evangelism conference are an evangelistic speaker, a dynamic music group, and a testimony delivered by a typical teenager. The speaker should be a gifted evangelist who relates well to youth and youth needs. The youth evangelism conference is not a discipleship event; the message should be evangelistic. It is not necessary to enlist a celebrity evangelist or one known to youth, but it is wise to review the material of any speaker before inquiring about his availability for the event.

Music is a major part of youth culture. Look for soloists and groups who appeal to youth with upbeat, versatile, and energetic music. You may want to investigate the possibilities of group singing as well.

The third element, the testimony, is no less important than the speaking and singing. Celebrity testimonies are a great drawing card and can have a tremendous impact on youth, but they are just as interested in hearing the testimony of teenagers like themselves. Remember that youth relate better with youth at this stage than with any other group. An average youth testimony should be limited to five minutes.

The program should be approximately one-and-one-half to two hours, and it should be conducted with a minimum of interruptions. The following is a sample program a simple one-evening rally.

Sample Youth Evangelism Rally Outline

Presession music:	15 minutes
Welcome:	10 minutes
(Includes introductions and announcements.)	
Concert:	30-40 minutes
Youth Testimony:	5 minutes
or	
Celebrity Testimony:	20 minutes.
Special Music	5 minutes
Message:	30-45 minutes
Invitation	

This chapter has merely suggested ideas for planning and implementing a youth evangelism conference; the methods of organization are not set in stone. They have worked for others with phenomenal success; however, this does not mean that an adaptation of the guidelines would not work as well. The key is creativity. Know the youth in your area and their needs, their interests, and motivations, then reach them on that level. A well-planned and executed youth evangelism conference can be an exciting, spiritually regenerating, life-changing event for youth in many areas. Where there are teenagers, there will always be the need for strengthening and equipping them with the truths based on the gospel of Jesus Christ, needs that for some only an evangelistic youth rally can begin to meet.

Ideas

The following ideas are to be the basis for generating other ideas. The best ideas will be found by allowing your steering committee to brainstorm about what can help make the evangelism conference a successful one.

1. As the teenagers are arriving have someone take instant developing slides of them. Prepare a multimedia presentation with some slots blank and drop the pictures of the youth into the presentation and show them during the conference.

2. Enlist the help of a mime or clowning group and have them

performing in the parking lot or around the auditorium before the conference begins.

3. Give all who attend a gospel tract or Bible as they enter. They can be reading this as they wait for the program to begin.

4. Enlist a group of adults and teens who will be responsible for personal evangelism during the conference. Provide some minimal training for them in presenting the gospel. Assign them the task of circulating among the crowd and look for youth who they can start a conversation with and present the gospel to.

5. Serve pizza and print tickets for every teen in the given area. Distribute these in the schools and teen hangouts.

6. Invite groups of teens to attend, (that is, rival football teams, cheer leaders). Show video clips from some of their activities.

7. Publicize a high-attendance contest between the schools and provide a banner or trophy for the one with the most.

8. Provide tickets for the conference. Each ticket when purchased is imprinted with; "We are glad that you are going to be involved in our youth evangelism conference. If you have a friend who does not attend church anywhere we will provide a free ticket for them if you will call phone number." Mail these tickets directly to the unchurched youth.

9. Use drama groups that begin their presentation spontaneously from seats scattered among the audience.

10. Ask several youth groups to prepare one-minute skits related to the theme of the night and mix these in the program.

11. Provide a three-by-five-inch card for everyone at the decision time and encourage them to make some kind of decision.

12. Encourage youth groups to witness between sessions. You might do this by providing them with a witnessing tracts to give away.

13. Include in your program a time to recognize the accomplishments of each junior high and high school in the past year.

14. Have a time for teacher, school administration recognition. Allow these people to sit on the platform as a group.

15. Have a march through town preceding or following one session of the conference.

16. Encourage churches to come to the rally with another church, all on the same bus.

17. Publicize the event on the radio through purchased or free spot announcements.

18. Have youth groups send in the names of lost youth they are bringing. The steering committee should use these to guide their prayer time.

19. Consider appointing youth groups certain places to visit during the conference for a witness experience. These might include parks, swimming pools, fast-food restaurants, malls, shopping centers, and so forth.

20. Have your meeting outdoors in a park or baseball field.

Resources

All of the following resources may be ordered from the Home Mission Board of the Southern Baptist Convention, 1350 Spring Street, Atlanta, GA 30367.

Counseling Guide (#211-02P) gives instruction in how to counsel with individuals responding to a public invitation.

Preparation Through Prayer (#211-07P) is a booklet with prayer ideas for preparation for revivals and rallies.

Area Crusade: Organization Manual (#211-05P) contains material on how to organize for a large-group meeting involving a number of churches.

Area Crusade: Committees Manual (#211-06P) contains other ideas and responsibilities that committees might want to do in preparation for a youth evangelism conference or rally.

Manual for Use and Care of Tents (#211-19P)

Personal Commitment Guide (#211-29P) is a brochure used by counselors in counseling. It gives help in dealing with salvation, recommitment, vocational service, and other decisions.

The Real Life Booklet (#212-04P) is a tract designed especially to be used by youth in personal evangelism. Order the following resources from Materials Services, 127 Ninth Ave, North, Nashville, TN 37234.

The Roman Road: A Witness Training Tool is a five-session study on how

to present the gospel to a non-Christian. It includes Scriptures that
have been put to music.

The Roman Road A video by Dean Finley and Curt Bradford which can
be used to teach *The Roman Road: A Witness Training Tool.*

"Have a Good Life!" is a gospel tract that uses the Roman Road Scriptures.

Existing Youth Evangelism Rallies

Some states already have significant youth evangelism rallies each
year. You may want to contact one of the following about an evangelistic youth rally in your state or in a neighboring state.

ALABAMA
Evangelism Department
Alabama Baptist State Convention
P.O. Box 11870
Montgomery, AL 36198-0001
Annual Date: June
Estimated Attendance 3,700

ARIZONA
Evangelism Department
Arizona Southern Baptist Convention
400 West Camelback Road, Suite 214
Phoenix, AZ 85013
Phone: 602-246-9421
Annual Date: June and December
Estimated Attendance: 2,000

ARKANSAS
Evangelism Department
Arkansas Baptist State Convention
P.O. Box 552
Little Rock, AR 72203
Annual Date: December
Estimated Attendance: 3,000

COLORADO
Evangelism Department
Colorado Baptist General Convention
7393 South Alton Way
Englewood, CO 80112
Annual Date: April
Estimated Attendance: 750

FLORIDA
Evangelism Department
Florida Baptist Convention
Florida Baptist Convention
1230 Hendricks Avenue
Jacksonville, FL 32207
Annual Date: July
Estimated Attendance: 3,000

GEORGIA
Evangelism Department
Georgia Baptist Convention
2930 Flowers Road, South
Atlanta, GA 30341
Annual Date: December
Estimated Attendance: 16,000

HAWAII
Evangelism Department
Hawaii Baptist Convention
2042 Vancouver Drive
Honolulu, HI 96822
Annual Date: Summer
Estimated Attendance: 500

ILLINOIS
Evangelism Department
Illinois Baptist State Association
Box 3486
Springfield, IL 62703-3486
Annual Date: Winter

Estimated Attendance: 4,500

INDIANA
Evangelism Department
State Convention of Baptists in Indiana
P.O. Box 24189
Indianapolis, IN 46224
Annual Date: Spring
Estimated Attendance: 400

KANSAS
Evangelism Department
Kansas-Nebraska Conv. of Southern Baptist
5410 West Seventh Street
Topeka, KS 66606
Annual Date: Winter
Estimated Attendance: 500

KENTUCKY
Evangelism Department
Kentucky Baptist Convention
P.O. Box 43433
Middletown, KY 40243-0433
Annual Date: Summer
Estimated Attendance: 5,000

LOUISIANA
Evangelism Department
Louisiana Baptist Convention
Box 311
Alexandria, LA 71309
Annual Date: December
Estimated Attendance: 2,000

MASSACHUSETTS
Evangelism Department
Baptist Convention of New England
P.O. Box 688

Northborough, MA 01532-0688
Annual Date: December
Estimated Attendance: 600

MICHIGAN
Evangelism Department
Baptist State Convention of Michigan
15635 West Twelve Mile Road
Southfield, MI 48076
Annual Date: Spring
Estimated Attendance: 1,000

MISSISSIPPI
Evangelism Department
Mississippi Baptist Convention Board
Box 530
Jackson, MS 39205
Annual Date: December
Estimated Attendance: 3,000

MISSOURI
Evangelism Department
Missouri Baptist Convention
400 East High Street
Jefferson City, MO 65101
Annual Date: July
Estimated Attendance: 10,000

NEVADA
Evangelism Department
Nevada Baptist Convention
406 California Ave
Reno, NV 89509
Annual Date: Spring
Estimated Attendance: 300

NORTH CAROLINA
Evangelism Department

Baptist State Convention of North Carolina
P.O. Box 1107
Cary, NC 27511-1107
Annual Date: Summer
Estimated Attendance: 12,000

OKLAHOMA
Evangelism Department
Baptist General Convention of Oklahoma
1141 North Robinson
Oklahoma City, OK 73103
Annual Date: December
Estimated Attendance: 7,500

OREGON
Evangelism Department
Northwest Baptist Convention
1033 Northeast Sixth Avenue
Portland, OR 97232-2049
Annual Date: Spring
Estimated Attendance: 500

PENNSYLVANIA
Evangelism Department
Baptist General Convention of Pennsylvania
4620 Fritchey Street
Harrisburg, PA 17109
Annual Date: Spring
Estimated Attendance: 800

SOUTH CAROLINA
Evangelism Department
South Carolina Baptist Convention
907 Richland Street
Columbia, SC 29201-2398
Annual Date: Summer
Estimated Attendance: 13,000

TENNESSEE
Evangelism Department
Tennessee Baptist Convention
P.O. Box 728
Brentwood, TN 37027
Annual Date: Spring
Estimated Attendance: 35,000

TEXAS
Evangelism Department
Baptist General Convention of Texas
Suite 1211, Baptist Building
Dallas, TX 75201-3355
Annual Date: Summer
Estimated Attendance: 20,000

UTAH
Evangelism Department
Utah-Idaho Southern Baptist Convention
P.O. Box 1039
Sandy, UT 84091
Annual Date: Spring
Estimated Attendance: 300

VIRGINIA
Evangelism Department
Baptist General Association of Virginia
P.O. Box 8568
Richmond, VA 23226
Annual Date: Winter
Estimated Attendance: 10,000

13
Youth in Revivals
Thad Hamilton

Introduction

Revival meetings may have been used to reach more youth for Christ in the twentieth century than any other single method of evangelism. Many adults and teenagers in our churches made their initial commitment to our Lord during a week of evangelistic services.

God is still using revival meetings today all across our land to reach youth for the Savior. Wise church leaders must grasp the urgency of this moment, seize the opportunity, and utilize this method of outreach now as never before.

There are two essentials to having revivals with an effective youth emphasis. First, a church's saved youth must be vitally involved in the initial planning of the meetings and in the carrying out of these plans. Secondly, the plans must be targeted to bring non-Christian teens into the services so they will hear about Christ. Youth want to feel they are important. When church leaders tell Christian youth they are needed, and when Christian youth tell non-Christian youth they are wanted, they will listen. When church leaders gain their attention, youth can be impressed upon to do what Jesus wants them to do.

Both types of teenagers can benefit from these revivals. Saved youth find the joy of being obedient to Christ in sharing their faith. Unsaved youth find the joy of receiving Christ as their Lord. How exciting it is to see youth reaching youth for Christ in revivals.

Biblical Basis

Our modern-day revival meeting has its basis in the Old Testament and its development in the New Testament. Although the term "revival meeting" is not found in the Scriptures, the pattern and plan for a series of services with this emphasis is clearly found in the Bible.

Old Testament

The Old Testament tells us of a number of mass gatherings especially planned to bring God's people back to Himself. The man of God called the people of God together. He then delivered God's message to them. The message normally was one of rebuke for their sins. God through His servant then offered His people forgiveness, cleansing, and restoration. The messenger climaxed his message with an urgent appeal for the people to respond positively to God. Usually those listening confessed their sins, turned from them, and recommitted themselves to God's purpose for their lives.

An excellent illustration of this is Elijah's meeting on Mount Carmel. The prophet told King Ahab to gather all of God's people on Mount Carmel. Elijah began his message with a stunning challenge: "How long halt ye between two opinions? if the Lord be God, follow him: but if Baal, then follow him" (1 Kings 18:21, JKV). He continued with another challenge, this one for a miracle to be performed by the false god. When no miracle occurred, Elijah said God would do what the false god could not do. God did, and the people were amazed. The prophet called for commitment. The people did what God said.

While most of these Old Testament gatherings were used to reclaim God's people, there is one especially notable account of a series of mass meetings which reached non-believers. God sent His prophet Jonah to Nineveh. The messenger delivered the words from heaven: "Yet forty days and Nineveh will be overthrown" (Jonah 3:4). Jonah preached this message all over the city. What God said had an arresting effect upon the metropolitan populace. The residents of the city turned from their sins. The Lord spared the people.

New Testament

When we examine New Testament instances of gathering people for God's servant to deliver His message to them, we discover the thrust is almost exclusively outreach. Both Jesus and those He called to announce His good news used mass meetings to great advantage.

Our Lord Himself utilized the method of feeding a large crowd of hungry people to preach to them. This is illustrated in the feeding of the five thousand, recorded by all four Gospel writers, and the feeding of the four thousand, recorded in Matthew 15 and Mark 8. After feeding them Jesus preached to them. His flawless logic was illustrated in a most practical way: before people can be preached to, they must be present. The Lord of the harvest showed us by His own example how to assemble a multitude of people together. This idea can help us build attendance in our revival services.

God directed Philip to conduct a mass-evangelism event. As a lay leader in the Jerusalem church, he conducted evangelistic efforts in nearby Samaria. As Philip told the Samaritans about Christ, God moved mightily among the people. Miracles, exorcisms, and healings took place as the spokesman lifted up the name of Jesus.

The modern-day revival meeting combines both emphases found in the Bible. The series of services is aimed at calling God's people to recommit themselves to Him and at calling non-Christians to make their first commitment to Christ.

The ideal situation is for the revival of God's people to occur before the actual week of the revival meeting begins. This often happens when God's people become obedient to Him in preparing for the week of services. When the church members pray and do what God wants them to do, they will do those things which help their non-believing friends and acquaintances come to know Christ as their Lord.

The majority of church members, both youth and adults, love Jesus. If asked for help and given something specific to do, they will do it. We must involve them in the revival.

Youth Culture

Youth in our day are moved to action by a number of forces, both around them and within them. If we can recognize these motivating influences which already exist and use them to our advantage, we can employ them to enlist youth in revival meetings.

Perhaps the greatest external factor which affects youth is their friends. If their *friends* like something, *they* like it. When their peers do something, they want to do it. The wise pastor and youth leadership realize this and seek to involve the youth group of the church in preparation activities. This is relatively easy, as many of the things which need to be done to get ready for a revival meeting are best done by a group. Asking the entire group to take part in the revival preparation uses this peer group influence beautifully.

Revival gets teenagers' attention by presenting a challenge. Youth want to be challenged. They will respond to a strong, positive, enthusiastic challenge. When young people are challenged to reach their friends for Christ, and the tremendous need is explained logically and intelligently, they will answer the call to become involved.

Youth are motivated internally by emotion. They want to do something fun and exciting. They want to have a good time. The mass meeting offers all of these elements. Sometimes these meetings have been criticized for their emotional level. However, an examination of the biblical text will show that it is the Holy Spirit that has moved people's emotions in these meetings. Nothing is more emotionally stimulating than having a part in seeing one of your friends come to Christ. The leaders of youth need to convey to them that it is a tremendously enjoyable experience to help their friends find the real answer to life. If youth can get a taste of this kind of emotional uplift, they will want to be involved in evangelism on a continuing basis.

Youth are also moved by the uncertainties they face. During their teenage years they will be making major decisions which can determine the course of the rest of their lives. Often teens will instinctively turn to God for the answers they need. Most people who receive Christ do so before their teenage years are over. The urgency to reach youth for Christ during this period in which they are open to God must be emphasized to our Christian teenagers.

Youth need to feel that what they are doing is important to others. We need to make much of all the commitments made by youth, whether salvation, recommitment to Christ, or answering God's call to full-time Christian vocation. Teens need to be encouraged to do the right thing, to follow Jesus. Youth need to hear that someone is proud of them for doing what God wants them to do. Revival meetings pose an excellent opportunity for many youth to make these commitments. We must be ready to encourage them.

Implementation

How then do churches have revivals with a youth emphasis? They do it in two ways. The youth leaders in that church must first involve their youth in the planning and preparation for the revival meeting. They must then focus on reaching lost youth during the revival meeting itself.

Youth Involvement

The first major task is the youth leaders getting their own youth involved in getting ready for the revival meeting. Detailed planning and thorough preparation are the keys to a revival meeting in which God works. The Holy Spirit uses the preparation as the channel through which He prepares hearts. The Christian youth of a church must become a vital part of the revival preparation. It is up to their leaders to get them involved.

The first area in which to involve the youth of the church in getting ready for the revival meeting is in the initial planning for the meeting. If the adults do all of the planning and then expect the youth to attend, the youth feel left out from the start. Yet, when the youth of a church are involved in the decision-making process, they are usually willing to supply the labor it takes to get the job done.

Youth Ideas

Another reason youth should be involved in the beginning is because of their unique viewpoint. Youth see things from a different perspective than adults do. Youth have a freshness about their ideas that we need. Often they have not yet grown negative and doubtful, as have many adults. They believe it can be done! This unique point of view needs to be incorporated into the planning of the revival emphasis.

One way to involve them in the revival planning is for the pastor and youth leaders to meet with the youth group for a brainstorming session. The pastor, youth director, or some other leader should explain to the youth that they see the need for the church to have a revival meeting. Then emphasize that the particular meeting will be different because the church wants the youth to help in the planning.

Youth should be assured their ideas are important and will be heard. The question should be asked, "What would you like to see us do about this upcoming revival meeting?" This may be all it takes to get them to talk freely about what they would like to see take place. If the teens do not speak up immediately, it may be because they do not know exactly why their opinion is being sought. The leader of the discussion might then say, "What do you think we should do about a speaker for the revival? What should he be like? Do you know of anyone you have heard speak you would like for us to invite?"

The youth may be stunned at first, but when they think about it they will think of people they would like to see come. Perhaps they heard a dynamic speaker at an area youth rally, youth camp, retreat, or during a revival at another church. It could be that they do not know a specific person, but that they could suggest qualities they would like to see in a revival speaker to invite. Then they can see that their wishes will enter into the choice, there will be discussion.

Other areas to explore are, "Are there any special musicians or singers you especially like that you want to invite? What kind of activities would you like to do during the revival week?" If there is a good degree of openness in communication between the youth and their leaders, fresh ideas will come forth.

Youth Involved in Leadership

Another way to involve the youth in the initial planning is to ask them to serve on the revival preparation committees. The youth would not only make a valuable contribution to the work of the committees but would receive valuable information and training in working with people to carry out projects and, in particular, spiritual tasks.

Some youth could be asked to serve as cochairman of a committee, along with an adult. If this is done, the church leaders will be able to identify youth who are walking with the Lord and who are developing as leaders. Natural leaders among youth who might serve as revival committee cochairmen with adults are those who have answered God's call to full-time Christian vocational service. These teenagers who have a special sense of God's hand upon their life should be encouraged to learn how to work together as believers in doing God's work. Serving as cochairman with a mature layperson would be a rich and valuable experience for the youth and the adult as well.

Perhaps a number of the church's youth could serve as regular members of the revival committees. The committee chairman should enlist them personally. As they meet with the committee they should be encouraged to speak up and share their ideas, being treated as equals by their adult counterparts.

Spiritual Preparation for Youth

One other way to involve the youth in the planning of the revival is to ask each of them to write a personal letter to the evangelist who has been invited to lead the campaign. In their letter they should share a number of things. They should assure him they are praying for him as he prepares to come. They could share with him what they hope God would do during the week of revival services. They should especially give him the names of their lost friends so he can be praying for them. These letters would really encourage the evangelist and give him knowledge of the situation before he arrived.

The second area where the leadership should involve the youth of the church is in praying for the revival. God loves the faith and fervency of the prayers of young people. He answers them. We need them praying for our revivals!

There are several ways in which leaders can get youth to pray for the revival. One way is to sponsor or set up special prayer events. The other way is to teach them how to pray better.

Some of the different kinds of prayer events which can be set up for youth are home prayer meetings, prayer retreats, after-school prayer snacks, and youth prayer cells. The home prayer meetings can meet once or twice each week for the two, four, or six weeks before the revival meeting. A prayer retreats could take place a few weeks before the revival. Parts of the prayer retreat program might include Bible study about prayer, its results, and its power. Also the retreat should include a prayer time, both in small and large groups with youth leading; devotionals about prayer led by youth; personal testimonies from youth about prayer. After-school prayer snacks in homes of church youth with light refreshments would be enjoyable. Youth prayer cells where two or three youth get together for prayer every day two weeks before the revival would give an urgency to the week.

Prayer involvement for the youth would also include teaching them how to pray. Leaders need to train youth who are leaders to conduct these prayer events for their friends. Youth need to be taught to pray for their lost friends by name. They need to be instructed how to claim a prayer promise from God's Word. They need to be shown how to make up a list of their friends to continue to pray for.

The third area where leaders of youth need to be involved is in spiritual preparation. If we can challenge our Christian youth to resubmit their lives to Christ before the meeting actually begins, God can really use them to reach a multitude of their friends for Christ.

Special Youth Emphasis

Special events can often be used to bring youth to see their need of renewed commitment to Jesus. A retreat six weeks before the revival begins could center around the theme of full commitment to Christ. A youth rally before the campaign could include Christian youth around the area. The rally format could include singing; youth testimonies, and a message on "Youth Winning Others to Christ." Youth can be challenged to make a rededication, do personal evangelism, and attend faithfully. At least a cookout for the youth with the visiting evangelist could take place the Saturday evening before the revival begins on Sunday morning. He would have a chance to challenge them to give their lives to Christ.

Often when the youth of the church catch fire it spreads throughout the membership. Spiritual preparation is usually the key. Because youth are at a point in life to question its meaning and purpose they are open to the gospel. This is the reason why revival preparation must include a youth emphasis.

Youth Publicity

The fourth main activity is which Christian teens need to be involved is in publicizing the revival. Youth are great communicators. Publicity says, "Here's what's happening and we need for you to be there!" Young people are naturals for publicity.

The youth should be involved in the designing and the artwork of the publicity. Perhaps the youth could have a contest to name a theme for the revival and a logo to go with it. They could have a poster contest and make posters to put up around the church and at school. If a youth night is designated, they might want to set up a special youth night publicity committee to design materials to publicize that night. There is some danger in publicizing a youth night. Avoid designating one of the revival services as a youth worship. The adults are likely to take this night off and not attend. Any youth-night publicity should be clearly related to activities outside the worship services. The worship services are for all. This does not mean to avoid having youth give testimonies in the services.

The teenagers should also be in the center of the efforts to get the publicity materials into the public. They should get permission themselves in their own junior high and high schools to announce the revival services, or at least the youth night. This should be done in every school in the area. They should pass out tickets to any youth meals planned to their friends. They should help stuff, stamp, address, and mail letters to the youth group of the church concerning the revival activities. The young people can take posters around to local businesses and put them up. They can give out smaller posters and or bumper stickers to church members to put on their cars. The could have a bike hike, going from one end of the town to the other as a group on their bikes, leaving a revival flier or handbill at every home in the community one week before the revival.

Youth Visitation

Youth should be involved in church-wide visitation for the revival. The teens know their friends and so are the natural ones to reach them for Christ. We must train them how to do it and give them every motivation we can to help them do it.

The church leadership should have witness training for the youth. The teens need role models for sharing their personal testimony and the gospel with a witnessing tract. Youth mission or discipleship groups are a good time for this training. If the revival meeting is held during the summer or other time when there is no school, witness training might be taught in the early afternoon with a time of visitation immediately afterwards. The youth should be challenged to witness every day, everywhere.

The group should be encouraged to share their faith by meeting weekly before the revival meeting for prayer and visiting. The week before the meeting, the youth could visit one night, every other night, or every night that week.

During the actual revival meeting, the leadership should organize a youth visitation program. This is commonly called *Crash, Youth Crash, Bring 'Em Back Alive* or *Go Get 'Em*. The youth need encouragement to bring their friends to the services. This program provides it. Many youth have received Christ over the years as a result of this effort.

The schedule for the program is for the youth to meet one hour before each revival service. They will go out in teams of two or three youth to each car with adult drivers from the church. They will go to their friends' homes and bring them back to the revival service with them. The number returning will build each night along with the excitement of the youth who are going out.

Begin preparation by enlisting drivers. People need to be asked who do not sing in the revival choir. Enlist plenty of drivers. Many individuals who have never been asked to do anything may be glad drive their cars so some youth can go get their friends. Use all available adults.

If the evangelist is to be the motivator, he should be enthusiastic. He should meet with the youth to promote it. If the revival starts on Sunday morning, he should meet with the youth for thirty minutes during Sunday School. If the meeting begins on Sunday evening, he should meet with them after the first service to promote it. Since the evangelist in this case should motivate them, let him also explain it. Simply tell the youth that it will be exciting and fun.

Attendance Emphasis

Akin to the visitation is attendance. The youth should again be involved. Most revivals have a Sunday School Night where high attendance is stressed. Give youth one or two names of absentees or prospects for their class to call and bring with them on Sunday School Night. Assign two youth a pew and ask them to fill it. Another attendance plan is to ask a number of the youth to serve as a host or hostess on one particular night. Each would be responsible for getting seven or more people, plus their own family, to the service that evening. A religious gift like a Bible, Christian book, or music tape could be given to the one who brings the most that evening. Youth respond beautifully to this kind of challenge. We should remember to commend them verbally when they do!

Youth should also be involved in the telephoning done for the revival. Give them the names of the absentees in the youth classes and asked to call them twice during the revival. Try giving them the names of the entire town's telephone directory cut up into twenty names each. It would be helpful in the latter case to write out a suggested wording of what you want them to say. Youth spend a lot of time on the telephone. They could use some of it talking about Jesus.

The music in the revival could involve many of your youth. Encourage them to sing in the revival choir. Getting to know the music evangelist or visiting music director personally would help make a lasting spiritual impression on them. The church's youth choir would sing at one service. Youth who sing would do solos, duets, or group singing. Those who play piano, organ, guitars, drums, brass, woodwinds, or stringed instruments could play instrumental numbers or accompany the congregational singing. Through involvement in the musical aspect of the revival many teenagers can make a real contribution to the revival.

Involvement During the Revival

There are several other avenues within the service itself through which Christian teenagers could serve the Lord. They could give their personal testimonies publically as to how they came to know Jesus Christ. They could read the Scripture and lead in prayer. They could be the ushers in a service. Each youth can feel useful and use his abilities, whatever they are.

Involve youth as revival counselors. Give them training. Choose youth mature enough in the Lord to counsel other teenagers as they come forward during the invitation.

Enlist Christian teens to be part of the follow-through efforts. Assign each young person who receives Christ to a team of one youth and one adult to help him grow in his new found faith. The youth/adult team would go to see the new youth convert. The new youth could come to church with the mature youth. The one sponsoring the new believer could show him around, introduce him to the other youth, and sit with him in the services. What a contribution our youth can make in helping other youth, newly saved, follow through with their commitment!

As you can well see, almost anything that an adult can do in the way of revival preparation, a youth can do, too. We, as leaders, must involve them in doing so.

Plan to Involve Non-Christian Youth

Once you have planned to involve Christian youth you will have an easier time of involving non-Christian youth. Plan activities that will carry out the objective of inviting teenagers to accept Christ.

Decide the focus of the revival meeting with reference to lost youth. What part of the efforts will be given to and directed toward reaching unsaved teenagers? Will the meeting be primarily devoted to reaching youth? Will this only be a part of the thrust?

Take two practical approaches in deciding about the focus on youth. One is to decide a numerical goal of how many youth you wish to seek to win to Christ. The second is to concentrate on reaching high-school youth and the junior high will follow along.

The Revival Leadership

The choice of an evangelist to reach youth is crucial. It does not take a young person to relate to youth. It does take someone who is really alive, both physically and spiritually. It takes someone who will let people know, and youth in particular, that they are loved and needed. It takes someone who will relate the gospel in a nonreligious language. It takes someone who is excited about his relationship to Jesus Christ and who is committed to bring lost youth to Him.

Close on the heels of the choice of the evangelist is the choice of musicians for the revival effort. Revival music should be gospel songs, sung by all the people, preparing the heart for God to speak. What kind of musicians can do this kind of music? Persons who understand and agree with your goals for the revival meeting. Persons who have a daily relationship with Jesus Christ. Persons who are willing to be cooperative in all areas, especially time in the services and the money to be given as compensation. If a visiting musician is not invited, perhaps a visiting youth choir could come. Instruct them to not use more time than allotted. Leave plenty of time for testimonies, preaching, and a time of invitation. High-school choirs are usually willing to sing for the services.

Publicity

Direct some of the revival publicity to the youth. It should be attractive, using colored ink and paper, as well as artwork or clip art. It should not look professional.

Ideas

1. Meals will draw a lost youth and give saved youth some help in getting them to church. Print tickets for the event. The number of pieces should be equal to the total number of the enrollment of all the junior high and high schools in your area. You will want every student, grades seven through twelve, to receive one. Exciting names for your activities will help like *Pizza Blast, World's Greatest Pizza Party, Youth Celebration, Jesus Happening,* or *Ice-Cream-Sundae Pig Out.* Keep the menu simple: pizza, spaghetti, hamburgers, tacos, banana splits. Keep the time short for eating so there will be time for a testimony and a few words from the evangelist. It is also helpful to put two times on your publicity, the time any meal or other activity starts and the time the revival service ends. This will keep them from going home in the middle of your service. Register everyone present on a three-by-five-inch index card with their name, address, where they go to church, and how often.

2. After-church fellowships will also draw unsaved teens. Have light refreshments: homemade cookies, cakes, ice cream, a bonfire with marshmallows, or a watermelon cutting. Use a cute name: *Chip, Dip and Sip, Yak-n-Snak, Scream and Cream, Ice Cream Galore,* or *Teen After-glow.* Keep them brief, just eat and sing before going home.

3. Having a designated "Youth Night" works if it is really special and planned to be so. Have a meal before the service. Tell the youth while eating, "Don't eat and run. Stay for the fun during the service tonight." Reserve a special seating area for the youth near the front of the auditorium. Tell those eating, "We have a Teenagers Up Front Club. Join Tonight! Sit in the area reserved for you." Perhaps you could ask the local high-school choir or chorus to sing. Invite a special person like an athlete to give his personal testimony. Direct the message to the youth.

4. Using delegations really works. Delegations are groups of youth who come as your special guests. Make a list of all the delegations you can think of in your area. Include sports teams, cheerleaders, bands, choirs, orchestras, scouts, all area church youth groups. Send a personal letter to their sponsor inviting them to be your special guest on a certain evening. Perhaps "Youth Night" is your best opportunity. Follow your letter with a call to confirm their coming. Give the pastor a note with the name of each group present and their sponsor. Recognize them in the service.

5. One final idea for reaching lost youth is to have an evangelistic time during the Sunday School period on the Sunday of the revival meeting. Go to classes, get records filled out, and assemble all youth classes. Have the evangelist share a basic presentation of how to become a Christian. Give an invitation for those present to receive Christ. Use the counselors who have been trained to help you talk with those who respond.

Resources

Bisagno, John T, *The Power of Positive Evangelism* (Broadman Press, Nashville, TN, 1968).

Cathey, Bill V., *A New Day in Church Revivals* (Broadman Press, Nashville, TN, 1984).

Phillips, Eugene *Ideas for Youth Outreach,* Volume 3, (Convention Press, Nashville, TN, 1972).

Promise of Life: Youth/Adult Partnership Revival Planbook (Home Mission Board, Atlanta, GA, 1984).

Slay, Lamar and Cathey, Bill V., *All Church Youth-Led Revival Preparation Manual* (Baptist General Convention of Texas, Dallas, TX, 1983).

The Work of an Evangelist (World Wide Publications, Minneapolis, MN, 1984).

YouthPlus Tell: Revivals for Youth and Adults (Baptist Sunday School Board, Nashville, TN, 1985).

Authors

Couch, Doug

Doug Couch is a graduate of West Georgia College and Southwestern Baptist Theological Seminary. He has been director of youth evangelism with the Georgia Baptist Convention since 1984. He has also served churches in both Georgia and Alabama as youth minister/ associate pastor and pastor. He has coordinated statewide youth evangelism conferences which have drawn over seventeen-thousand youth from six-hundred churches and has initiated regional conferences, as well. Couch is also the director of Georgia's SuperWOW Summer Youth Conferences, as well as founder and coordinator of the Advanced SuperWOW School of Evangelism for youth.

Cox, Bill

Bill Cox is married to Cathy Cox. He is the associate in the Evangelism Department of the General Board of South Carolina Baptist Convention. His primary emphasis is youth evangelism and includes directing various regional and statewide youth conferences and rallies. For six years Bill was the director of "Bill Cox Abundant Life Ministries, Inc." and traveled with Cathy throughout the country leading conferences, revivals, retreats, youth rallies, and camps. His unique ministry includes special-effects chalk drawings, three-screen multiimage presentations, music, puppetry, and drama, as well as preaching and teaching. He has authored several books and magazine articles, and composed numerous songs, including a musical drama. For five years he was minister of youth at Taylors First Baptist

Church in Greenville, South Carolina. Bill and Cathy have two sons, Christopher and Taylor, and live in Columbia, South Carolina.

Everett, Richard

Richard Everett has served as director of personal evangelism for the North Carolina Baptist Convention since 1974. He has served as a pastor in Tennessee and North Carolina. He is a graduate of Carson-Newman College and Southeastern Baptist Theological Seminary.

He is married to the former Linda Hicks of Sweetwater, Tennessee. They have one daughter, Beth.

Finley, Dean

Dean Finley is the national evangelism consultant with youth in the Specialized Evangelism Department, Evangelism Development Division, Evangelism Section, Home Mission Board of the Southern Baptist Convention. He has served in this position since 1982. He has also served in five different churches as a minister with youth, one church as a minister to college students, a campus minister at Campbellsville College in Campbellsville, Kentucky, and as a professor of world religions. He has traveled and spoken to over five-thousand youth and college leaders and one-hundred thousand junior high, high school, and college students.

He lives in Stone Mountain, Georgia, with his wife Beverly and two daughters, Dawn and DeAnn. He grew up in Springfield, Missouri. His parents, George and Opal, and two brothers Dennis and Davy Finley still live in Springfield. He is a graduate of Southwest Missouri State University with a teaching degree in mathematics. He also holds a Masters of Arts in Christian Education, Master of Divinity, and Doctor of Education degrees from The Southern Baptist Theological Seminary in Louisville, Kentucky.

Hall, Clyde R.

R. Clyde Hall, Jr. is manager, youth section, Church Training Department, the Sunday School Board of the Southern Baptist Convention, Nashville, Tennessee. He has led in the development of youth discipleship materials and programs for use in Southern Baptist Churches since 1976. He is co-compiler of *Disciple Youth I* and *Disciple Youth II Kits, DiscipleHelps: A Daily Quiet Time Guide and Journal,* and *DiscipleNow Manual.* He has directed discipleship conferences for more than one-hundred thousand youth and youth leaders.

Hamilton, Thad

Thad Hamilton is associate director of mass evangelism for the Home Mission Board of the Southern Baptist Convention. He has also served as a full-time evangelist. He lives with his wife in Atlanta, Georgia.

Lagrone, James W.

James Lagrone is associate director of evangelism for the Arkansas Baptist Convention. Jim has a Master of Divinity degree from the Southwestern Baptist Theological Seminary. He is also a graduate of Arkansas State University in Jonesboro, Arkansas. He has served as a pastor and youth minister in Arkansas and Texas.

Jim and his wife Rebecca live in Little Rock. They have two children, James and Janna. Jim began a statewide youth evangelism school in Arkansas.

Mattingly, Don

Don Mattingly is manager of the program services section of the Church Recreation Department of the Baptist Sunday School Board. He has served in the Church Recreation Department for twelve years. He is a graduate of Baylor University with a B.S. degree in Church Recreation, and the Southwestern Baptist Theological Seminary with both the Masters of Religious Education and Doctor of Education degrees.

Don is married to the former Cathy Hubbard of Fort Worth, Texas, and they have two teenaged sons, Robbie and Chad. He enjoys playing golf and water skiing with the family.

Hunter, Phillip

Phillip Hunter is the associate in the Evangelism Department of the Missouri Baptist Convention. He plans, coordinates, and directs the youth evangelism schools and the youth evangelism conference. He has served in this position for three years.

Phillip does evangelistic preaching, teaching, and musical concerts in churches.

He received the Bachelor of Arts degree from Eastern Washington State University. He received the Master of Music degree from Southwestern Seminary in Fort Worth, Texas. He also attended Golden Gate Seminary where he received the Master of Divinity degree and the Doctor of Ministry degree.

Phillip has served churches in Washington, Oregon, Texas, and California as a minister of youth and music, an associate pastor, and a pastor.

He and his wife, Roni, have three sons, Phillip, Joshua, and Matthew. They live in Jefferson City, Missouri.

Poe, Harry L.

Harry L. Poe serves as associate director of evangelism for the Kentucky Baptist Convention. He formerly served as pastor of the Simpsonville Baptist Church in Simpsonville, Kentucky and as Chaplain of the Kentucky State Reformatory. He holds the Master of Divinity degree and the PhD in Evangelism from The Southern Baptist Theological Seminary.

Riley, Lonnie

Lonnie Riley has been a full-time evangelist since 1987. He formerly served as the associate director of the Evangelism Department for the State Convention of Baptists in Ohio for nearly six years. He has also served as assistant to the president of Cumberland College in Kentucky. In addition, he has pastored for six years and worked with youth in high schools and colleges. He has led many youth revivals in Indiana, Kentucky, West Virginia, and Ohio.

Woods, Larry

Larry Wood is associate director of the Evangelism Department, Florida Baptist Convention in Jacksonville, Florida. Serving in that capacity since June 1983, a major part of his task is youth evangelism. He also served in a similar position for three and one half years as evangelism associate for the Missouri Baptist Convention. In addition to youth work, Wood worked with vocational evangelists in these states. He served for nine years in full-time evangelism prior to coming to the Missouri post. He has also served as pastor and as minister of youth in Arkansas. Wood has majored on communicating to youth during his ministry.